GAY PLAYS

Submariners *by Tom McClenaghan,* The Green Bay Tree *by Mordaunt Shairp,* Passing By *by Martin Sherman,* Accounts *by Michael Wilcox.*

Selected by the playwright Michael Wilcox, the four plays in this volume all feature homosexual characters but are also concerned with wider issues than homosexuality itself. Included are Tom McClenaghan's hilarious *Submariners,* concerning a young naval rating who feigns homosexuality to get a discharge from the navy; the classic Mordaunt Shairp play, *The Green Bay Tree,* in which a wealthy bachelor has taken care of the education of a young, working-class boy; *Passing By* in which Martin Sherman treats a casual gay relationship with humanity and compassion; and Michael Wilcox's own *Accounts,* about a widow with two sons, one of them homosexual, struggling to survive on a hill farm in the Scottish Border country. *The Green Bay Tree* is introduced by Peter Burton, and the other plays by their respective authors, while the volume itself opens with an introduction by Michael Wilcox.

D1287855

A METHUEN THEATREFILE
in series with
OTHER SPACES: NEW THEATRE AND THE RSC
by Colin Chambers
THE IMPROVISED PLAY: THE WORK OF MIKE LEIGH
by Paul Clements
THE PLAYS OF EDWARD BOND
by Tony Coult
ALL TOGETHER NOW: AN ALTERNATIVE VIEW OF
THEATRE AND THE COMMUNITY
by Steve Gooch
DARIO FO: PEOPLE'S COURT JESTER
by Tony Mitchell
UNDERSTUDIES: THEATRE AND SEXUAL POLITICS
by Michelene Wandor
PLAYS BY WOMEN : VOLUME ONE
(*Vinegar Tom* by Caryl Churchill; *Dusa, Fish, Stas and Vi* by Pam Gems;
Tissue by Louise Page; *Aurora Leigh* by Michelene Wandor)
Introduced and edited by Michelene Wandor
PLAYS BY WOMEN: VOLUME TWO
(*Rites* by Maureen Duffy; *Letters Home* by Rose Leiman Goldemberg;
Trafford Tanzi by Claire Luckham; *Find Me* by Olwen Wymark)
Introduced and edited by Michelene Wandor
PLAYS BY WOMEN: VOLUME THREE
(*Aunt Mary* by Pam Gems; *Red Devils* by Debbie Horsfield;
Blood Relations by Sharon Pollock; *Time Pieces* by Lou Wakefield
and The Women's Theatre Group)
Introduced and edited by Michelene Wandor

GAY PLAYS

SUBMARINERS
by
Tom McClenaghan

THE GREEN BAY TREE
by
Mordaunt Shairp

PASSING BY
by
Martin Sherman

ACCOUNTS
by
Michael Wilcox

Edited and introduced by
Michael Wilcox

A Methuen Theatrefile
Methuen . London and New York

A METHUEN PAPERBACK

This volume first published as a Methuen Paperback original in 1984 by
Methuen London Ltd, 11 New Fetter Lane, London EC4P 4EE
and Methuen Inc, 733 Third Avenue, New York, NY 10017, USA.

Submariners copyright © 1984 by Tom McClenaghan
The Green Bay Tree first published in 1933 by Allen & Unwin Ltd.
Copyright © 1933, 1984 by Mrs Margaret Williams
Passing By copyright © 1984 by Martin Sherman
Accounts copyright © 1984 by Michael Wilcox

British Library Cataloguing in Publication Data

Gay Plays.—(A Methuen theatrefile)
   1. Homosexuality—Drama   2. English
drama—20th century
   I. Wilcox, Michael
   822′.912′080353   PR1259.H6

ISBN 0-413-52330-6

Printed in Great Britain by
Redwood Burn Ltd, Trowbridge, Wilts.

CAUTION
All rights whatsoever in these plays are strictly reserved and application for performance,
readings etc, must be made before rehearsal to the authors' agents as follows:

Submariners: Goodwin Associates, 19 London Street, London W2.
The Green Bay Tree: Margery Vosper Ltd., Suite 8D & E, 26 Charing Cross Road,
London WC2H 0DG.
Passing By: Margaret Ramsay Ltd., 14a Goodwin's Court, St Martin's Lane, London
WC2N 4LL.
Accounts: International Copyright Bureau, Suite 8D & E, 26 Charing Cross Road,
London WC2H 0DG.

No performance may be given unless a licence has been obtained.

CONTENTS

INTRODUCTION

One thing the four plays included in this volume have in common is that some or all of the characters in each are homosexual. That is the only sense in which they should be regarded as 'gay plays'. My selection for this anthology has deliberately avoided plays that are concerned with gay politics. Here are not plays written by a minority for a minority audience. Each play stands with confidence and independence. None is an apologia for homosexuality.

The earliest play included is Mordaunt Shairp's *The Green Bay Tree*. This was produced first in London in 1933 and was staged in New York later that year with a cast including Laurence Olivier, Leo G. Carroll, James Dale and Jill Esmond. At that time, the Lord Chamberlain had to approve all play scripts prior to production in the United Kingdom. In New York, the police had recently closed down a production of Bourdet's *The Captive* for being an affront to public decency. Mordaunt Shairp's play treads as near to the edge of his subject as the times would permit. If the homosexual relationship between Dulcimer and Julian had been mentioned unequivocally in the text of the play, it would not have reached the public stage on either side of the Atlantic. Whilst one might wonder precisely why the subject of homosexuality should arouse such keen official antagonism, confronting a forbidden subject in the theatre creates substantial dramatic tension. The London critics had a marvellous time. A.E. Wilson in *The Star* (26 January 1933) headed his review with an extended headline; 'TWO UNPLEASANT PEOPLE – WHICH WOULD YOU KICK THE HARDER? – A WRETCHED YOUTH – AND A GUARDIAN WHO WAS CORRUPT'. After a vitriolic condemnation of the characters and their actions in the play, Wilson concludes; 'if the object was to arouse powerful detestation for two abominable people a kind of success may be concluded. But that is all.' At no point does he use the word 'homosexual'. Nor do any of the critics I have read. If they had done so, is it reasonable to suppose that the play would have been closed down? It is interesting to note that A.E. Wilson stopped short of sticking his knife into the play's heart by *not* mentioning unequivocally the play's homosexual theme.

The West End theatres of 1933 were full of frothy musical comedies. You could take your choice between Noël Coward at the Adelphi or Ivor Novello at the Criterion and the Playhouse. Plays by Ben Travers and A.P. Herbert were in preparation (with huge casts). To see middle-class characters as objects of fun or romance was one thing, but to see them as vicious and perverse was quite another matter. The play was brilliantly acted by Frank Vosper, Hugh Williams and the rest of the company, and it was a huge success and a major talking point of the season.

When *The Green Bay Tree* opened in New York in October 1933, its reputation had already aroused the keenest anticipation. The first night received a marvellous set of reviews, but as in London, none of the reviewers mentioned, directly, the homosexual theme. The memory of the fate of *The Captive* was too fresh in their minds. A week after the opening, Robert Garland of the *New York World-Telegram* reviewed the play for the second time in a week (his second string had reviewed the opening night). He decided to be more explicit than his colleagues; 'My brothers of the First Night Garden, remembering the bad luck of *The Captive*, are prone to pretend that Mr Shairp's play deals with a couple of other things. Mr Dulcimer's admiration for Julian's wavy hair, for instance. Or the manner in which that personable young fellow occupies a couch, purring like a cat in the lap of luxury. Reading the reviews printed while I was out of town, I gather that *The Green Bay Tree* has nothing to do with the way of a man with a man. If it has nothing to do with that (and 'that' is an incident not unknown to the public in general and to patrons of revues in particular) Mr Shairp's play is the most meaningless play ever written by anybody. But Mr Shairp's play *isn't* the most meaningless play ever written by anybody . . .'

Looking back at the play 50 years later, possession seems a more central theme than homosexuality. The struggle to possess Julian, body and soul, between Mr Dulcimer, Leonora Yale and the young man's father is what holds the play together. And Mr Dulcimer is a wonderful, theatrical creation. While he is on stage, which is most of the time, the play sizzles along most entertainingly.

The three other plays in this collection come from the 1970s, a decade that saw a proliferation of plays with homosexual themes on both sides of the Atlantic. In Britain, the Gay Sweatshop theatre company performed a series of plays the length and breadth of the country, dramatising social, political and personal aspects of homosexuality. I encountered one of their productions in a down at heel gay night club in Newcastle upon Tyne in the North East of England. The company acted out a series of problems encountered by their gay hero such as 'coming out' at home and being discriminated against at work. A hundred and fifty gay 'Geordies' in the audience appreciated the performance greatly, but I imagine the play was more useful in performance in appropriate venues than on paper.

My own experience of politically motivated theatre, based mostly on observation and occasional professional participation with companies based in the North East of England, suggests to me that for all the skill of the staging and the brilliance of many of the artists involved, political considerations seem to smother the more durable, dramatic instincts of most of the playwrights. And where plays were created by committee, for all the educational value to those directly concerned with the creative process, the final agreed upon script was a disappointment. Long before the end of the decade, the description 'devised by the company' seemed to me a guarantee of a poorly-crafted play. In spite of the large number of plays with homosexual themes written in the 1970s, finding plays that had not already been published and which were worth publishing in 1984 was not easy.

Martin Sherman wrote *Passing By* in the early seventies before the AIDS outbreak, and the innocent attitude of Simon and Toby to their shared illness contrasts harshly with present day fears of transmitted sexual diseases. Getting ill together is a great inconvenience, but the way the two men are able to nurse each other back to strength displays their good humour and kindly natures. Sherman's play is free of guilt and misery. The lives of Simon and Toby are not confused with notions of abnormality and their homosexuality is the least remarkable aspect of their encounter. This play is a welcome antidote to plays in which the luckless homosexual is shown to be socially and professionally disadvantaged.

In Tom McClenaghan's *Submariners,* young 'Cock' Roach tries to convince his fellow submariners on a nuclear submarine that he is gay in the hope of getting a discharge from the navy. He adopts the camp mannerisms of a young queen with great ease. He is shocked to discover at the end of act one that his antics break through the defences of a genuine homosexual, who has managed to keep his preferences private and secret. But more important than this domestic drama is the fact that the nuclear submarine is the carrier of immense destructive forces itself. Throughout the games of young Roach, the announcements of the ever present tannoy intrude as the real voice of authority. The seriousness of HMS *Superior's* mission and its vast capability for nuclear destruction, set against the triviality of the daily lives of its men, is at the heart of the play. 'Cock' Roach's bid for freedom at the end is wonderfully anarchic and a far more effective strike at the heart of authority than his gay posturing of act one.

Accounts is that rare theatrical beast, a rural rather than urban play. A widow and her two teenage sons have moved from their traditional family farm in Northumberland, where they have been tenants, to a new farm near Kelso in the Scottish Borders, where, for the first time, they are landowners. The action is spread over the first year of their occupation of the new farm. The emerging homosexual nature of Donald, the youngest brother and an exceptionally talented rugby football player, is just one of many events in the play. The family has always lived in a remote, isolated location and has formed living habits away from the influence of neighbours, or of television. Their world consists primarily of the family, sheep and the wild creatures of the fells. They don't read many books. They rarely talk things over outside the family circle. There is a primitive innocence in which the brothers eat, work, fight and sleep together. When Donald tells his brother that he is homosexual, he talks in terms of sheep: 'I'm more interested in tups that yows just now, like.' In view of this, should the boys continue to share the same bed? This is just one of many decisions and adjustments that have to be made by all the family during the course of the play. As with the other plays in this volume, although the homosexual theme is present throughout, there is a larger theme of which is is a part. In the case of *Accounts,* this is survival, which has domestic, social and economic manifestations.

In addition to making four interesting plays widely available, I hope that this anthology will encourage writers who wish to portray homosexual characters to do so without any special pleading for the way they have been programmed sexually, and also to remember that in the theatre, as in everyday life, a person's sexual inclinations are only a part of a much greater complexity of character. In so many 'gay plays', you'd think that homosexuality was the only thing in the world that mattered. In a realistic scale of things, a person's sexuality is by no means the most important factor in his or her survival.

You may wonder why all the plays deal only with homosexuality in men and not in women. The fact is that of all the plays sent to me, whether by the publishers or as a result of articles about this anthology that appeared on a number of occasions in the gay press, not one play about homosexuality in women was submitted for consideration. If there is a worthwhile, durable play about gay women that hasn't been published, I should like to know about it.

Finally, I should like to have found some other title than *Gay Plays* to head this collection. 'Homosexual plays'? 'Plays with homosexual characters'? These looked clumsy to me. Then the publishers pointed out that many high street bookstores were unlikely to stock a book with 'homosexual' in the title, but 'gay' was acceptable! That settled it! If there is to be a second volume (and I already have two excellent plays from different playwrights ready for inclusion) this edition has got to sell. But the next time anyone complains about the misuse of that useful word 'gay', in addition to using the familiar arguments about the abuse by heterosexuals of the words 'queer' and 'bent', I shall also now point out that the great God Commerce demands that poor overworked, abused 'gay' must labour in the galleys for a few more years yet.

Michael Wilcox
December 1983

SUBMARINERS

Submariners was first presented at the Royal Court Theatre Upstairs on 11 September 1980, with the following cast:

CHAPLAIN	Donald McKillop
COCK	Philip Davis
HOUSEY	Andrew McCulloch
SPIDER	David Beames
SPLASH	George Sweeney

Directed by Antonia Bird
Designed by Mary Moore
Lighting by Gerry Jenkinson

Some words and phrases used in the play

forad, forward the front part of a ship
aft towards the stern of a ship
starboard the right-hand side of a ship
klaxon mechanical horn with a rasping sound
lanyard a cord for hanging a knife or whistle around the neck, but also a regular item of naval uniform
Asdic apparatus for detecting and locating a submarine or other underwater object by means of ultrasonic waves echoed back from the object
Number One suit best dress, going-ashore uniform
Number Eights working uniform (pale blue shirt and dark blue trousers)
NB. Naval uniforms are numbered: the higher the number, the less formal the uniform.

Submariners

In 1979 I was commissioned by CVI, a Coventry-based theatre group attached to the Belgrade and administrated by Caroline Hunt. After an initial meeting it was decided to concentrate on a low budget project with two acts and a cast of five.

At a later date I travelled to Coventry where I met Ron Hutchinson and was shown around the studio theatre. It struck me at the time as being long, dark and very claustrophobic. I made the profound remark, 'You could be in a submarine here'. (Although my time in the navy was spent on surface ships, I have on numerous occasions visited various 'boats', enough to realise where I was better off!) Ron got very enthusiastic and we sparked off on different comic and manic situations under the waves.

My original idea was that due to defence cuts the submarine never actually ventured on patrol but lurked just off the Scottish coast. After doing some research (drinking in Gosport pubs), I realised there were more exciting avenues to explore – with a nuclear reactor, it makes no difference if you steam fifty miles or around the world. I started off with two topical lower deck themes, claustrophobia and homosexuality, then encased both under a nuclear umbrella.

When the first draft was completed I was informed by CVI that although they liked the script they unfortunately could not mount a production for financial reasons.

The Royal Court was first to pick up on *Submariners* and after it had successfully negotiated their intricate system I had a discussion with Rob Ritchie, their literary director. He gave me sound constructive advice regarding changes for a Royal Court production. Hence, after numerous rewrites and meetings, Max Stafford-Clark introduced me to Antonia Bird as a possible director, and a schedule was planned.

The major problem that Mary Moore, the designer, had to overcome was how to build a set looking like the lounge of a public house yet also saying 'We are inside a Polaris submarine'. This she achieved excellently in the natural claustrophobic surroundings of the Theatre upstairs.

Thanks to Antonia's pacey direction the actors added their polish to the characters. A special thanks to Andrew Brown for his invaluable advice throughout.

Tom McClenaghan

ACT ONE

Scene One

HMS *Superior, a nuclear submarine, is
getting underway from Faslane to begin its
eight week patrol. It will remain
submerged throughout the trip. The Chiefs'
annexe is empty and untidy. On the left
are bunks in tiers of three and some metal
lockers. On the right is a recreation space.
This consists of a bar, table, chairs, built
in seats, more lockers, sink and typical
naval decoration, crests, etc. Empty
glasses and beer cans are scattered
around. Off centre is a large steel door
which is locked by clips. On the bulkhead
are two tannoys, one is square with a grill
– this is the entertainments tannoy which
can be switched off; the second, shaped
like a megaphone, is operated by the
control room.*

Opening Tannoy in darkness:

TANNOY: Now hear there. Ship to shore
telephones are now being disconnected:
the gangways will be removed in three
minutes' time as sea checks are now
being carried out. Stand by to test
reactor shut down. Officers and their
ladies kindly leave by the forad
gangway, ratings and their wives by the
aft.

Lights up and banging on the door.

COCK (*off*): Knock, knock.

Pause.

Who's there?

Cock?

Cock who?

Cock Roach.

*The door swings open and in he comes,
da dumming a fanfare with a hoover.
Disappointed!*

Nobody at home?

*He is about eighteen years old and
dressed in Number Eights. He half
closes the door and when he sees he's
alone checks the left-overs. He picks up
a half filled beer glass and takes an
appreciative drink. He moves a chair
towards another, spies a glass of
spirits. He takes a sip, savours it and
spits it out. He picks up another one,*

sniffs it and, happy, sees it off. He leafs
through a pile of magazines and selects
a girlie one. He goes to the chair, sits,
and puts his feet up on the other. He
opens the magazine, takes a pull from
the beer glass. He settles into leafing
through the magazine. Suddenly the
bosun's pipe comes over the tannoy. It
is ear splitting and COCK reacts to it.*

TANNOY: Hands fall in for leaving
harbour.

COCK (*jumps up and launches into a
song and dance act*):
Wish me luck as you wave me goodbye,
Cheerio here I go on my way.
Give me a smile I can keep all the while
In my heart and never stray.

*He flops down again and resumes
flicking through the magazine.*

TANNOY: Casing party close up. Assume
NBCD state three condition zulu alpha.
Close all red openings.

COCK (*to the* TANNOY): Hey, keep it
clean.

TANNOY: Shut all watertight doors.
Assume ventilation state three.

*COCK dives at the door through which
he has entered and throws his body
against it and makes a great thing of
securing the clips. Then he turns and
leans his back against the door,
panting.*

COCK: Made it, sir. We may be trapped
down here, but at least we're dry. And
while there's air there's life. (*Mimics
officer.*) Well done, AB Roach. You've
saved us all again. There's a medal in
this for you. (COCK's *own voice.*) Can
I have a tot instead, sir, before it's
locked up? (*Mimics.*) Help yourself, lad.
You've earned it. (COCK.) Thank you
sir.

*He dashes behind the bar and pours
himself a double rum. He makes a
toast.*

HMS *Superior.* The world's first
nuclear prison. God bless her and all
who sail in her.

He knocks back the rum.

TANNOY: Casing party remove gangway.

COCK: Aye, aye, sir.

TANNOY: Special sea duty men to your
stations.

COCK: Aye, aye, sir.

TANNOY: Panel parties man your panels.

COCK: Aye, aye, sir. And cleaners man your Hoovers.

TANNOY: Cast off the forward head rope.

COCK (*marching around the mess, sings*):
Goodbyee, goodbyee, never fear wipe the tear from your eyee.
Though it's sad to part I know
I'll be tickled to death to gooo.
Don't cryee, don't cryee . . .

TANNOY: Let go aft. Slow ahead both engines.

Gradually the sound of the engines increases. COCK *slumps into a chair. He looks around the mess and yells in frustration and real anger.*

COCK: Eight weeks of this. I'll go mad.

TANNOY: Attention to starboard.

COCK *jumps to attention and salutes to starboard.*

Flag Officer Submarines. (*The bosun's pipe sounds.*) Carry on.

COCK: Will do, sir. (*He goes back to cleaning.*)

TANNOY: Attention all officers and ratings.

COCK (*leaps to attention*): What is it now, sir?

TANNOY: A silver identity bracelet has been handed into the Regulating Office. It can be claimed when hands fall out.

COCK: If it's an identity bracelet, how is it you don't know who it belongs to?

COCK *plugs in the Hoover and begins vacuuming. Another ear piercer from the bosun's whistle comes over the tannoy.*

You're pushing your luck, chum.

TANNOY: The Captain will now address the ship's company

COCK: Oh, the Captain.

COCK, *with mock enthusiasm, pulls up a chair in front of the tannoy. He sits with arms folded and looks at it expectantly.*

CAPTAIN (*voice over*): As we are proceeding down the loch, I feel it is as good a time as any to have a few words

with you all. To the ratings new to *Superior* I'd like to say, 'Welcome aboard' and that goes for all the old hands as well.

COCK: Thank you, sir.

CAPTAIN (*voice over*): And as those who have sailed with me before already know, any problems, worries, questions of any kind, I hope you'll come to me, and I want to assure you I'll help in any way I can. If there is anything you want to know, just ask.

COCK (*shoots his hand up like an excited schoolboy*): Sir, sir. Where do you dump the gash on a submarine?

CAPTAIN (*voice over*): . . . with me in my cabin. (*He pauses to clear his throat.*) I have the coveted Polaris Trophy, which was awarded to *Superior* for accurate firings during work-up. To achieve this we had team work, dedication and a devotion to duty. I expect the same during this patrol. I have our sealed orders which no doubt will be routine. But bearing in mind the present political tension we must be prepared for anything.

COCK: Like good Boy Scouts.
(*He salutes.*)

CAPTAIN (*voice over*): Therefore I expect that little bit extra from everyone on board. Be alert and on the ball.

COCK *suddenly comes to and dashes around at high speed with the Hoover.*

COCK: Very good, sir.

CAPTAIN (*voice over*): We're a professional team on *Superior*.

COCK: You said it, sir.

CAPTAIN (*voice over*): Now I'd like to introduce you to the Royal Naval Chaplain for Faslane*, the Reverend Ian Butler who besides looking after the spiritual welfare of those on board has also volunteered to be entertainments officer. It is the chaplain's first time in a submarine and I'm sure you'll all join me in welcoming him aboard.

---

*The Chaplain's 'parish' would be made up of all the submarines in the Faslane area as well as the shore base. He has just recently taken up the appointment and has chosen *Superior* to familiarise himself with his 'flock'.

A bit of a splutter as the CHAPLAIN *takes over.*

CHAPLAIN (*voice over*): Thank you, Captain. Captain Ackery told me that we will dive to a depth of 800 feet if the need arises. If hell is down below that's as close as I want to get to it. (COCK *groans.*) Perhaps I should have joined the Air Force. (*A few chuckles in the background.*) Seriously though, I feel honoured to be on board and I look forward to playing my part.

COCK: Yeah, shark bait.

CHAPLAIN (*voice over*): I've just about everything you can think of to help pass the time. Twenty-eight new films. Westerns, horrors, comedies, everything but *Emanuelle Goes to Sea*.

COCK: Everything, I hope, but *Morning Departure*.

COCK *goes to a mirror and takes a lipstick from his pocket. Maybe it's best if we don't see what he is doing. The mirror is small and all the audience should see is the back of his head.*

CHAPLAIN (*voice over*): If that isn't enough there are games, competitions and quizzes. Tombola, bridge, backgammon. Then there are classes. Surprise your wife or girlfriend by learning how to cook, learning how to say it in French, knitting her a bikini. Keeping in trim for your next leave. Get a suntan. Could you win the sponsored slim?

COCK: Sponsored Swim.

COCK *puts the lipstick away and takes out an eyebrow pencil.*

CHAPLAIN (*voice over*): . . . Read away the time, there are hundreds of paperbacks in the library. Grow the best beard, don't forget there are prizes. Work up an act for the Sod's Opera. There are crates of beer for the most original, and for the most entertaining.

COCK *finishes with the pencil and takes out mascara.*

Who will be the darts champ?

COCK: Me.

CHAPLAIN (*voice over*): Which mess will win the Brains of the Boat award?

COCK: Mine!

CHAPLAIN (*voice over*): Who will guess the boat's mileage?

COCK: Me!

CHAPLAIN (*voice over*): Think of the next eight weeks as a magical mystery tour.

COCK: You said it, sweetheart.

Music: 'That's Entertainment'. COCK *turns. The sight is astonishing for he has done an expert job. He goes into a routine to the music. All very clownish, but not at all draggy or camp.*

He sings: The clown with his pants falling down, etc.

He switches off the tannoy still singing: That's bloody awful!

He doesn't notice the door behind him opening. One of the clips has been opened when he turns mid-dance to see the other being moved. COCK *dashes to the door and begins closing the clip that has been opened. It continues as one is opened from the outside, another is closed from the inside.*

SPIDER (*off*): What the fuck's going on?

COCK: You can't come in.

SPIDER (*off*): Stop pissing about. Open up.

COCK: Are you sure you're ready for it?

SPIDER (*off*): Stop fucking about or I'll start.

COCK: Now you're talking.

The door opens. SPIDER WEBB *enters.* COCK *has his back turned.* SPIDER *shoots him a look and goes to his locker.*

SPIDER: Dozy pillock.

He turns to COCK *and just stands there, amazed.*

COCK: Well?

SPIDER: Bugger me.

COCK: No. The idea is for you to bugger me.

SPIDER: Look Roach –

COCK: I'm Cock to my friends, Spider.

SPIDER: Chief to you, Chief Petty Officer Webb. Got it.

COCK *nods in mock humility.*

SPIDER: What's on your face, Roach?

COCK: It's called 'Water Babies'.

SPIDER: Fuckin' stroll on. Get it off.

COCK: But it's by Mary Quant.

SPIDER: You can't ponce about like that.

COCK: Why not?

SPIDER: You can't.

COCK: There's no regulations about it.

SPIDER: There's got to be. Nothing has been overlooked.

COCK: Make-up has. I checked.

SPIDER (*not taking him seriously*): You'll give everyone the wrong impression.

COCK: Or the right one.

SPIDER: What are you trying to tell me?

COCK: Isn't it obvious?

SPIDER: But you're in the bloody navy, on a bloody patrol of eight weeks with a hundred odd sailors.

COCK: One hundred and thirty. Plus thirteen officers and I'm not superstitious.

SPIDER: They'll lock you up.

COCK: There's nowhere. Anyway what harm is there in lending a little colour.

SPIDER: What are you up to?

COCK: I've come out of the closet.

SPIDER: Well I'd get back into it. And fast.

COCK: This is the nineteen eighties, Spider.

SPIDER: Chief to you, Able Seaman Roach. What's the nineteen eighties got to do with it?

COCK: Liberation. I'm glad to be gay.

SPIDER: You won't be when the old man hears about it.

COCK: Are you going to tell him?

SPIDER: I don't have to, Roach.

COCK: Cock.

SPIDER: 'Cause you're making it obvious, without any help from me. You only need to step outside that door looking the way you do and the old man will know before your feet touch the deck. So wash the lot off your face, that's an order. I don't want to be seen alone with you.

COCK: Why not?

SPIDER: Because you get up my nose.

COCK: That's not the real reason.

SPIDER: It's the only reason. Now get that off, then get this mess squared off.

COCK: No.

SPIDER: 'Roach'.

COCK: Let them put two and two together. After a few weeks at sea half of them will be green with envy. I don't care, why should you?

SPIDER: I wouldn't touch you if I was wearing rubber gloves.

COCK: Good I'm not into rubber either.

SPIDER: Do you want the shit knocked out of you?

COCK: Do whatever you fancy?

SPIDER: I fancy my missus.

COCK: On board is she?

SPIDER: No way are you a substitute.

COCK: The real thing never is, Spider.

SPIDER: Chief.

COCK: Spider.

SPIDER: Chief.

COCK: All right, sweetheart. Chief.

SPIDER: You'd get a thick lip if I didn't think this was a joke.

COCK: What makes you think it's a joke?

SPIDER: Poofs don't join the navy, they just follow it.

COCK: There's nothing like being on the inside.

SPIDER: Is that why you joined up?

COCK: Exactly.

SPIDER: Why are you telling me all this?

COCK: Because out of all the crew you are the one.

SPIDER *laughs uproariously.*

I got to know you on the last patrol. I'd watch you coming in from the engine room, covered in perspiration and grease. Your overalls unzipped to your naval. You made me so nervous that I dropped over a dozen plates. Even the galley boy can have dreams. Then came my lucky break. A job change. It was a miracle. Me in here looking after you. Airing your sleeping bag. (*Gives a little orgasmic shake.*) Doing all those little things that mean a lot.

SPIDER (*smiling*): You dirty little brown hatter.

COCK: I hope in time you'll come to love me.

SPIDER: You're raving nosh.

COCK: That's right. Then what are you going to do about it? Slap in a complaint?

SPIDER: I should.

COCK: Well?

SPIDER: I don't want to see anyone at your age kicked outside.

COCK (*begins to sing, very torchy*): You always hurt the one you love.

SPIDER: Jeesus. Two months of this.

COCK: It's not too late. We haven't dived yet. A quick complaint and I'd be ashore tonight. (*He sings.*) I let my heart fall into careless hands. Careless hands.

SPIDER: You'd like that, wouldn't you? You cocky little . . . I'm beginning to sus you out. You don't want to do the patrol.

COCK: How do you know?

SPIDER: Because I don't want to either and that's why I can see through you.

COCK: Why don't you do something about it?

SPIDER: None of us like it, Roach.

COCK: No, none of us like it. How many draft requests have you had turned down?

SPIDER: Keep your shunk out.

COCK: Two isn't it. (*He indicates the make-up.*) Put some of that on and we could go to the Mother Superior as a double act. That would crack it.

SPIDER: I just want to get out of Faslane, not out of the navy.

COCK (*dead serious*): That's the difference. I want to get out.

SPIDER: Then buy yourself out.

COCK: That's not my style. The challenge. It's all a game on here. I'm bored with playing theirs, they're going to have to play mine.

TANNOY: Clear the casings, clear the casings. Hands to diving stations.

SPIDER: That's me. And your chance. It looks like you've blown it.

He locks up the bar.

COCK: No way. This will keep me sane and scheming for the next eight weeks. I'm going to plan every detail. You won't give the game away, chief?

SPIDER: No. Half your nerve.

He's about to go.

COCK: Just a minute, Spider. Why don't you join in?

SPIDER: You mad? What could I do?

COCK: Spread it around that I've turned. I'll break down and confess.

SPIDER: Who to? Your DO?

COCK: He'll never swallow it. But there's someone new on board who will.

SPIDER: Who?

COCK: The chaplain.

SPIDER: He sounds like a right wanker.

COCK: Exactly. The modern navy. This is a fucking nuclear boat and it's full of planks like that. Here we are, Spider, waiting to start the ultimate holocaust. Us. We're the finger on the trigger for oblivion.

SPIDER: Because we're the finger on the trigger it'll never start.

COCK: That's the propaganda. We've got to have it so it won't happen. Alice in submarine land, Spider. A war-mongering paradox.

SPIDER: Get off the soap box, Cock. I'm not interested in Polaris, Cruise, Trident or any other stupid missile. I'm doing a job. (*He points at the tannoy.*) And they pay me.

TANNOY: Chief PO Webb close up at the rush.

SPIDER: Bloody Ada, gotta blow.

COCK: So you'll help me? It'll break the monotony.

SPIDER: What's in it for me?

COCK: You want to get off boats. If you're serious, I'll help.

SPIDER: How?

COCK: Leave it to me.

SPIDER: No brown hatter stuff?

COCK: Sure. I'll think of something, and it'll be diabolically clever. So is it a deal?

SPIDER: I'll think about it. You really had me worried for a while.

He goes. COCK *stands smiling.*

TANNOY: Dive, dive, dive, shut the lower lid, open main vents, take her down to sixty feet, up periscope.

The klaxon sounds twice.

COCK (*begins to sing as he mops up. He alters the words to 'Yellow Submarine'*):
We all live in a nuclear submarine,
a polaris submarine,
an unclean machine.
One thing for sure;
I'm going to blow the scene
going to blow the scene,
going to blow the scene.

Scene Two

It's a week later. After eight o'clock in the evening. Three of the chiefs are in the mess. SPIDER WEBB, SPLASH BRADY *and* HOUSEY HOUSEMAN. *Tombola is being played over the tannoy.*

TANNOY (*in darkness –* CHAPLAIN's *voice*): Now to continue the house. Eyes down and look in.

The sound of numbers being shaken.

On its own, number two, unlucky for some thirteen. Sixty-six clickety click. Four and five half way, one and seven old Ireland.

Lights up.

SPIDER *is filling in his own ticket as well as* SPLASH's, *who is the keep fit freak on the mess. Physically he's in great shape. You can see because he's wearing only a singlet and shorts and classy running shoes. He skips all the while counting each turn. He's well into the seven hundreds when the scene*

begins. HOUSEY HOUSEMAN *has text books open in front of him but he is more interested in his tombola ticket.*

All the eights . . .

SPIDER: Bishop's bollocks –

TANNOY: Eight-eight. All the fours.

SPIDER: Pompey whores.

HOUSEY: Dirty drawers.

TANNOY: Fourty-four. Number Ten.

SPIDER: } Maggie's den.
TANNOY: }

TANNOY: Legs eleven.

Everyone wolf whistles.

TANNOY: Let's have a little shake then.

SPLASH *skips over to* SPIDER.

SPLASH (*still skipping*): Am I sweating yet?

SPIDER: Yeah, all over me.

SPLASH (*skipping away*): Remember fifty-fifty if I win. Seven hundred and sixty, sixty-one, sixty-two, sixty-three . . .

TANNOY: Eyes down again my lucky lads, it's the biggy night. The house stands at twenty pounds. Someone somewhere must be close to winning.

HOUSEY: Yeah, I am. So get on with it.

TANNOY: All the twos.

TANNOY (*with everyone in unison*): Two little ducks. Two and six. Half a crown.

MESS (*in unison*): Was she worth it?

TANNOY: Nine 0.

ALL IN UNISON: As far as we go.

HOUSEY: Just one to go. Come on seven.

TANNOY: On it's own. Number three.

HOUSEY *throws his pencil down in disgust.* SPIDER *exchanges a glance with* SPLASH.

SPLASH: Eight hundred, and one and two and three.

HOUSEY: Shut up Splash, I'm trying to get the bloody numbers.

TANNOY: All the fives.

TANNOY: } Beehives.
SPIDER: }

TANNOY: House has been called, on

number three.

HOUSEY: Bloody hell. I was one number away.

TANNOY: A short break while we check the ticket.

HOUSEY: One miserable bloody number.

SPIDER: Not good enough, Housey.

HOUSEY: Cut your cackle as well.

SPIDER: What are you so steamed up about?

HOUSEY: And that everlasting fucking skipping.

SPLASH: I'll stop when I get to a thousand.

HOUSEY: Then what'll you start?

SPLASH: On your face if you keep manking.

SPIDER: What's the matter? Can't you crack the angle of the dangle? Don't worry. Cock'll have the answers.

SPLASH: Yeah. (*In a sing-song voice.*) One and one are two-oo. Two and two are four-or. Three and three are six-x. Shit I've lost count. So I'll start again, there's all the time in the world.

HOUSEY: Aren't you fit enough yet? Are you going to keep on exercising for the next seven weeks?

SPLASH: I've got to keep my heart rate up.

HOUSEY: Why don't you settle on keeping it normal then maybe we can have some peace.

SPLASH (*starts skipping*): I'll skip quietly, OK? You're as bad as my missus always dripping.

HOUSEY: It's not only the counting, it's the draught you make.

SPLASH: Think of it as a sea breeze.

TANNOY: The house has been won by MEM Porter from the After mess.

HOUSEY: I know that jammy little get.

TANNOY: Tomorrow night's house will be a double. I hope you'll all join in the fun. Now in ten minutes we'll be showing tonight's film in the dining-hall. Clint Eastwood stars in *Every Which Way But Loose*. So if you're off watch come along and enjoy the show.

SPLASH: I saw that. It's shit hot.

HOUSEY: Why don't you see it again?

SPLASH: I've got to keep to my schedule. Tear yourself away from your maths and you go, Housey.

HOUSEY: Don't think I wouldn't like to.

SPLASH *does some more exercises.*

SPLASH: Shh . . . Shh . . . Shh . . .

HOUSEY: This is a Lunatic Asylum.

SPIDER: Not like home?

SPLASH: Thank God. I'd be at a dinner-dance in some poncy Scottish country club.

SPIDER: Like the old quick quick slow, does she?

SPLASH (*nods*): The Bossa Nova washed down with sweet Martini is the missus' idea of heaven. A rumba or two to shake down the prawn cocktail and chicken in the basket. Give me hard naval tack any day. (*He throws a few furious punches.*) Makes you fit and strong.

SPIDER: What would you be up to this evening, Housey?

HOUSEY: Pottering about the garden maybe.

SPLASH: In mid-winter? In Faslane?

HOUSEY: There's always something . . .

SPLASH: You'd be doing what you're doing now if I know your wife.

HOUSEY: But you don't.

SPLASH: I've seen enough to know who wears the trousers. Don't kid yourself, Housey. You'd be studying and I'd be at a fucking dinner-dance.

SPIDER: . . . and I'd have my feet up in front of the TV with a jug of home brew getting nicely legless.

SPLASH: What would your old lady be doing, getting dolled up for a heavy night?

SPIDER: No Splash, she'd be on the phone to her mother in Gosport complaining about Faslane, know what I mean?

SPLASH: That's life in a Blue Suit on Polaris.

The door swings open. There is a pause and COCK steps in. He is balancing a

tray high up on one hand, and makes the grand entrance once more. They all react as if his behaviour is typical. He is wearing bell bottoms and a T-shirt. On the front is printed:
'SUBMARINERS DO IT DEEPER'.
There is no response so –

COCK (*sings*): From the moment I stepped into the mess, I could tell you were chiefs of distinction. Real big spenders. (*He grabs* SPIDER's *tombola ticket and throws it into the air.*) Good lookin' (*Tweaks* SPIDER's *cheek.*) and so refined. (*Shimmies past* HOUSEY *and puts down the tray and jumps in and skips with* SPLASH.) So how about telling me what's going on in your mind? (*He jumps out from the skipping rope.*) Tea for three? (*He takes a teapot and spoons in tea and goes to the jackson boiler and fills it.*) I've got a special treat tonight boys. There I was lined up for the spam sarnies when the chef momentarily turned his back, with a sleight of hand, read officers' ham for chiefs' spam. (*He sings.*) What I did for love, what I did for love.

SPIDER: Well done, Cock.

COCK: I'd eat them quick before the search party gets here. Come on muscles. Feed your brain Housey. I want my student to pass with honours.

HOUSEY: Just a pass will do.

COCK (*makes a grab at* HOUSEY): Do you mean this sort of pass? (HOUSEY *treats it as a joke.*) You'll pass Housey, no sweat. Do you all know that up there you can see the milky way. It's a hot, balmy, sensual, Caribbean night. The steel drums are beating, with an urgency (COCK *does a bit of reggae*) the rum punches are cool and intoxicating, out of the darkness comes a dusky maiden, the only thing she wears is a hibiscus behind her ear. The sweat glistens on her heaving breasts. She runs her tongue around her panting mouth and says (*like a parrot*) Hello sailor, new in town?

They all groan.

SPIDER: You've been peeking through the periscope.

COCK: It's my vivid imagination. Now how are you doing with your test paper, Housey?

HOUSEY: I'm stuck and it's cracking me.

SPLASH: He can't concentrate. There are too many distractions.

HOUSEY: Like skipping, weight lifting, press-ups, push-ups, sit-ups, pull-ups.

SPIDER: Throw-ups.

COCK: But won't we be proud of him when Muscles here wins the Inter-Services Boxing Championship? I'm going to be proud of you all. One an officer, one a boxer and what can I do for you, Spider? I think I know, and it'll be our secret.

HOUSEY (*registers this*): Cut the skylarking. Finish your work then you can help me.

COCK goes to him and looks over his shoulder.

COCK: It's basic.

HOUSEY: It may be to you. But I left school a long time ago.

COCK: You've got the brackets in the wrong place. It's a simultaneous equation. Multiply by four there. Then multiply this one by two and there's your answer. No problem.

HOUSEY: But . . .

COCK: No buts. If you want to be an officer, chief, you've got to master the basics. Like I'm doing. Not that I want to be an officer.

HOUSEY: What do you want to be?

COCK: In charge . . . of the world.

HOUSEY: Beats me why you joined up.

COCK: Ever lived in Bedford?

SPLASH: I got my leg over there once.

COCK: In Bedford, are you sure?

SPLASH: Yeah.

COCK: And it hasn't dropped off.

SPLASH (*stops skipping, feels around for it*): Where is it? Wait a minute, that's my meat but where are the potatoes?

SPLASH goes to his locker. He wraps a towel around himself. He ticks off a list stuck on his locker door. He checks his pulse.

SPLASH: Good recovery. (*He checks the schedule.*) I'm getting too fit. (*He fills in.*) 100 press-ups, 200 abdoms, 50 birpees and another 50 for luck. Three sets of chin-ups and fifteen minutes skipping. Boy am I in good shape!

He comes out shadow-boxing and is ignored

COCK: Here drink your steroids. (*He hands him a cup of tea.*)

SPLASH: Thanks kid.

HOUSEY: God I wish I could fathom this out. Listen – (*He reads.*) Four grey socks and two blue socks are kept in a drawer. If two socks are taken out at random in succession and without replacement, find the probability that (a) the first sock is grey (b) both socks are grey and (c) both socks are the same colour.

SPLASH: On here after a few weeks they'd all be grey.

COCK: I told you, it's easy. With probabilities you use a tree diagram, Housey.

HOUSEY: It's hopeless. One lousey GCE.

COCK: If I could give you one of my seven, I would. You should've picked something easier than maths.

HOUSEY: I've got all the easy ones.

SPIDER: When's the exam?

HOUSEY: The week after we return.

SPIDER: So you've got seven weeks to boff up.

TANNOY: Nine o'clockers are now being issued in the galley.

Housey walks across and shuts off the tannoy muzak.

HOUSEY: How can you concentrate on anything down here?

SPIDER: So what's so important about being an officer?

HOUSEY: Ask my wife.

COCK: A dragon is she?

HOUSEY *nods.*

So is my mother. I'm glad to say it broke her heart when I ran away to sea. I was only following in my father's footsteps.

SPIDER: Was he a matelot as well?

COCK: I don't know. He just ran away. So the missus wants you to be an officer?

Bit late in the day isn't it?

HOUSEY: Next year it will be. That's why this exam is so important.

COCK: Too old at thirty-four. (HOUSEY *nods.*) And once you've made it, all your problems will be solved?

HOUSEY: The marital ones.

COCK: You should've tried before.

HOUSEY: I have. So this is make or break.

COCK: You're worrying about it too much, chief. Every time you get bogged down give me a yell. You'll find me scrubbing somewhere.

HOUSEY: I'll take you up on that, Cock.

COCK: It'll cost you.

HOUSEY: What?

COCK: You can be part of my act for the Sod's Opera. Look, I've got him smiling already.

TANNOY: Tonight's movie is about to start.

COCK: Why don't you go to the movies? Relax and enjoy yourself. While you're at it take Splash.

SPLASH: No, I'm off for a bath and dhobi.

COCK: There's someone in it who looks like you.

SPLASH: Yes, Clint Eastwood.

COCK: No, the Orang-Outang.

SPLASH (*flicks his towel at him*): Cheeky sod. Remember your place as the lowest form of life down here and don't throw that tea away. I'll be back.

SPLASH *leaves.*

HOUSEY: Are you coming to the movies, Spider?

SPIDER: No, I'll give it a miss. I want to get my head down before the middle watch.

HOUSEY *leaves.*

COCK *collects up the mugs and teapot and begins singing.*

COCK: Chiefly put me day work, you have my tot. Chiefly put me day work, you can drink the fuckin' lot.

SPIDER: For someone who hates the navy

you seem pretty cheerful to me.

COCK: It's all an act.

SPIDER: That's the trouble with you, I never know when to take you seriously.

COCK: Keep 'em guessing.

TANNOY: Bible classes are now being held in the wardroom.

COCK: But nothin's changed. The day we get alongside I'm going to walk away from this boat and the navy.

SPIDER: Was all that true about running away to sea?

COCK: Maybe. Now I want to start running again.

SPIDER: Why? The navy's a cushy number. Look at the unemployment outside.

COCK: I'll tell you a little story, Spider. I did my basic training at Raleigh and out of forty in my class there was only one other OD as bright as me. We became good oppos. It was us against all those morons. It was a push-over and we enjoyed it. I went to Pompey and did a sonar operator's course which exercised the grey cells for the first time, and my mate Ginger wangled a transfer to the marines. He did all the courses, unarmed combat, diving, became a top sniper, sailed through the exams and do you know where that led to?

SPIDER: Northern Ireland?

COCK: No, being a cleaner to a Rear Admiral. There was Ginger, a trained killer, vacuuming, dusting, running errands, picking up the kids after school and baby-sitting for them at night and he was stuck with it. He couldn't get drafted, so out of desperation he went on the trot. Five days later they picked him up. It took two shore patrols to put him in the meat waggon. He was court-martialled and got ninety days in Pompey DQ's. That was a lesson to me. So it's different tactics. The navy's going to have to dump me.

SPIDER: Wait until you get back to your proper job on the sonar, or slap in for a job change.

COCK (waves his finger at the tannoy): They'd like that. (He mimics an upper class voice.) Had enough, eh, Roach, learnt the hard way eh?

Yes, sir, I'm sorry, sir, I'll never speak out of turn again. (He turns to SPIDER.) No way am I going to toe the line.

SPIDER: You're too impatient, Cock.

COCK: Youth always is.

SPIDER: You've got an answer for everything.

COCK: I've got an answer for you if you want to get off boats.

SPIDER: As long as it doesn't land me in Pompey DQ's.

COCK: No. It's going to be sympathy all the way, Spider. It's called claustrophobia.

SPIDER: Come off it.

COCK: It's perfect. Act a nuke spook.

SPIDER: I don't want that on my docs.

COCK: Why not?

SPIDER: It'd be a black mark.

COCK: Hell it will. It'll just mean you won't get submarines. They'll feel sorry for you, Spider. You won't be blamed for anything.

SPIDER: But I'll have to go in front of a medical board.

COCK: So. The symptoms are all in your head, and you only get them when you're down here. You can still be the thrusting young CPO, but up there (he indicates) in the sunshine after this patrol.

SPIDER: I'd get drafted back to Pompey.

COCK: There you are. A couple of years ashore then a nice little frigate that potters around the south coast.

SPIDER: She would love that, back down amongst her friends. She's really threadbare being stuck up in Haggis land.

COCK: She's right you know, Spider. There's nothing there but fucking heather. And the Scots, they're another race, know what I mean?

SPIDER (nods): You want to hear her go on about them.

COCK: So find someone to pick on. But not me, OK? Some little steamie in the engine room. Give him a hard time. You're never going to keep still. This mess will be like a cage, and you're going to pace around. After you've pulled that off we might stage something a little more spectacular. A blackout at the right psychological moment.

SPIDER: I couldn't handle that.

COCK: Yes you could, it's the only answer.

SPIDER: It's over the top.

COCK: It has to be.

SPIDER: They'll never believe me.

COCK: Yes they will. In a situation like this you get the benefit of the doubt.

SPIDER: What about my future?

COCK: Isn't that what we're sorting out? How much do you know about boats?

SPIDER: Too much. This is my fourth patrol.

COCK: But psychologically, how much do you know?

SPIDER *shrugs.*

SPIDER: How much does anyone know?

COCK: Exactly, and they won't tell us what they do know. I know this much. We're all guinea pigs when we are at this depth. And here we are, no day, no night, breathing recycled air for eight weeks and it's causing havoc to our metabolism.

SPIDER: How do you know?

COCK: I can read and I can see, Spider. And most of all I can think. I know there's a great veil of secrecy over nukes. They call it security. Well that's their story. In fact it covers a hell of a lot of ignorance. Who knows what the long term effects are. Leukaemia, brain damage, sterility, impotency.

SPIDER: No.

COCK: It's all well within the realms of possibility and we're the victims.

SPIDER: You're imagining all that.

COCK (*dead serious*): If that's what you think maybe there's a bit of brain damage already.

SPIDER: Why are you doing this, Cock?

COCK: We're helping each other.

SPIDER: No. It's more than that, sure you're not using me?

COCK *realises he is almost correct.*

COCK: I'm not using you, I'm helping you.

SPIDER: No shit?

COCK: No shit. You have nothing to lose.

SPIDER: OK. When do we start?

COCK: We've started. The next thing is to find your victim, persecute him till he cracks, and slaps in a drip chit. Then you spread the word about me.

SPIDER: But why pretend you're a brown hatter?

COCK: It's the one thing the navy could never come to terms with.

SPIDER: But you're not, Cock.

COCK: You spread the word. The navy'll do the rest. (*He begins to sing as he cleans up.*)

SPLASH *enters.*

When this lousy trip is over,
No more submarines for me.
When I get my civvy clothes on,
Oh how happy I shall be
No more cleaning heads on Sundays,
No more stoppage of my pay.
I shall kiss this boat goodbye
How I'll miss it how I'll grieve.

SPLASH: And very nice too, Cock.

COCK: Thanks, Muscles. (*He gives him a wink.*) We're going to work up an act together for the Sod's Opera.

SPLASH: But I can't sing.

COCK: You don't have to, Splash. With me on stage everyone else is going to fade in to the background. Remember there's only room for one star in this dressing-room. And it's me. Right, Spider?

SPIDER: Too right, Cock.

COCK: Too right indeed. Keep the middle watch steady. OK boys. See you in eight hours.

He goes out with the tray.

SPLASH *plugs in his suntan lamp and begins to get under it. He dons his sunglasses.*

SPLASH: Cheerful little sod, isn't he?

SPIDER: Sod's the word.

SPLASH: What do you mean?

SPIDER: Cock's raving.

SPLASH: How do you know?

SPIDER: He propositioned me.

SPLASH: You're having me on.

SPIDER: Straight up.

SPLASH: I don't believe it.

SPIDER: I'm telling you, Splash.

SPLASH: Little Cock Roach, eh?

He smiles to himself. He puts on the sunglasses and lies under the lamp.

SPIDER (*checks him briefly and paces the mess*): This mess is like a bloody cage.

SPLASH *doesn't react.* SPIDER *goes to the bulkhead and smashes his fist against it.*

A fucking cage.

Scene Three

It's the third week.

When the lights come up the occupants of the mess are lined up behind SPLASH. In fact, it is the rehearsal for COCK ROACH's number for the Sod's Opera and is his version of the Judy Garland number that ends the film 'Summer Stock'. At first COCK is not seen for he is behind the line of chiefs. They are all dressed in normal working attire, except COCK.

COCK: OK. Once more from the top. Try and get it right, Housey, or there'll be no help with the homework. One . . . two . . . hit it, Splash.

COCK *beings a rhythmic clicking of his fingers.* SPLASH *moves to one side, leans out and freezes. Then HOUSEY moves in the opposite direction and tries to hold a similar pose.*

Freeze, Housey.

SPIDER *then moves and reveals COCK wearing a black fedora and still clicking. He is wearing a chief's jacket stuffed with two tennis balls, blue shorts, fishnet stockings and black high-heels. He moves down-stage*

stepping nimbly through his chorus, and singing.

Come on along everyone, get happy
blow all your cares away.
Come on along everyone get happy
get ready for the judgement day.

For fuck's sake. Spider, that's when you're supposed to move.

SPIDER: Where?

COCK: Up stage. Out of my way.

SPIDER (*does so*): Here do?

COCK: Yeah, and freeze.

When he does so, COCK *resumes clicking and, after a few beats, singing.*

The sun is shining, come on get happy
Let me take you by the hand.

Pause.

Well take it, Splash.

SPLASH *does so.*

I said take it, not break it.

COCK *does a twirl and bends backwards over* SPLASH's *arm, and kicks one leg in the air.*

Come on along everyone get happy
Get ready for the Promised Land.

(*He counts to himself.*) One, two, three. (*Then straightens up.*) Now this is where you all fall down.

They fall to their knees and bend backwards with their arms outstretched.

Tremble them, Housey.

HOUSEY: I am trembling them.

COCK: No you're not. You're waving them about.

SPIDER *is hamming it up.*

Stop hamming Spider. I'm the star of the show. You're just the star fucker. (*He gives a conspiratorial wink.*) Ready boys?

HOUSEY: Get on with it.

COCK: Start trembling and I will.

They do so. COCK *begins an elaborate cake walk, hands up and down as he steps over the others and sings.*

We're goin' cross the river, up the river, dum de dum
It's going to be peaceful on the other side.

Are you all ready?

HOUSEY:
SPIDER: } Ready.

COCK: And this time don't drop me, Housey.

(*He begins clicking, then:*) So. (*He dives forward and lands on the joined arms of* HOUSEY *and* SPIDER.) Good. Now bounce me.

They do so, and he is caught by SPLASH *and lifted high in the air.*

Mind the tennis balls, Splash. Slowly.

SPLASH *lets him down slowly.* COCK *sings.*

Come along everyone get happy
Throw all your cares away.

SPIDER *and* HOUSEY *pick him up by his arms and carry him across the mess and sit him on the bar.* COCK *goes into the finale.*

Come along everyone get happy
Get ready for the judgement day.

COCK *sits there with his legs crossed and his hands up in the air, while the three chiefs go down on one knee at his feet.*

Didn't I ask someone to wipe this bar dry?

HOUSEY: I thought that was your job.

COCK: Getting this act together is my job. Well not bad. Another week –

HOUSEY: You're kidding –

COCK: – of hard work and we could just about be ready.

HOUSEY: We're making total fools of ourselves.

SPLASH: Isn't that the general idea in a Sod's Opera?

TANNOY: Through lack of interest Bible classes tonight are cancelled.

COCK: Let the others make fools of themselves. We're going to be a sensation, what with the costumes, lights, make-up.

HOUSEY: That's where I'm drawing the line.

COCK: Make-up.

SPLASH: Forget it.

COCK: Dissension in the ranks.

SPIDER: You wear the make-up.

SPLASH: I don't think they sell it on board, Cock.

HOUSEY: They don't need to, Cock's thought of that.

COCK: Right on, Housey.

HOUSEY: No make-up, OK?

COCK: Aren't I winning you a crate of beer?

HOUSEY: They'll take one look at us and it'll be Babycham. Why don't I operate the lights? You can get by with Splash and Spider.

COCK: Now it's shirker in the ranks. I don't know if I will have time for that maths tutorial tonight, Housey.

HOUSEY: Don't joke about it.

COCK: I'm not.

SPIDER: Come on, Housey, you'll have to be a good sport in the wardroom, so you can start here. And Cock is going to win that first prize for us.

HOUSEY: Without me and make-up. If I get a slipped disc from all this poncing about I'm going to ram those tennis balls down your throat.

SPLASH: Think of it as exercise.

HOUSEY: I knew you'd be the one to bring that up.

SPLASH: You could do with it. A flabby body means a flabby mind.

HOUSEY: There's nothing flabby about my mind.

SPLASH: What is the matter then?

SPIDER: It's just a bit on the slow side.

COCK: They won't be saying that when you've got the gold braid. OK Housey so let's have another run through. We'll take it from where you fall down.

HOUSEY: Why can't we just perform the 'Zulu Warrior'?

SPLASH: Or sing the 'Eton Boat Song'?

COCK: That's old hat. What this boat needs is a breath of fresh air – literally? Don't forget to open your legs this time. OK, with a one and a two.

We're goin' cross the river, up the river,

dum de dum
It's going to be peaceful on the other side.

TANNOY: Dining-room party close up.

COCK: Spoilsport.

SPLASH: Where did you learn all this poncing about?

COCK: My mother was stage struck. When I was four she'd sit me on top of the piano and I'd sing 'Mad About the Boy' at her Avon parties.

SPLASH: No wonder you ran away.

COCK: A one, two, a one, two, three . . .

TANNOY: Leading Seaman Jones report to the sick bay at the rush.

COCK: You keep interrupting. That's enough.

(*He starts clicking.*) One two three.

We're goin' across the river, up the river, da da dum
It's going to be peaceful on the other side. Soooo.

COCK *dives onto the linked hands of* SPIDER *and* HOUSEY. *They bounce him up and he is caught and lifted by* SPLASH. *Just then the* CHAPLAIN *enters carrying boxes of games and books. He stands in the doorway enjoying the rehearsal and beating time with his foot.*

Come along everyone get happy.
Throw all your cares away.
Come along everyone get happy,
Get ready for the judgement day.

COCK *is carried across the mess and sat on the bar. The* CHIEFS *get down on their knees. The* CHAPLAIN *puts down his boxes and books and applauds.* COCK *acknowledges and begins to walk down-stage.*

COCK (*to himself*): Applause, applause.

When he reaches down-stage he raises his hands to stop the imaginary applause. The CHAPLAIN *stops as well.*

CHAPLAIN: Very good. One of the best I've seen.

COCK: *The* best, sir.

CHAPLAIN: I don't know about that. The PO's are doing Snow White and she has about twenty dwarfs.

COCK (*out of the corner of his mouth to the others*): And they're all fucking her. (*To the* CHAPLAIN.) That's not all, sir. (*He begins a speech to the imaginary audience.*) Before my encore of Alma Cogan's 'Bell Bottom Blues' I'd like to say a few words.

SPLASH: Get on with it, Cock.

COCK: A few words to all the like-minded on this boat. The movement for Gay Equality will meet every Friday, officers willing, in the wardroom.

CHAPLAIN (*treating it as a joke*): I don't think they will be.

SPIDER: Why not, sir? Half of them are.

The CHAPLAIN *forces a laugh.*

SPLASH: He's only taking the mick, sir.

SPIDER: If young Cock Roach had his way, sir, there'd be Gay Power stickers all over the boat.

COCK: I've decided to be honest about my inclinations, why not?

CHAPLAIN: This is a joke?

COCK: They all think so, sir. Every time I come in here to clean I get snide remarks.

SPIDER: He's a tasty bit of skin, eh, sir?

COCK: See what I mean?

SPLASH: Is that it, Cock?

COCK: Yeah, take five boys. (*To* CHAPLAIN.) They'd do anything to win a case of beer.

SPIDER: You should have a word with him, sir. The old helping hand. (*He winks.*) But seriously he could do with sorting out.

SPLASH: Bath and dhobi time again. (*He collects his towel from his bunk.*) A clean body means a clean mind.

HOUSEY: You should be a saint by now.

SPLASH *gives two fingers and leaves.*

COCK: Could we have a talk now, sir?

CHAPLAIN: This is hardly the time, or the place –

SPIDER: Give us the nod and we'll thin out, sir.

CHAPLAIN (*distinctly uncomfortable*): That's good of you, but at the moment I've got my entertainment officer's hat on. There are Tombola tickets to sell, library books to collect.

SPIDER: They'll keep, sir. A word from you would help him, and help us. It'll be a much happier mess. You agree, Housey?

HOUSEY: No skin off my nose.

SPIDER: So let's go, give Cock a break.

TANNOY: The gash disposal unit will be in operation for the next ten minutes.

HOUSEY and SPIDER go. There is an uncomfortable silence.

The CHAPLAIN is wary for he is not quite sure if it is a leg-pull. He is lost for words. COCK looks like butter wouldn't melt in his mouth. The CHAPLAIN picks up the tennis balls and begins to juggle with them. He drops one and makes a thing of retrieving it. COCK smiles in encouragement, then offers the CHAPLAIN a chair. Rather than sit, the CHAPLAIN stands behind it.

COCK (*takes the tennis balls. All innocence*): Would you like a seat, sir?

CHAPLAIN: Well, AB Roach, this is all rather a surprise. Personally I'd put it down to youthful exuberance.

COCK: You think I'll grow out of it, sir?

CHAPLAIN: Yes, I do. Don't you think you should change out of that?

COCK (*begins to peel off his stockings*): Yes, sir.

CHAPLAIN: Put your trousers on, Roach.

COCK does so.

CHAPLAIN: I realise the circumstances down here are unusual. We're all on top of each other as it were. It's all in the mind, isn't it . . . Well isn't it? (*COCK hangs his head.*) I mean nothing . . . There's no one.

COCK: Haven't you ever been attracted to anyone –

CHAPLAIN: Of course –

COCK: Of your own sex?

CHAPLAIN: Now look here, Roach.

COCK: I wasn't suggesting anything, sir. I just want you to understand what it's like.

CHAPLAIN: You're doing a lot of beating around the bush.

COCK: I know, sir. But it's difficult to talk about something seriously. And it is my future at stake.

CHAPLAIN: Don't you like the navy?

COCK: I love it, sir. I've always wanted to be a submariner. I'm a five year man.

CHAPLAIN: Good, good. And these inclinations, that's all you have?

COCK: So far.

CHAPLAIN: When I see you with a black eye I'll know you've gone too far.

COCK looks reproachful.

I was joking, lad. In the navy there is a tradition of tolerance. It doesn't matter what we are, or what we do, as long as we don't overstep the mark. Sit down, lad. I'll give you an example from my own experience. I was on the *Tiger* one Christmas in Malta. Between duties I looked in at a bar, and there were lots of sailors dancing with each other. No one thought anything of it. For the explanation was obvious.

COCK: They preferred each other to the Maltese women?

The CHAPLAIN frowns.

COCK: Just a joke, sir.

CHAPLAIN: There simply weren't enough women to go around. That's all. Maybe one or two beers too many, away from home, but that's as far as it went. Good clean fun. Like your act for the Sod's Opera.

COCK: But what if I gave in to the temptation?

CHAPLAIN: You'll get the rebuff you deserve. And you'll have learnt the hard way. (*Warming to it.*) Every mess deck thrives on sexual banter and innuendoes. I know I'm called the Sin Bosun but it's part of the way of life. We are living in a totally male environment and there can be an inordinate amount of stress and tension, especially in our present situation. We are all down here together, working efficiently, doing a job, ignoring personal animosities and petty differences. When we are troubled we have to get it off our chests. Sometimes just a talk is enough, like the one we're having. Some find relief by exercising. And others, and you'd be surprised how many, find it in prayer. You might try it, Roach. Ask God to help you in your present difficulties. When you find yourself tempted, pray for help, and you'll be given it, because you've made the effort. God understands.

COCK: Like He says in the bible. No greater love hath man than for his fellow man.

CHAPLAIN: Not quite right, and don't take it too literally.

COCK: Thank you, sir.

CHAPLAIN: Splendid. And whenever you want to chat you'll find that I'm available. You feel better?

COCK: It's nice to know you understand, sir.

CHAPLAIN: You enjoy your naval life. Make it your career, and all will be well. These unwelcome thoughts that bother you from time to time can be controlled.

COCK: Will you tell the Captain, sir?

CHAPLAIN: Certainly not. I regard our talk as confidential and I wouldn't dream of breaking a confidence.

COCK: So it's all right to be gay and stay in the navy?

CHAPLAIN: If you put it that way, I'd have to say no, it isn't all right. But I believe you are going through a phase. You're not the only troubled soul who has confided in me; it's very true that we all have a cross to bear. Now I'd like to put on my psychiatrist's hat, as it were, and give you a little advice of a different sort. If you follow these inclinations, remember one thing. Don't get caught. It's a slur on the navy, and on yourself, and we just don't like it.

COCK: So if I can't be good, be careful, as it were?

CHAPLAIN: That's right, keep your mind occupied.

COCK: With what?

CHAPLAIN: I'll think of something. Now putting on my entertainments officer's hat once more, can I sell you a book of Tombola tickets? Remember the House now stands at thirty pounds.

COCK: No thanks, sir.

CHAPLAIN: Helps to keep you busy.

COCK: And off the streets, eh?

CHAPLAIN: I know the chiefs like to play, so tell everyone in the mess that I'll be back. Now I must round up those scrabble sets. (*He goes to the door.*) By the way, there's an excellent film on tonight. *Watership Down.* You've read the book, now see the film and then eat the stew.

He leaves laughing at his own joke. The door closes.

COCK: And choke on it. And fuck off and, as it were, take all your hats with you.

He throws a shoe at the door.

Scene Four

Week four.

The mess is empty except for COCK *who is taking his make-up off in front of the mirror. He sings to himself. He has his bell bottoms over his Judy gear.*

COCK:
There's no people like show people, they smile when they are low,
Even with a turkey you know will fold,
Still you wouldn't change it for a sack of gold.
Let's go on with the show.

SPIDER *enters wearing a bow tie.*

SPIDER: Well, you can't win them all.

COCK: I hate losing Spider, especially to a sub-lieutenant acting the 'Death of Nelson'. I mean could you believe it, he didn't even say 'Kiss me, Hardy'. 'Shake hands, Hardy' doesn't have the same sort of ring.

SPIDER: Housey thinks he's dislocated his shoulder.

COCK: Trust Housey. I'm sorry I didn't win you the case of beer. It occurred to me during the luke-warm applause, they don't like drag to be good. It touches too many raw nerves. They just want it to be grotesque. It knocked the wind out of my sails.

SPIDER: Well it did pass the time, Cock.

COCK: From now on we're going to do more than just pass the time. We're going to escape from all this . . .

SPIDER: Yeah, I've been working on it. (COCK *shoots him a look.*) Honest, I've been giving that Frisb a hard time.

COCK: What Frisb?

SPIDER: McNally. The poor little steamie was rolling himself a crafty smoke, one of the things I normally turn a blind eye to. I came down on him like a ton of bricks.

COCK: Good. You're taking it seriously.

SPIDER: Why can't I just throw a wobbly and get it over with?

COCK: That's the climax. You work up to it. But first there's two weeks of irritability.

SPIDER: Then what?

COCK: A couple of temper tantrums, at me if you like. Anything. I haven't cleaned properly. Pick on something small. No over-acting OK?

SPIDER: Claustrophobic's honour. I'll move when the mess is full. Plenty of witnesses.

COCK: You're catching on. Then you go to the coxswain and complain.

SPIDER: What'll I say? You don't clean properly, that sort of thing?

COCK: No. You say to the coxswain, this. There's a brown hatter on board and he's been leaving me little notes under my pillow. I'll write half a dozen of them for you as evidence. I can't take my eyes off you. Love from an admirer.

SPIDER: Rotate, Cock. That's a bit strong, isn't it?

COCK: The plan is you don't know who they're from. The coxswain then sets a trap. No one will hold it against you. There'll be an investigation, I'll confess, I mean they're not going to need a handwriting expert.

SPIDER: I couldn't do it.

COCK: Why not?

SPIDER: I couldn't pull it off.

COCK: All you have to be is bewildered. Come on, Spider.

SPIDER: I agreed to spread the buzz, a word here. Sure Cock Roach's a brown hatter. But he keeps us entertained.

That's as far as I can go.

COCK: Who do I have to fuck to get out of the navy?

There is a noise at the door, COCK *and* SPIDER *exchange looks.* COCK *goes to the door and assists* HOUSEY *through the door. He is dressed in a similar fashion to* SPIDER.

HOUSEY: My bloody back. I've ricked it.

SPIDER: Cock will give you a massage. I'm off to the flicks.

HOUSEY: You mean we have the mess all to ourselves. No more poncing around, OK.

COCK: Sure. Get out your books and oil your slide rule, and let's get down to it.

HOUSEY *goes to his locker, still rubbing his back and gets out his maths textbooks.*

COCK: I thought you performed like a real trouper, Housey.

HOUSEY: Wasn't bad, was I?

COCK: Let me get you a beer.

He does so.

HOUSEY: You're all right, Cock.

COCK: Thanks, Housey. How are you getting on with it?

HOUSEY: I'm worrying myself sick about it. I'm even taking pills to help me sleep. I knocked off some of the wife's valium.

COCK: Highly strung, is she?

HOUSEY: Sort of edgy. She's always pushing, if it's not me, it's the kids. She was a teacher before we married.

COCK: So she likes to be obeyed?

HOUSEY: She'd be a headmistress by now, as she keeps reminding me.

COCK: Straight up?

HOUSEY: Listen, Cock. Let me read you the last familygram I got from her. Forty words she's allowed, right?

COCK: Right.

HOUSEY: So get an earful of this. (*He reads.*) 'I hope you're concentrating on your exam, you know how important it is to pass.'

COCK: Sixteen so far.

HOUSEY: 'The children are going to your

mother's while I house-hunt.'

COCK: Twenty-seven.

HOUSEY: 'I'm sure I'll find something. Car failed its MOT again. Study hard. Cynthia.' (*Looking up.*) And that's an order.

COCK: Literally from above.

HOUSEY: Forty words and not even room for 'I miss you'.

COCK: Sounds like she doesn't. You're better off down here.

HOUSEY: Sometimes I wonder. Never marry a woman from Guz, Cock.

COCK: Why not?

HOUSEY: Because it means you're too lazy to wank. There's nothing wrong with the house we've got. But there's no satisfying her.

COCK: So becoming a sub-lieutenant is just a step to becoming Admiral of the Fleet?

HOUSEY: That's how she sees it. I suppose the trouble is that I know my limitations. But I tell you, I've got two great kids. So she's right about wanting the best for them.

COCK: Is that why you're in boats? For the extra money?

HOUSEY: It's one reason.

COCK: Sounds like the only reason.

HOUSEY: For her it is. You know what I miss most after the kids?

COCK *waits.*

The garden.

COCK: Got green fingers have you?

HOUSEY *nods.*

HOUSEY: I try and grow all the weird things she likes to cook. Courgettes, green peppers, and I manage to.

COCK: Pity you can't get an O level in horticulture.

HOUSEY (*sighs*): A wife with aspirations.

COCK: Housey, there's one way to guarantee passing.

HOUSEY: Yeah, steal the exam papers.

COCK: I have something in mind that is even more audacious.

HOUSEY: What?

COCK: Bribe someone to sit the exam for you.

HOUSEY: Don't be stupid.

COCK: I'm not. Have you ever seen the examiner? Has he ever seen you?

HOUSEY: Who would do it? You?

COCK: Try me.

HOUSEY: Why?

COCK: Because you can do a favour for me.

HOUSEY: So what's on your mind, Cock?

COCK: A deal. I'll sit the O level and pass it and no one will be any the wiser.

HOUSEY *is intrigued.*

We've both got to recognise that there is an element of risk, but that'll keep us on the ball.

HOUSEY: It's impossible.

COCK: No it isn't. How many were in the examination room when you failed last time?

HOUSEY: Thirty or so.

COCK: I'd get away with it. It's wide open.

HOUSEY: I'm not convinced.

COCK: You don't have to be. Just a little less cautious.

HOUSEY: You said earlier bribe someone. So what's the bribe?

COCK: It's more of a favour.

HOUSEY: I'm listening.

COCK: Report me.

HOUSEY: What for?

COCK: Being gay.

HOUSEY: Why?

COCK: I want to get out of the navy.

HOUSEY: It's a messy way to go about it.

COCK: The end justifies the means.

HOUSEY: Let me get it clear. You want me to go to the Mother Superior and say there's a brown hatter in the mess and he should be off this boat and out of the navy?

COCK: Why not?

HOUSEY: I'll tell you why not. I don't care what you are, Cock. What you do, or who you do it with. That's your business, but I tell you what I'm not going to do and that's shop you and then face the rest of the crew.

COCK: Then go one step further. Say I've been propositioning you, up till now you've been treating it like a joke, but the joke's over. Say I've given you no alternative.

HOUSEY: And for doing that you'll sit my O level?

COCK: Sure, a deal's a deal.

HOUSEY: And where will you sit it from? Detention Quarters Portsmouth?

COCK: They won't put me away, Housey. They'll just get rid of me.

HOUSEY: You'll never get away with it.

COCK: Yes I will.

HOUSEY: You're too young, Cock.

COCK: I'll age up. Grow a beard. They won't be looking for an imposter.

HOUSEY: Sorry.

COCK: Why not?

HOUSEY: It just won't work.

COCK: What's the volume of a sphere?

HOUSEY: Oh, Jesus.

COCK: Come on.

HOUSEY: Something like two thirds pi –

COCK: Four thirds times pi times R to the power of three.

HOUSEY: Yeah. That's it.

COCK: Can't you remember anything? What is the cosine rule?

HOUSEY: I know that one.

COCK: Come on then. A squared equals . . .

HOUSEY: B squared plus c squared . . .

COCK: Yes. I'm waiting . . .

HOUSEY: Shit.

COCK: That doesn't come into it.

HOUSEY: Don't be such a clever dick.

COCK: I can't help it Housey. Plus c squared come on. Minus two b. c cosine A. Remember?

HOUSEY: Yeah, minus two b.c. cosine A.

COCK: You'll have to do better than that.

(*He grabs one of* HOUSEY's *books*.) What about a simple arithmetic question. Divide £120 ratio of five to four to three.

HOUSEY: I can't work it out in my head.

COCK: Come on it's easy. Remember what Cynthia said, study hard, so think, Housey.

HOUSEY (*eventually*): £120 let's see. Fuckin' hell what use is all that?

COCK: Don't ask me, ask the examiners, then ask Cynth. Divide £120 in the ratio of –

HOUSEY: I know, I know.

COCK: If you know give me the answer.

HOUSEY: Seventy pounds sixty.

COCK: Sorry, Housey. It's fifty pounds forty pounds and? . . . Come on.

HOUSEY: Thirty?

COCK: You sure?

HOUSEY: No.

COCK: Well I am. Try this one –

HOUSEY: For fucks sake, Cock, no more.

COCK: Good. So I'll have my evenings free from now on.

HOUSEY: You're really tying me up in knots.

COCK: You only have to do one thing for me.

HOUSEY: I can't.

COCK: Why not? You can speak.

HOUSEY: I don't want to.

COCK: Then fail. Because without me that's what's going to happen.

HOUSEY: What is it you want, Cock?

COCK: Like I told you.

TANNOY: The ice cream machine is out of use till further notice.

HOUSEY: That fucking ice cream machine again. That's my part of ship.

COCK: You'd better go then; we don't want strawberry ripple all over my clean decks.

HOUSEY: Have a heart, Cock. Don't ask me to get involved.

COCK: So spend your life fixing the ice cream machine. Changing fuses and keeping toasters popping.

HOUSEY: You've got to help me.

COCK: Ask someone else.

HOUSEY: It's not that easy.

COCK: No, nothing is for you.

HOUSEY: I'm desperate.

COCK: So am I.

HOUSEY: We made a deal.

COCK: I know.

HOUSEY: And now you want to make another one.

COCK: That's right.

HOUSEY: It's not on. I've got to go.

COCK: Then piss off.

HOUSEY: I can't do it.

COCK: You would have if I just tapped you up.

HOUSEY: If you had have tapped me up . . . I don't know.

COCK: Filled me in?

HOUSEY: Maybe.

COCK: And I would have reported you. Then the shit'd hit the fan.

HOUSEY: What really is the matter with you, Cock?

COCK: Stuck down here. Having to clean up for you lot.

HOUSEY: It's more than that.

COCK: You said it.

HOUSEY: I didn't make the rules.

COCK: Neither will you break them.

HOUSEY: No I won't . . . I can't.

They both face each other. After some moments, SPLASH comes in. He is whistling 'Come on everyone get happy'. He is still dressed in white shirt, bow tie.

SPLASH: What's this then – a post mortem?

HOUSEY: No.

SPLASH: I've just come from the stokers' mess, Cock. They're drooling over you, there's talk of starting a Fan Club.

COCK: We didn't win.

SPLASH: It's no good crying over lost

beer anyway. I enjoyed it. Didn't you, Housey?

He slaps him on his back.

HOUSEY: My fuckin' back, you big ape.

He storms out of the mess.

SPLASH: What's eating him?

COCK: Housey just can't get his sums right.

SPLASH: If he can't take a joke he shouldn't have joined.

SPLASH begins to undress. He removes the bow tie and shirt, then does some arm stretching.

What this boat needs is a gym. It doesn't have to be large, just enough room for a couple of benches, a bike and some weights.

COCK: Put it in the suggestion box, Splash. Why don't you ask for a sauna and jacuzzi while you're at it?

SPLASH: Yeah and heat it all from the reactor.

COCK: Why not? The navy seem to think of nothing else but new ways for us to kill time.

SPLASH does a few squats, his attention is really on his own body. He removes his trousers with his back to COCK. COCK watches him very carefully. Then the plan occurs. He takes off his bell bottoms and still in his fish net stockings gets into his high heels. He goes to the door and closes all the clips then begins to sing and dance. It is all focussed on SPLASH who is sitting on his bunk undoing his shoes.

(Sings):
Whatever Cock Roach wants, Cock Roach gets
And Chiefy, little Cock Roach wants you.

SPLASH stops and watches COCK in amusement.

SPLASH: Is this the encore?

COCK: Could be. Like it?

SPLASH: Very professional. Did you sing this on top of the piano as well?

COCK *(sings):*
Make up your mind to have no regrets,
Recline yourself, resign yourself, you're through.

The dance is entirely directed at
SPLASH. COCK *is at his most*
seductive.

I always get what I aim for
And your heart and soul is what I came for.

He gives SPLASH's *arm muscle a*
playful squeeze and dances away.

Whatever Cock Roach wants, Cock Roach
gets
No use to fight, don't you know you can't
win.

The amused smile goes from
SPLASH's *face.* COCK *sees what*
could be anger replacing it. He gets
ready for the kill.

You're no exception to the rule
I'm irresistible you fool.

(*He's right up against* SPLASH *now.*)

Give in, give in, give in.

Instead of the expected punch SPLASH
lets out a strangled cry and grabs
COCK *in his arms and buries his face*
in COCK's *neck.*

SPLASH (*rocking* COCK *and sobbing*):
Baby, baby. My baby.

COCK: Bleedin' hell.

COCK *struggles to free himself – he is*
absolutely horror-struck.

ACT TWO

Scene One

Superior *has now been submerged for five*
weeks and it is off-duty time for SPLASH,
SPIDER *and* HOUSEY. *There is an*
increasing degree of listlessness and
irritation with each other. Keep fit is
coming over the tannoy. The only one
following it is SPLASH *who is physically*
far beyond its demands. He's doing it for
no apparent reason. HOUSEY *watches*
him with unconcealed anger and
mechanically drums a pencil end over end,
tapping it monotonously. The inevitable
text books are open in front of him.
SPIDER *is sitting on his bunk seemingly*
engrossed in a game of patience.

TANNOY (*in darkness*): Lift up and
lower, lift up and lower. That's good,
deep breaths now, suck that lovely air
down into your lungs. Lift and lower, lift
and lower. You feel good now, loose and
relaxed. Terrific. OK, keeping your feet
apart I want you to stretch down and
touch the deck. Not too far at first, we
don't want any pulled muscles, the
missus wouldn't like it. OK boys, nice
and steady does it. Stretch down, feel
those hamstrings tightening. Down right,
down now . . .

Lights and . . .

(*sing-song voice*): Down, right down
now. Back. Forward. Side, and up.
Keep those backs straight. Now that's it
in a slow time, now follow my timing as
we speed up slightly. Ready . . . and . . .
back, forward, side and up. And back,
forward, side and up. More speed. Back,
forward, side, up, back, forward, side,
up.

SPLASH *is mouthing along with the*
tannoy and keeping perfect time.
SPIDER *goes to the tannoy switch and*
turns it off.

HOUSEY: Thank God.

SPIDER *returns to his bunk and*
resumes his cards. SPLASH *hasn't*
broken his stride and the mouthing and
the exercises continue.

SPLASH (*exercising*): Up. Your fat arse.
Up your fat - arse. Spider - is - a prick.
What -are - you - Spider? You - are - a-
prick. Now for something new.

He turns on the tannoy.

TANNOY: That wasn't too difficult, was it?

SPLASH: No. It was kid's stuff.

TANNOY: OK, you *Superior* ratings, the next exercise is slightly tougher. Hands on the chest, then stretch, then chest, knees, toes and back to chest again. We'll do ten of these, stand by and . . . hands on chests, then stretch, on toes, then down and down and back. Again. Stretch and down and back. Stretch and down and back. Stretch and down and back.

SPIDER *gets up again and goes to the tannoy and switches it off. He returns to his bunk and the cards.*

SPLASH (*keeping time*): You - can't - crack - me. You - can't crack - me. You -

SPIDER: Shut up. You sound like a fucking parrot.

SPLASH: Spider's - got - a - widgy - on. Spider's got a widgy on.

SPIDER: That's right so wrap it up.

HOUSEY: Amen

SPLASH *continues to exercise.*

SPLASH: I must, I must improve my bust, I must, I must improve my bust!

SPIDER *gives him a look and he shuts up.* HOUSEY *continues drumming and turning over the pencil, tapping it each time he does so. He doesn't realise but* SPLASH *is now exercising to the beat of* HOUSEY's *pencil. It's the only sound and it continues.* SPIDER *leaves his cards and walks around the table, takes the pencil out of* HOUSEY's *hand, snaps it, and puts the two pieces back on the table.*

SPLASH *picks up his skipping rope and begins.*

HOUSEY: That's a shit house trick.

SPIDER: Would you rather it was your neck?

He goes back to his cards.

HOUSEY (*to* SPLASH): What's he so chokker about?

SPLASH *just looks mystified.*

SPIDER: That endless fucking tapping, professor.

HOUSEY: What tapping?

SPIDER: The tapping that goes on every time you sit at that table with your books. You never stop fucking tapping, and it's driving me up the fucking bulkhead.

HOUSEY: Oh, that tapping. Get on your wick, does it?

SPIDER: Yeh.

HOUSEY: Well do you know what gets on my wick?

SPIDER: What?

HOUSEY (*getting up and crossing to the bunk*): You're doing it now.

SPIDER: What am I doing.

HOUSEY: Flicking your cards. You've been doing it for the last five weeks and I can't stand it anymore either.

He sweeps all the cards off the bed. They face each other momentarily.

SPLASH: That's it. No more tapping, Housey. And Spider, no more flicking. OK?

HOUSEY: OK.

SPLASH (*to* SPIDER): OK?

SPIDER: OK.

He hauls a knife on the end of his lanyard, opens the blade, takes SPLASH's *skipping rope from the table and cuts it in two.* HOUSEY *and* SPLASH *are on the move around the table.*

SPIDER: OK?

SPLASH: What's up with you?

HOUSEY: You're always at it, Splash. Anyway I thought skipping was for girls.

SPLASH: Who pressed your starter?

HOUSEY: It's not a bloody gym. It's our mess.

SPLASH: You want a mouthful of baldy gums?

HOUSEY: It's Spider you should be having a go at. I didn't cut your stupid skipping rope. I'm just the voice of reason.

SPLASH: The voice of what? You can't even reason your way through the multiplication table. And you an electrical mech striving for greater things.

TANNOY: Yoga classes are now being held in the senior rates rec space.

SPLASH (*sings*):

Housey Housey the battery boy,
He's a walkie talkie toy,
Press his switch see his light,
But don't expect it to be too bright.

HOUSEY: You're a typical engine room steamie, Splash.

SPLASH: You'll make an officer all right.

HOUSEY: And when I am, you'd better make yourself scarce.

SPLASH: Yes, sir, I will, sir.

HOUSEY: Skipping your way through life. It's pathetic.

SPLASH: Sorry, sir. Can I carry your books?

HOUSEY: When I'm in the wardroom.

SPLASH: Yeh, sweeping it.

HOUSEY: Very funny. But I'll have the last laugh on you lower deck morons.

SPIDER: Always assuming you pass. And if you don't pass what happens then Housey?

SPLASH (*singing*): D-I-V-O-R-C-E.

HOUSEY: That's good coming from you.

SPLASH: What do you mean?

HOUSEY: I've heard the buzz.

SPLASH: What buzz?

HOUSEY: You know.

SPLASH: What are you on about?

HOUSEY: Your sex life.

SPLASH: What about it?

HOUSEY (*winks*): Nudge, nudge. I've heard.

SPLASH: Who from?

HOUSEY: It's common knowledge.

SPIDER: Stop manking you two. Wind your necks in.

They ignore him.

SPLASH: What are you insinuating?

HOUSEY: Your missus.

SPLASH (*relieved*): What about her?

HOUSEY: She's had more pricks than a pin cushion.

SPIDER: That's true, Splash. As soon as we get alongside what do you do?

SPLASH: The same as everyone else.

SPIDER: No, instead of doing your press up's on top of your wife, you're off on a sky diving course. Rock climbing course. Any course.

HOUSEY: Except intercourse.

SPIDER: Don't you poke her enough?

SPLASH: You two have been sitting in on too many coffee mornings.

HOUSEY: She's got to get it where she can. How's your wife's new car?

SPLASH: What's it to you?

HOUSEY (*to* SPIDER): She got a new car and he thinks the money came from selling tupperware.

SPLASH: She got it on HP.

HOUSEY: She got it on her back, on her hands and knees, behind the Mecca. You name it.

SPLASH: You're in a bad way, Housey. Take a day off. Cock will get you through.

HOUSEY: There's another one.

SPLASH: Leave him out of it.

SPIDER: He's the best mess man we've ever had.

HOUSEY: Keep you entertained all right. I've seen the two of you.

SPIDER: What do you mean?

HOUSEY: I've got eyes.

SPLASH: But what good are they without the brains to back them up?

SPIDER: Me and Cock? Are you thinking what I think you're thinking.

SPLASH: He's not thinking, Spider. He's got the IQ of a rocking horse.

HOUSEY: I don't give a fuck what you and Cock do.

SPIDER: You really are hallucinating.

HOUSEY: The little raver's been trying it on with everyone.

SPIDER: Who's everyone?

HOUSEY: Well me. Has he tried it on with you, Splash?

SPLASH: No, but I live in hope.

SPIDER: As usual poor old Housey is getting his equations all wrong. Won't you ever learn?

HOUSEY: Cock's raving.

SPIDER: Come on board, Housey. Don't be a prick all your life.

SPLASH: All this because you broke his pencil.

SPIDER: Cock was only pretending to be a snapper.

SPLASH: Yeh, it was an act and he got tired of it.

SPIDER: He was passing the time of day.

HOUSEY: What do you think I am? The village idiot?

SPLASH: You've got all the qualifications to be.

SPIDER: Housey, Cock wants to get out of the navy.

HOUSEY: Because he's queer.

SPIDER: No, like Splash said it was all an act. And he dropped it last week. Hadn't you noticed that either?

HOUSEY: So why did he give it up?

SPIDER: Ask him.

HOUSEY: You really are an ungrateful sod, Housey. After all the help the kid's given you. You're going to be a real officer, a pig's orphan.

The door opens and COCK *enters. He has a tin of dried milk. He looks around then breaks into Al Jolson. It is directed at* HOUSEY.

COCK (*sings*):
I'm sitting on top of the world
I'm rolling along, yes rolling along.
I'm quitting the Blues of the World,
I'm singing a song, yes singing a song.
Glory Hallelujah I just told the parson
to get ready to call . . .

HOUSEY: For God's sake.

COCK: Don't you like it?

HOUSEY: I'm not in the mood. I've had enough from this lot without you flashing up.

COCK: Poor Housey. Climb upon my knee Housey Boy, though you're only . . . what is it . . . thirty-three Housey Boy.

HOUSEY: Fuck off.

He pushes COCK *away.*

COCK (*on his knees*); Look at me! Don't you know me. I'm your little Cock. I'll crawl a million miles for one of your smiles my Housey.

HOUSEY: I preferred you as a brown hatter.

COCK: Did you? I had to give that up.

HOUSEY: Why, someone bother you did they?

COCK: No such luck. I couldn't even convince the Sin Bosun and boy did I try.

HOUSEY: If you're here to clean, get on with it.

COCK: You could cut the atmosphere with a knife. What's got into you all. (*He picks up the two halves of the skipping rope.*) I suppose you just snapped it in two. You don't know your own strength, Splash. You should get a job in a circus.

HOUSEY: Yeh, as a clown. He could team up with you, a right pair.

COCK: How about it, Splash?

SPLASH: You be the clown. I'll be the straight man.

COCK: Now you're talking. I've got a bone to pick with you, Spider.

SPIDER: What is it?

COCK: It's about McNally.

SPIDER: That little skate.

COCK: He's stopped wanking, now he cries himself to sleep.

SPIDER: Good. I might get some work out of him.

COCK: If you keep persecuting him he'll crack, and you'll be responsible.

SPIDER: Then you can stand by. There are too many Jack-me-Hearties on here.

HOUSEY: Bloody right.

SPIDER: Get turned to. Chop, chop and then give us your impersonation of the disappearing man.

COCK: You'll get that the day they put the

gangway down. You're all turning into monsters. It's as if some mysterious force has taken over the boat.

SPLASH: The invasion of the mind snatchers.

COCK: They wouldn't get much joy on here.

HOUSEY: Don't you ever let up.

COCK *walks across to the tannoy and switches it on.*

CHAPLAIN (*voice over*): Whoever you are and whatever you are doing I'd like you all to join me in prayer asking God to look down on our loved ones this evening.

HOUSEY *kills it.*

SPLASH: Jesus – it must be Sunday.

COCK: He's still at it. There is tannoys going off in every mess throughout the boat.

SPIDER: Probably talking to himself by now.

HOUSEY *is pacing around.*

COCK: How does he know it's evening, think he's had a peek?

SPLASH: As far as I'm concerned it's been five weeks of night.

HOUSEY: It's been five weeks of hell.

COCK: Three weeks to go Housey, things could get better . . . or worse.

HOUSEY: You're a little pest.

COCK: I know, so do you want the good news or the bad news first?

HOUSEY: You're bad news period.

SPLASH: What is it, Cock?

COCK: The bad news is we have run out of Long Life milk . . .

SPIDER: Don't tell us it's . . .

COCK: The good news is we have powdered milk.

Holds up tin.

HOUSEY: Not that stuff.

SPLASH: It'll upset my metabolism.

COCK: Sorry boys, I forgot to leave a note for the milkman.

SPIDER: Dried milk! It'll be bromide in the tea next.

COCK: Funny you should say that, the doc was in the galley just now.

HOUSEY: He's always doing rounds in there. Hygiene, cleanliness. (*He indicates the sink.*) Understood?

SPLASH: Yeh he's looking for the chef who picks his nose.

SPLASH: Bromide . . . I wonder . . .

HOUSEY: Don't talk wet.

SPLASH: When was the last time you had a hard-on, Housey?

HOUSEY: Piss off.

COCK: We could have a 'Ban the Bromide' march.

SPIDER: A protest.

SPLASH (*chants*): Bromide out. Bromide out.

COCK: Should I chain myself to the reactor or a war-head?

HOUSEY: You two grow up and Roach just play the mess man.

COCK: I'm not playing at anything anymore.

HOUSEY: You'll get filled in.

COCK: I've got a theory, do you want to hear it? It's novel.

HOUSEY: Have we a choice?

COCK: You'll like it, you might learn something Housey.

HOUSEY: I'm all ears.

COCK: My theory is we're approximately ten nautical miles from Faslane.

HOUSEY: Bollocks.

COCK: One thing the navy does have is cunning. So here we go, for eight weeks somewhere. But no one knows where. Of course everyone speculates. The north pole, is favourite, the Med.

SPLASH: I reckon we're in the Gulf – that's the hot spot.

COCK: Too obvious. I maintain we go nowhere. What would be the point of leaving this loch. The whole thing is an elaborate charade. Peace time in the services is playing games, the RAF have their Red Arrows.

SPLASH: Which they keep crashing.

COCK: Nice . . . The army their massed

bands, and the dear old navy have nuclear boats playing hide and seek in their own back yard.

HOUSEY: What a load of codswallop.

COCK: You've got no imagination, Housey. My theory is, as watertight I hope, as this boat.

SPLASH: Ingenious.

COCK: Isn't it? What do you reckon, Spider?

SPIDER: You don't know what you're talking about.

COCK: I know a lot more than you think.

SPIDER: That superior brain of yours putting two and two together?

COCK: Do you know what this boat is ultimately? (*He has their attention, and he uses it for dramatic effect.*) A black steel coffin.

SPIDER (*gives him a wink to egg him on*): I don't want to think about it.

COCK: It's about time we all did. Above us are thousands and thousands of tons of water. We might as well be inside an egg, and you know how easy it is to crack an egg. We are Britain's first line of defence, that's got to be a joke. But the fact is we are. Did you know there are missiles trained on us that we couldn't dive deep enough or go fast enough to avoid? So what's the point of going to sea for eight weeks? Polaris is totally obsolete.

SPLASH: That's why Mrs T. is spending £500 thousand million.

HOUSEY: You should keep all your crackpot ideas to yourself.

COCK: The wardroom speaks.

SPIDER: How safe are we, anyway?

HOUSEY: Completely.

COCK: Oh really. Have you heard of the *Threasher*?

SPIDER: Yes it disappeared in 1963. Two hundred miles out of Boston.

COCK: Right. Have you heard about the *Scorpion*?

HOUSEY: Of course we have. Another US nuclear boat that disappeared.

COCK: She was found in millions of tiny pieces all over the sea bed. One thing about nuclear subs, no one has ever lived to tell the tale.

SPLASH: You're a morbid little bugger, Cock.

COCK: Of course we don't know how many the Russians have lost, but we do know that about fifty miles off the coast of Scotland there is a pocket of radiation coming from the sea bed. Something's down there so keep the kids off the fish fingers – they could be contaminated.

HOUSEY: You're talking nonsense Roach. There hasn't been an accident on a British nuke.

SPIDER: There's been enough on ordinary boats.

COCK: Yeh remember the *Thetis*?

SPLASH: Yeah.

COCK: Yet another example of the Admiralty hiding their incompetence behind a wall of secrecy.

HOUSEY: It happened before the war.

COCK: That's no excuse. Ninety-nine men trapped, only four escaped.

SPLASH: And the navy learned by that mistake. That's why we have Thetis clips now.

COCK: Everyone knows how it happened. The fuck-up was, why weren't those men rescued?

SPLASH: They couldn't find them, could they?

COCK: What? The stern was sticking out of the water and it still took them seventeen hours. Then they sat around and waited for the poor sods to escape by themselves.

HOUSEY: They were early days.

COCK: It was a balls-up, they should have saved them.

HOUSEY: You could be on a subversion charge.

COCK: For knowing too much?

HOUSEY: For talking too much.

COCK: Would they throw me out?

HOUSEY: After they'd locked you up.

COCK: What's all this constant niggling that you're handing out, Housey?

HOUSEY: You're beginning to get up my

nose.

COCK: Am I? I never used to. But then you needed my help.

HOUSEY: I've never been able to count on that.

COCK: No, there's a price for everything. When is the dummy examination?

HOUSEY: How do you know about that?

COCK: The vicar told me.

HOUSEY: He had no business to.

COCK: Take it up with him.

HOUSEY: I will.

COCK: I personally think it's a good idea.

HOUSEY: I'm sure everyone who sits it will be delighted to know.

COCK: I hope so. Because the vicar asked me to help set it.

HOUSEY: No way –

COCK: Ironic for you, isn't it? After all I'm the brightest rating on board.

HOUSEY: So you keep telling us. But not the most qualified – there are more degrees in that wardroom than you've had hot dinners.

COCK: Remember, Housey, a little knowledge is a dangerous thing. Anyway it's next week. I'll dream up some problems that will make your brain reel.

SPLASH: Like what do four and four equal.

COCK: Yeh, along those lines, Splash. I better not make them too difficult because guess what?

SPLASH: No, what?

COCK: I'm correcting them as well.

HOUSEY: You're full of shite Roach.

He leaves.

SPLASH (*calls after him*): Going for a breath of fresh air, Housey?

He goes to his locker and begins sorting out laundry into a pillow case.

SPLASH: I'm worried about Housey, he's like a bear with a sore head.

SPIDER: He'll be all right. It's the exam.

SPLASH: I hope he passes it. Reckon he will, Cock?

COCK: I'll make sure of it. But it does him good to sweat on it.

SPLASH (*to* COCK): You can swing it for him?

COCK: Splash, no problem. I'll arrange it.

SPLASH: That's decent of you, Cock.

COCK: He's going places he doesn't want to go, but he's going.

SPLASH: As long as he appreciates what you are doing for him.

COCK (*shrugs*): It'll be a secret. I'm good at keeping them.

SPLASH *understands the implication.*

SPIDER (*finally getting back to his game*): Lying on my bunk. Staring up and thinking about all the water. It's enough to drive you around the twist. Three more weeks of it.

COCK: How many of these patrols have you done?

SPIDER: This is the fourth.

SPLASH: You're an old hand at it.

COCK: And has it worried you before?

SPIDER: Not really.

COCK: So it's building up. Getting worse?

SPIDER: Yeh, something like that. (*Getting up from his bunk.*) I get so restless.

He begins pacing around.

SPLASH: You want to try exercising, Spider. It's not only physical, it's mental discipline as well.

SPIDER: With you flogging your body and Housey flogging his mind there's more than enough discipline in this mess all ready. I need fresh air. Not yesterday's farts recycled.

SPLASH: You want to get it out of your system. Exercise.

SPIDER: Skipping isn't going to help. What I want to see is daylight.

COCK: Feel the wind.

SPIDER: Yeh, all that. The sun. Some blue sky for Christ's sake.

SPLASH: Blue sky this time of the year? You've got to be dreaming. It's thermal underwear time up there.

SPIDER: You know what I mean.

Anything's better than this.

SPLASH: Maybe you're right. I'm off. Anyone got any dhobi dust?

SPIDER: In the bottom of my locker. But it'll cost you.

SPLASH: I'll buy you a new pack of cards.

He leaves with his laundry and SPIDER's Daz.

SPIDER (*waiting till the door closes. He jumps around in glee*): How was that?

COCK: Not bad.

SPIDER: Not bad? It was terrific! (*Mimicking himself.*) How safe are we? I get so restless. I want to see daylight. Fucking magic. (*He begins to really overact. He grabs the bunk and thrashes around like someone possessed.*) I'm going mad, I tell you, sir. Look how it shakes. (*He holds out his hand and vibrates it.*) See. And at night it's worse. I have to gag myself not to scream out.

COCK: That's the next stage.

SPIDER: When? When? (*Tweaks COCK's cheek.*)

COCK: When you've got an audience. Witnesses. And when I say the word.

SPIDER: Have we got time for a rehearsal?

COCK: Splash'll be back.

SPIDER: A quick one.

COCK: All right. A quickie. And a quiet one. I'll lead off with my Captain Nemo impersonation of Nautilus caught in the maelstrom. Or is the giant octopus attack better?

SPIDER: It's your show.

COCK: Which you're going to upstage. Maybe the last scene from *Morning Departure* would be more appropriate. When they pray and wait to die in their watery grave. Anyway, whatever it is I'll get the atmosphere right with a story and your cue will be when I say, 'Hasn't it got cold all of a sudden', then pause. (*Pause.*) Then you're on. (*Pause.*) 'Hasn't it got cold all of a sudden.'

COCK *sits and critically watches* SPIDER. *He gives him a nod of encouragement.* SPIDER *collapses onto the floor sobbing and making*

incoherent noises.

COCK: A rehearsal I said. Give it the works when you do it for real.

SPIDER: Sorry. I got carried away. (*He continues.*) Is that better?

COCK: Roll around a bit more. (*He does so.*) Scare me. (SPIDER *gets his knife out.*) Give me the odd, 'I've got to get off this boat'. 'I'm going mad cooped up down here.'

SPIDER (*quietly*): 'I'm going mad cooped up here get me off. Please get me off.'

COCK: Not bad.

SPIDER: 'Get me off, get me off, get me off.'

COCK: You're spoiling it.

SPIDER: How?

COCK: You sound like a record that stuck. You're supposed to be mad. So go bananas.

He does so.

Quite impressive.

SPIDER: How will I know when to stop?

COCK: Someone will knock you unconscious.

SPIDER: Hang about, Cock.

COCK: I'll do it.

SPIDER: Can't I just run out and lock myself in the heads?

COCK: Where's your sense of drama? No you have to be knocked out. So unless you want your jaw rewired make sure that I'm always between you and Splash. I don't plan to hit hard. I might damage my hand. Fake it, like you faked the rest. When you're out cold I'll do my man in charge of the situation number. We'll get you on the bunk and tie you to it. Then the doc will come along and give you an injection which really will knock you out. The next day you'll wake up not remembering what happened but full of fears. It's a cinch.

SPIDER: I . . . don't know Cock.

COCK: You can. It's too late for half measures.

SPIDER: Let's not lose our heads over this. (*Pause.*) I wonder about you, Cock. You behave as if the way it is down here has already got to you.

COCK: I'm the only sane person on this boat.

SPIDER: You could fool me.

COCK: I know.

The CHAPLAIN *enters.*

CHAPLAIN: Evening chaps.

SPIDER: Is it?

CHAPLAIN: Take the chef's word for it. I've just eaten beef stroganoff so it can't have been breakfast. At the moment I have my postman's hat on. There's a familygram for you chief.

SPIDER: Thank you, sir. (*He takes it.*)

CHAPLAIN: And one for Chief Houseman. Is he about?

SPIDER: Somewhere, sir. These always make me uneasy. (*He gives* COCK *a conspiratorial wink.*) Know what I mean?

CHAPLAIN: It can only be good news.

SPIDER (*reading*): It's no news. What can you say in forty words.

CHAPLAIN: It's the thought that counts, chief. How are you getting on, young Roach?

COCK: I'm wrestling with my conscience.

CHAPLAIN: Time for another talk, eh? I've been meaning to get back to you. I'll leave this. Now don't forget that tomorrow night is quiz night.

COCK: Why don't you stay for cocoa, sir? (*He gives* SPIDER *a nod.*) I'm about to make it.

SPIDER: Yes, sir. Stay. Make you sleep like a top.

CHAPLAIN: That's thoughtful, chief. But I have to finish my rounds.

COCK: Come back when you've finished, sir.

CHAPLAIN: Right. I shall. I've just got to pop these in the PO's mess and I'll be back in a brace of shakes.

He leaves.

COCK: While he's drinking his cocoa, I'll tell the story of the Affray, and at the end of it you go bananas.

SPIDER: I don't know, Cock. Sure it's not too soon?

COCK: First night nerves. Do it, it's the perfect opportunity.

TANNOY: The reactor tunnel is now open.

COCK *begins to make the cocoa.* SPIDER *looks at the familygram again.*

SPIDER: I can read between these bloody lines. It's not what she says that gets me, it's what she doesn't say.

COCK: All the more reason, Spider.

SPIDER: She really hates it up there. She can't drive of course, so she's stuck in the marriage patch all the time. In fact she hates leaving the house. Babs has this mate who picks up the odd bit of shopping for her. I think she'd rather starve than catch a bus to town.

COCK: That bad is it?

SPIDER: Yeh, the doc says she got agoraphobia. I should do something about it.

COCK: Just as soon as you get off here. So make it convincing.

SPLASH *and* HOUSEY *enter.*

COCK: Cocoa up team. We've got a guest coming so it's smiles all around. The vicar. There's a familygram for you, Housey.

HOUSEY *reads his familygram,* COCK *watches him and pours the cocoa.* HOUSEY *folds the familygram and puts it in his pocket.*

SPLASH: What's the news about the house.

HOUSEY: We lost it.

SPLASH: At least she can't blame you for it.

HOUSEY: Cynth'll find a way to. 'If only you had been here it wouldn't have happened.' I can hear her already. How can she do it?

SPLASH: Do what?

HOUSEY: Make me feel guilty down here.

SPLASH: Don't worry about it. Have a cup of Cock's cocoa.

HOUSEY (*taking it*): Cheers.

SPLASH: Take his mind off his troubles, Cock. Tell him a bedtime story.

COCK: OK. You want to hear a story, Spider?

SPIDER: Why not?

COCK: What about you, Housey?

HOUSEY: Please yourself.

COCK: Are you all sitting comfortable? Then I'll begin. This one doesn't knock the navy, Housey. So it won't get up your nose. It happened in 1951, a submarine left Portsmouth on a routine training exercise. There were seventy men on board. The plan was to be away for three days. She had been at sea a few hours when she signalled she was diving. That was the last that was heard of her.

The CHAPLAIN *enters.*

Here's your cocoa, sir. I was telling the mess about Affray.

CHAPLAIN: Yes, a tragic business. I remember once . . .

SPLASH: Go on Cock. What happened next?

COCK: Do you mind, sir?

CHAPLAIN: Carry on by all means. Very little has ever come to light.

COCK: She just vanished. She was due to surface the following morning and signal, but she didn't. (SPIDER *gets off his bunk and begins to pace about.*) The biggest sea search ever got underway. They pulled out all the stops, but it was like looking for a needle in a haystack. She could have gone down anywhere in the channel. The search went on for three days but nothing, not a survivor, wreckage, marker buoy, nothing. But they kept looking didn't they, sir?

CHAPLAIN: Yes I believe it went on for months.

COCK: Two months, sir. Two months, and then they found her.

CHAPLAIN: Yes the extraordinary thing was she was over thirty miles off course. In the vicinity of the Channel Islands, if my memory serves me.

COCK: Right, sir. Near Alderney.

CHAPLAIN: Yes, Alderney.

COCK: And what was so strange was that there was no sign of damage. The hatches were closed, no one tried to escape. (COCK *keeps an eye on* SPIDER *who is pacing unobtrusively.*) Why? No one will ever know, because it is still down there. Seventy-five bodies in an iron tomb.

CHAPLAIN: It does no good dwelling on that. You are allowing your imagination to run riot, lad.

COCK (*ignoring him*): Think about it, those seventy-five men waiting to die, and being unable to do anything about it.

CHAPLAIN: It must have been quick. God in his mercy would have seen to that.

COCK: It takes a long time to die and there is nothing to do but wait for it to happen.

CHAPLAIN: That's enough. Something of an authority on naval mishaps, are you?

COCK: As a matter of fact I am, sir. I've specialised in disasters. I've read everything available. What I'd give to read the Admiralty files. But they're locked away for ever, aren't they, sir?

CHAPLAIN: I don't know. And if they are, you can be sure there is a good reason.

COCK (*watches* SPIDER): So no one will ever know why those men died. (*Almost to himself.*) I wonder what it looks like in the Affray now? (*Pause.*) Floating skeletons I expect. (*Pause.*) Hasn't it got cold all of a sudden? (*He takes a sip of his cocoa and waits.*) But this will warm us up. (*He sips the cocoa.*) But it is cold all of a sudden.

SPIDER *is about to start.* HOUSEY *shows signs of agitation, but no one is aware of it.*

CAPTAIN (*voice over*): Hands to action stations. Hands to action stations. This is the captain speaking. We are in a red alert situation. Repeat, red alert. I want everyone's attention.

SPIDER, SPLASH *and* HOUSEY *change rapidly into their overalls and run out of the mess.*

CAPTAIN (*voice over*): I have just received a priority signal from NATO headquarters informing me that a prototype missile UVU4 has gone out of control . . . in our vicinity. *Superior* is the nearest vessel to its present position. We will be there first and wait for a salvage team to arrive. I cannot give you any further information at present. I'm sure I don't have to spell out the significance and the importance of this mission. An undreamt of opportunity for the NATO allies. Hands to action stations. Assume NBCD state One Zulu Alpha. Three hundred feet. Alter course to one seven zero maximum revolutions.

Bells ring. The CHAPLAIN *leaves. The bells stop ringing.* COCK *walks around the mess picking up the cups.*

COCK: Shit.

Scene Two

It is twenty-four hours later. Above the steady and constant rumble of the engine is heard the sonar ping coming at five second intervals. COCK *is sitting at the table with his feet up. A pile of sandwiches is in front of him and he is munching his way steadily through them. He is dressed in his Number Eights and around his neck he is wearing his white cotton anti-flash head cover. The door opens and* SPIDER *enters. He is wearing dark blue overalls and white gloves. His respirator is over his shoulder. He begins to peel off his white anti-flash hood.* COCK *turns and acknowledges him.*

COCK: All burning and turning back there, Spider?

SPIDER: What are you doing here?

COCK: I'm cleaning.

SPIDER: Looks like it.

With his gloved fingers he wipes the surface and shows the dirt to COCK.

COCK: I keep wondering myself where it could possibly come from.

SPIDER: Do something about it.

COCK: Amazing isn't it, Spider? Here we are on the eve of the third world war. Everyone wetting themselves with excitement. Fingers poised on destruct buttons. Half the navies of the world converging on one spot. And what am I supposed to be doing? The dishes.

SPIDER: Those our sarnies you're seeing off?

COCK: Yeh. It's compensation, for lack of having anything worthwhile to do.

SPIDER: You'd rather be in charge?

COCK: It would be safer if I was.

SPIDER: Ours is not to reason why, ours is but to do or die.

COCK: I hope you're not speaking on my behalf, Spider. What's got into you?

SPIDER: It's for real.

COCK: What's the buzz?

SPIDER (*pours himself some tea*): We've been going like the clappers for the last twenty-four hours, so we can't be far off now.

COCK: If I was designing a submarine I'd put in windows so we could all see where we are. Then we wouldn't have to rely on that.

The ping continues at five second intervals.

SPIDER: Last night was a washout. I was all tuned up. The funny thing was that story you told really got us all.

COCK: It was supposed to.

SPIDER: I don't know when we'll get another opportunity.

COCK: What do you mean? We're in the middle of one. All this red alert. The tension, the responsibility. It's perfect. We'll wait for the right moment and I'll give you the lead in – it's turned cold all of a sudden –

SPIDER: It's not time for playing games, Cock.

COCK: It's a game now. I thought we were getting you a cushy shore number so you could get away from the wilds of Scotland and save your wife's sanity and your marriage.

SPIDER: I can't throw a wobbly in the middle of a situation like this. Come on, Cock. You know what I mean. I'm a senior rate.

COCK: I know. But you're not going to lose it. You'll get sympathy, not a reprimand. You can recover in a couple of days and be determined to get back to duty, they'll love you for it.

SPIDER: It's a question of priorities.

COCK: Absolutely. Your marriage is the priority. Throw a little one, enough to get them concerned. (SPIDER *nods.*) I'm right.

SPIDER: Yeh.

COCK: The end justifies the means, Spider.

SPIDER: OK, but don't let it go on for long. I'll do it during this off watch period so make sure you stick around.

COCK: I'll keep myself busy cleaning.

SPIDER: You'd better. Housey's out to win points. He'd kill to get into that wardroom.

SPLASH *enters dressed in a similar fashion to* SPIDER.

SPLASH: God, it's harry hotters in that engine room. I've sweated pounds. Tea's up?

COCK: Any time.

He pours a cup while SPLASH *gets out of his gear.*

SPIDER: All steady.

SPLASH: A couple of bearings overheating but nothing to worry about yet.

TANNOY: Damage Control Parties will exercise at fourteen hundred hours.

SPLASH: For five weeks we've been sitting around and at last we're doing something. I've heard on the grapevine that another signal's come through.

COCK: Heard what it is?

SPLASH: No. Have you heard the rumours that are flying around?

COCK: All day.

SPIDER *begins to pace around.*

SPLASH: I'd love to know what's going on. Are the Russians really going to let us photograph and even salvage one of their missiles? And all in their backyard.

COCK: Is that where we're supposed to be?

SPLASH (*nods*): The north coast of Russia.

SPIDER: Some say the Red Sea.

COCK: As long as it's not the Dead Sea.

SPIDER: Only Mother Superior and the navigator know our exact position.

SPLASH: The Baltic's doing the rounds. That's all I can tell you.

COCK: I'm too young to be a prisoner of war.

SPLASH: What war?

COCK: The one Mother Superior's going to start. (*Mimicking the captain.*) An undreamt of opportunity for the NATO Allies. (*His own voice.*) One advantage about being the mess man. When we're caught, I'm going to get the lightest sentence. That's if we're not blown out of the water first.

SPLASH: What's up, Spider? You're like a cat on a hot tin roof.

SPIDER: Am I? (*He sits but locks his hands together and displays all the signs of agitation. To* COCK *irritably*): Doesn't working agree with you?

TANNOY: Now hear this. There will be no rounds tonight.

HOUSEY *enters. He looks around but doesn't speak. He is dressed in a similar fashion to the other chiefs.*

COCK: Like a cup of tea, Housey?

HOUSEY (*watches as* COCK *begins to pour it*): I'll help myself when I'm ready.

COCK: Be like that.

HOUSEY: Like what?

COCK: Ungrateful.

HOUSEY: Just get on with your duties and less cackle. And you two are as much to blame. You should be setting an example.

SPLASH: Stop manking, Housey. Let's just relax for four hours. It's been one hell of a watch.

HOUSEY (*enthusiastic but a bit strange*): It's been a terrific watch. History is being made around us. *Superior* will be famous and we're part of it. Like the *Amethyst* escaping down the Yangtze. Do you know that story, Roach?

COCK: 'Fraid not.

HOUSEY: No you wouldn't. That was one to be proud of. And there are hundreds of others. *Cambletown, Kelly, Upholder, Glowworm, Hood.*

Renown . . .

COCK: Hold on, Housey. Some of those were sunk. You're not making any comparisons?

HOUSEY: Don't you take anything seriously? Don't you know what's going on out there?

COCK: Frankly no. And that's the trouble.

HOUSEY: Nor do you care.

COCK: Of course I care. What do you expect me to do? Jump up and sing 'Hearts of Oak'? I care all right. Starting with number one.

HOUSEY: Typical . . . Where did the navy ever find you?

COCK: Maybe you volunteered for submarines, Housey, but I had no choice. I was drafted, and for five years. I sat the exam which no one ever failed, because if you fail it deliberately they know and they pass you anyway. If you don't sit the exam you get court-martialled so that's why I'm here and I'm fucking petrified by the way the lot of you are reacting. This is life or death. Not a Butlin's outing. We're not just going home after a few beers and a knees-up.

HOUSEY: What you're saying is mutinous.

COCK: Are they going to blindfold me and make me walk the plank?

HOUSEY: You'd crack jokes at a funeral.

COCK: I'd crack jokes at yours.

SPLASH: OK that's enough. Cool it. Take it easy, Housey. If you're going to pick on Cock there's no way you can win.

COCK: Unless you pull your rank.

HOUSEY: I might just do that.

COCK: If you do make sure there are no loopholes, because if there are, I'll find them.

SPLASH: OK, Cock. The point's taken. Don't push your luck.

SPIDER: All this bitching is getting on my tits. Why should Boris worry about us. The British navy versus the Russian. That's a farce.

HOUSEY: The only thing you lot are good at is dripping.

COCK: I'd just like some reassurance. What sort of lunatic situation are we getting ourselves in? Is it unreasonable to want to know that?

HOUSEY: You're in good hands.

COCK: Jesus, Housey. Is that what you really believe? That's what lemmings say as they follow the one ahead. We are here as a deterrent. Got that? Once we take the initiative we fail.

HOUSEY: Who says we are taking the initiative.

COCK: Aren't we going somewhere we shouldn't?

HOUSEY: We could be anywhere.

COCK: OK. But we're going after something that's not ours. When we find it let's hope they don't mind too much.

HOUSEY: We're not alone.

COCK: That's no comfort. When everything else has failed it's us. We're the last resort.

HOUSEY: Like I said we're in good hands.

COCK: Who are you kidding? With everyone going on about being covered in glory and history being made around us, the whole thing is just an exercise in heroism.

HOUSEY: That's important for morale.

COCK: I personally would like more logic and less emotion.

HOUSEY: You can always stay down here with your broom and knowing you, you will.

COCK: Right first time, Housey. That makes a change. I know what you want. A re-run of Boy Cornwall VC. Me manning the gun and blazing away before dying at my post.

HOUSEY: Always the smart Alec.

COCK: There's nothing more vulnerable than a submarine. I've told you some of the stories.

HOUSEY: And we don't want to hear anymore. You're destructive, Roach.

COCK: I just have a different point of view.

HOUSEY: The navy doesn't want to hear it.

COCK: You speak for the navy now?

SPIDER: Have you two finished?

HOUSEY: I'm putting him in his place. It's about time someone did.

COCK: And I'm just getting underway.

HOUSEY: You're a little Jack Strop. In a dog watch and thinks he knows it all.

COCK: So what are you? You're still working yourself up the ranks and you're hardly on the first rung. The navy promises to use talents you never knew you had, I suppose that's partly true. I didn't know I had a talent to clean.

HOUSEY: You haven't, but that's all they want from you. You've got nowhere and you'll get nowhere. (*He points at the tannoy.*) They're on to you, you don't have to work your ticket, they will give it to you. You're not navy material and they know it. (*He points at the tannoy.*) They don't want you for all your so-called brains. You are this boat's idiot. You've left your mark all right. AB Cock Roach – the perfect name, something to be stamped on and squashed. Vermin. (*He shakes his head, a little bit mad.*) Vermin and dirt.

SPLASH: That's it, you two. Roach, out.

COCK: I haven't finished using my talent.

SPLASH: You haven't started yet.

COCK: I'm about to.

SPLASH: Tomorrow.

COCK: If we live that long.

HOUSEY: Get out!

SPIDER: Shut up, shut up, shut up.

It's really intense. Is it really an act? SPIDER has been behaving in a restless and agitated way throughout this scene.

TANNOY: Now hear there. No smoking throughout the boat until further notice. No smoking throughout the boat.

SPIDER *and* HOUSEY *are smoking.*

SPIDER: Bloody typical. Just when you need one most.

TANNOY: Missile officer report to captain.

HOUSEY (*taking a last long drag*): Something's happening.

They stub out their cigarettes. After a pause the CHAPLAIN *puts his head around the door.*

CHAPLAIN: I'm wearing my teacher's hat at the moment. (*To* HOUSEY.) Finally the two text books you've been waiting for, returned.

HOUSEY: Thank you, sir.

CHAPLAIN: Isn't it marvellous? Suddenly a real purpose to this patrol. Walking through this boat tonight you could sense the expectation. In every mess the men are keyed up. Hardly anyone can sleep, so in case you can't, chief, I thought I'd bring these myself. I'm sure you'll find them a great help.

HOUSEY: I'm sure they will be, sir.

CHAPLAIN: So you don't need to worry. Between myself and our young genius here, we'll get you through with flying colours. Isn't that right, Roach?

COCK: Miracles do happen, sir. But that's more your department.

CHAPLAIN: Always cheerful, no matter what the situation.

COCK: What's happened to the muzak, sir?

CHAPLAIN: Shut down due to the red alert, it's standing orders.

HOUSEY: I would have thought that was obvious.

CHAPLAIN: We're all learning, chief. It's also new to me.

The tannoy bursts into life with the sound of the bosun's pipe.

CAPTAIN (*voice over*): This is the captain speaking. I want to bring you all up to date on the present red alert situation. We now have an accurate fix on UVU4 and we're rapidly closing on the area. In preparation I'm stepping up to a higher state of readiness. Keep your voices low and movements throughout the boat to a minimum. All unnecessary machinery will be shut off. It goes without saying that I expect you to carry out your duties quietly, and be prepared for any emergency. That is all for now.

NUMBER ONE (*voice over*): Now hear there, all quiet throughout the boat.

The noise of the engine winds down and half the lights are extinguished. The ping of the ASDIC continues.

CHAPLAIN (*quietly*): Not knowing the procedure I'd better wait here. Out of harm's way. No one minds?

HOUSEY: No, sir.

CHAPLAIN: We're all in the same boat, after all. (*He moves a chair to sit at the table and scrapes it. Everyone gives him a look.*) Sorry.

COCK *moves around quietly and pours tea. He gives a mug to* HOUSEY *who accepts it. Then he goes to* SPIDER.

COCK: More tea, vicar? (*He sniggers nervously.* SPIDER *takes the cup.*) Are you ready?

SPLASH: Listen to it. (*The ASDIC signal begins to change.*) It's bouncing off something. Listen. (*They all do. After a long pause they look at each other. No one is sure about what to do.* COCK *folds his arms across his body and begins to rub his upper arms. He looks across at* SPIDER *who is avoiding him*). Do you think it's the missile?

COCK: What else could it be?

SPLASH: We've found it.

There is a dramatic change in tone as the signal bounces back. It reaches a crescendo then stops. The only sound is the motor at half-speed. More of a purr. They are all perfectly still looking from one to another for a confirmation, except HOUSEY, *who has moved to his locker. He opens it and brings out his number one suit and lays it on his bunk. He begins to change.*

COCK: I wish someone knew what was . happening.

CHAPLAIN: It's obviously going to plan. The missile has been located.

COCK: I wonder what it looks like? We must be on the sea bed. How deep do you think we are, Spider?

SPIDER: I don't know.

COCK: When the last patrol was over, do you know what I noticed first? The smell of the fresh air in the Loch. It was like new mown hay in a barn, warm and sweet and I took in gulps of it.

The CHAPLAIN *gives him an indulgent look and puts a finger to his lips. They wait for some moments.* COCK *is nervous. Eventually:*

What happens next?

SPIDER: I don't know.

COCK: Hazard a guess.

SPIDER: Stop asking all these questions, keep the noise down.

COCK (*after a long pause*): It's got cold all of a sudden hasn't it? (*Pause.*) Well hasn't it?

SPLASH: I'm sweating neaters.

COCK: I think it's cold, don't you, Spider?

SPIDER *doesn't answer. By now* HOUSEY *is seated on his bunk. He is now in his complete uniform and is tying his shoe-laces.*

SPLASH: With the air conditioning off and you're cold.

He turns to look at HOUSEY *and is astonished.* HOUSEY *stands and gets his cap.*

Spider. (*He nudges him.*) Look.

They all do. HOUSEY *is filling his brown holdall. He finishes and turns to the mess. He speaks in a normal voice. It sounds unnaturally loud for the others have all talked in whispers.*

HOUSEY: I'm off now, lads. I hope you all have a nice weekend.

SPIDER (*whispers*): Fuck's sake, shit in it.

SPLASH: What's got into you? Where are you going.

HOUSEY: I'm off home. Cynth is on the jetty and she doesn't like to be kept waiting.

He picks up the holdall and crosses to COCK *who like the rest is transfixed.* HOUSEY *holds out his hand.* COCK *takes it.*

Thanks Cock, for all your help.

COCK (*whispering*): Are you mad?

HOUSEY (*ignoring it*): I couldn't have passed without you. You were right, it was no sweat. I only hope one day I can return the favour.

COCK: Housey. You're not going anywhere.

HOUSEY: Yes. It's my weekend off. Well lads, must rush. We're house-hunting, something bigger with a decent-size garden. I've put my foot down there. I want room for an asparagus bed. I've always wanted to try my hand at growing them.

He goes to the door and knocks a clip off. It clangs. SPIDER *and* SPLASH *run and grab him.*

SPIDER (*whispering*): You can't go anywhere, we're at the bottom of the fucking ocean.

HOUSEY: No.

He makes a desperate grab at the clips.

SPLASH (*whispering*): Shut up. Come in and sit down. Come on, vicar. Do something.

HOUSEY (*shouting*): Get your hands off me. I'm late. I'm adrift. I've got to go. You can't keep me.

SPLASH: Cock, go get the doc.

CHAPLAIN: Come and sit down, chief. It's all right. We're all safe.

HOUSEY: No we're not. We're stuck here. We're running out of air. We're all going to die, like the *Affray.* (*He breaks free and charges around the mess.*) I don't want to die. Not like this. God I don't want to die. (*He falls on his knees and pounds the deck.*) Let me go home.

The CHAPLAIN *goes to him.*

CHAPLAIN: It's all right chief.

HOUSEY: It's not all right.

The CHAPLAIN *tries to restrain him and* HOUSEY *lashes out, knocking him down.*

TANNOY: All quiet, For'd.

COCK *has the door open and* HOUSEY *goes to charge through it.* SPLASH *and* SPIDER *try to restrain him but he fights as if possessed.*

HOUSEY: Get out of my way. All of you. I'm an officer. An officer. You hear me. I did it. She's so proud of me.

COCK *stands at the door.* HOUSEY *pushes* SPLASH *away and knocks* SPIDER *onto his bunk.* SPLASH *jumps on his back and there is a melée.*

SPLASH: Fuck, he bit me.

SPIDER: Hit him, Splash.

SPLASH *does so and* HOUSEY *slumps.*

SPIDER: Let's get him to the sick bay, quick.

They manhandle him out.

TANNOY: I repeat all quiet for'd.

SPLASH: OK you lot, back to your messes, the show's over.

The CHAPLAIN *hauls himself back onto his feet. They're all back to whispering again.*

CHAPLAIN: The poor man. The strain. Who had any idea?

SPLASH *comes into the mess. He slumps into a chair.*

SPLASH: Fucking Ada, could you believe it? (*He examines his hand.* SPIDER *comes in.*) How could he get in a state like that?

SPIDER (*to the* CHAPLAIN): Are you OK?

CHAPLAIN: Yes, chief.

SPIDER: Then what are you doing here?

CHAPLAIN: What should I do?

SPIDER: Report it. I'll go if you like. It'll sound better coming from you.

CHAPLAIN: Quite right, chief. The captain will want to know the details.

He nods at them all and goes. SPIDER *follows him to the door and closes it after him. He then walks towards* COCK *and faces him.* COCK *defiantly returns the stare.*

The tannoy comes on.

CAPTAIN (*voice over*): We have reason to suspect that an unidentified vessel is nearby. For the time being we are going to maintain our present position. There will be a state of ultra quiet throughout the boat. Any noise will reveal our position. We are going to lie deep, stationary and silent. Only watch-keeping personnel may leave their mess. All others turn in.

SPIDER (*whispering*): You'd better get back to your mess.

COCK (*whispering*): I'll stay here.

SPIDER: I don't want you here.

There is a long pause then SPIDER *cuffs* COCK. *A longer pause.*

COCK: OK. If it makes you feel better, blame me. You didn't take your opportunity but I'm going to take mine.

SPIDER: What does that mean?

COCK *puts his index finger to his mouth and:* 'Schuuuu'. *He leaves the mess.*

NUMBER ONE (*voice over*): Ultra quiet throughout the boat. Ultra quiet throughout the boat.

All the lights are extinguished leaving the red night lights. The noise of the machinery stops and for the first time there is complete silence. SPLASH and SPIDER go to their respective bunks and turn in. Thirty seconds go by. Then the entertainment tannoy crackles into life.

COCK (*voice over*):
On the good ship Lollipop
It's a sweet trip to a candy shop
Where bon bons play – on the sunny beach of Peppermint Bay
Lemonade stands everywhere, cracker-jack bands fill the air
And there you are – happy landing on a chocolate bar
See the sugar bowl do a tootsie roll with the big devil's food cake
If you eat too much ooh! ooh!
You'll wake with a tummy ache
On the good ship Lollipop
It's a night trip into bed you hop
With this command and dream away –
All aboard for candy land.
On the good ship Lollipop –

SPIDER and SPLASH sit up and stare at the tannoy. COCK continues singing and behind it can be heard banging on the door. The banging increases and finally the door breaks. A struggle ensues and then silence, when the tannoy is switched off. SPLASH and SPIDER look at each other then the ping starts quietly. It is different from the first ASDIC for it is more of a screech.

SPIDER: Is that us?

SPLASH: Someone else. Jesus Christ we've been caught.

The tannoy bursts into life. Lights go on blindingly.

CAPTAIN (*voice over*): Stand by to surface. All hands to emergency stations. Blow main ballast.

SPLASH and SPIDER scramble off their bunks and run off at the double. The screech gets louder and louder until it is deafening. Then everything goes black and silent. After some seconds a light comes on revealing COCK dressed as a British Airways steward.

COCK: Housey got a medical discharge, but he's still in uniform handing out parking tickets. Nothing too taxing and he gets lots of fresh air. I'm still in uniform as well but flying the flag instead of showing it. I'm an airline steward. Jumbos on the Jo'burg run. When it really gets me down I work on my plan for the ultimate hijack. Unfortunately there is no airport at Utopia.

Anyway I got a dishonourable discharge after the court-martial and after eighteen months in DQ's. I was told it would've been a longer sentence but they took into consideration the fact that there was no missile. *Superior* was only on an exercise. The Royal Navy was playing a bigger game than I was. I fell for it, hook, line and sinker. Sometimes I wonder if it was a game I was playing. Submarines really do weird things to your mind. In my defence the chaplain said I had the devil in me. Funny, people have been saying that all my life. Before I joined up I read that there are three kinds of people. Those who are alive, those who are dead and those who are at sea. At first I didn't understand it, but I do now. Anyway, (*he sings*) Come fly with me, float off in the blue, etc.

COCK *continues to sing as the lights fade.*

THE GREEN BAY TREE

The Green Bay Tree was first presented at St Martin's Theatre, London, on 25 January 1933, with the following cast:

TRUMP	Henry Hewitt
MR DULCIMER	Frank Vosper
JULIAN	Hugh Williams
LEONORA YALE	Catherine Lacey
MR OWEN	Herbert Lomas

Produced by Milton Rosmer
Designed by Molly McArthur

The Green Bay Tree subsequently opened in New York at the Cort Theatre, on 20 October 1933, with the following cast:

TRUMP	Leo G. Carroll
MR DULCIMER	James Dale
JULIAN	Laurence Olivier
LEONORA YALE	Jill Esmond
MR OWEN	O.P. Heggie

Directed by Jed Harris
Designed by Robert Edmond Jones

Act One
Scene One: Mr Dulcimer's flat in Mayfair. May.
Scene Two: The same, some hours later.

Act Two
Scene One: Mr Owen's house in Camden Town. August.
Scene Two: Mr Dulcimer's, the same evening.

Act Three
Scene One: Mr Dulcimer's, the next morning.
Scene Two: The same, six months later.

The Green Bay Tree

First presented at St Martin's Theatre, London, on 25 January 1933, Mordaunt Shairp's somewhat melodramatic play, *The Green Bay Tree*, ran for a respectable six months, later transferring to Broadway (with the young Laurence Olivier). And *The Green Bay Tree* flourished; almost twenty years later it was revived in London (Playhouse Theatre, 1950) and in New York (Golden Theatre, 1951). Even as late as the mid-sixties, *The Creeper*, a play by Pauline Macaulay, showed every indication of being in direct line of descent from Shairp's moral tale about the dangers to facile young men from rich and predatory homosexuals.

The word homosexual is nowhere used in Shairp's play, but from the first scene it is obvious that it is the central theme of the piece. Mr Dulcimer, a confirmed bachelor of Wildean aspect, possessing great wealth, fussily arranges the fresh flowers sent up from his country estate. In an exchange which echoes the opening of the third act of *An Ideal Husband* (Lord Goring and his manservant Phipps discussing buttonholes), Dulcimer and his valet Trump converse about tulips and irises.

Whilst Wilde was aiming for wit, Shairp is setting up Dulcimer ('Dulcie' to his friends) as the epitome of effeminacy. This brief exchange quickly telegraphs the information to the audience that 'Dulcie' is not a 'real man', that he must therefore be decadent and, thus, is not to be trusted. The scene also adroitly establishes the slightly sinister bond between Dulcimer and Trump, whose obsequiousness makes him a rival to Uriah Heep.

With the entrance of Julian, Dulcimer's twenty-three-year-old adopted son, the play begins to gather speed. Beautiful, languid and pampered, Julian represents a younger image of Dulcimer (interestingly, the late Hugh Williams was cast as Julian in the 1933 London production and as Dulcimer in the 1950 London revival). Julian exists for luxury and attention, but is about to throw the well-ordered Mayfair household into a state of refined turmoil. He is in love, he declares. He wishes to marry.

By cunningly abbreviating names, Shairp distorts established gender values. Mr Dulcimer is diminished as a man when he is referred to as 'Dulcie' (decidedly feminine): Leonora Yale, the object of Julian's attentions, is enhanced when she is referred to as 'Leo' (decidedly masculine). It is a virtue when a woman (Leonora) is possessed of masculine 'strengths'; to both dramatist and audience, it is patently a vice when feminine 'virtues' are adopted by a man (Mr Dulcimer, Julian, Trump).

In 1933, the attitudes of society towards homosexuality differed very little from those which prevailed at the time of the Oscar Wilde trials, still then within living memory and due to be recreated on the London stage in Sewell Stokes's biographical play (with Robert Morley, Gate Theatre, 1936). That Dulcimer had the same tastes as Wilde was obvious to any audience – and Shairp's stagecraft fully endorsed the audience's fears and prejudices.

Nor were the responses of the critics of the day any more enlightened. Though the play itself garnered good reviews ('I cautiously predict that *The Green Bay Tree* will be one of the three best plays of 1933.' – *Evening News*; 'One of the best plays we have had for a long time.' – *Time and Tide*; 'He has enriched the world with a most remarkable play.' – *Sketch*), the character of Dulcimer came in for a sound trouncing (*The Times* described 'Dulcie' as 'Evil'; the *New Statesman* called him '. . . a wealthy degenerate').

The Green Bay Tree is a very simplistic play about the battle between good (Leonora, Mr Owen – Julian's rather boring actual father) and evil (Dulcimer, Trump) fought over a rather worthless battleground (Julian). Quite why the intelligent and fastidious Dulcimer and the commonsense Leonora should be so infatuated with Julian is a mystery. He is a callow youth, living only for sensation; almost certainly devoid of any genuine feeling or emotion. Both 'Dulcie' and 'Leo' could do better for themselves.

Though perhaps Mr Dulcimer is simply following a convention (in fiction and in real life) of homosexual men of his class and historical period: the need to act as a father substitute to a youth from the working class, often unworthy of their attentions and often maintained because of the misery they cause their keeper – this latter state indicating the level of guilt and self-loathing many gay men appear to have felt about themselves – thus, love equals suffering equals expiation of guilt.

Perhaps the most extraordinary thing about *The Green Bay Tree* is the conclusion. Anyone reading the play would be fully justified in anticipating a full-blown virtue triumphant ending – Julian and Leonora clasped for ever in each other's arms. But this is not to be. One traditional convention at least is adhered to: the death of the homosexual villain (in this instance, Dulcimer). Yet, in the end, it is Dulcimer who is triumphant.

The final scene brings the play full circle. Dulcimer is dead – but Julian is now in possession of his fortune. Believing Julian's inheritance to be tainted, 'Leo' refuses to have anything further to do with him. Trump – who in an off-stage scene has resigned because he doesn't want any truck with the female servants he feared would accompany Leonora – withdraws his resignation. As the curtain fall, Julian and Trump are arranging flowers. Julian's dialogue echoes that of Mr Dulcimer from the first scene. Truly, 'Dulcie' has created Julian in his own image and, in time, we can imagine Julian as 'Julie', worrying about some young man he too wishes to mould into his own likeness.

Will Julian be happy? Supremely so, almost certainly. And Trump? Undoubtedly. Leonora? She will find another young man to dominate and settle into boring married bliss. And Mr Dulcimer? From whatever heaven he has entered, he must be smiling.

Now celebrating its fiftieth birthday, *The Green Bay Tree* can only really be read as a historical curiosity. But do not sneer too quickly or form too hasty a judgement; pause for a moment and ponder. Have attitudes really changed very much? Think on it . . .

All that said, are there any good reasons for reprinting the play more than fifty years after its inception? Perhaps just three reasons will serve – firstly, *The Green Bay Tree* is both historically interesting and historically important as possibly the first contemporary drama about homosexuality. It should be remembered that for all the circumlocution of Shairp's language, the play is actually very direct in the treatment of its subject. Secondly, the piece makes for stunningly effective theatre and even on the printed page grips the attention of the reader. A third – and perhaps slightly sentimental – reason would be the rehabilitation of the reputation of a minor but unjustly forgotten dramatist.

A word of thanks to Debbie Collins; Denholm Elliott for his memories of the 1951 New York revival of *The Green Bay Tree* in which he appeared as Julian to Joseph Schildkraut's Mr Dulcimer; Guy Larrington for his research in the library of Sussex University; Colin Mabberley, Curator of The Raymond Mander and Joe Mitchenson Theatre Collection; Hugh Miller and Timothy d'Arch Smith.

Peter Burton

ACT ONE

Scene One

At MR DULCIMER's *flat in Mayfair, London. An evening in May.*

The atmosphere of the room is one of luxury and fastidiousness. The owner is an artist in the sense that everything in the room has been chosen for its intrinsic value and given its absolutely right position in the general scheme of decoration. He never puts up anything because of its associations, nor leaves anything about because the room has been well-used. To the outsider the room is artificial, but it excites curiosity about the owner. To him, it is a constant source of pleasure. It reflects his personality, his sensitiveness, and delicate appreciation of beauty.

The room has a large semi-circular window on the right. This is curtained and fitted with cushioned seats, and looks out on to the tops of trees of a London Square. In the centre of the back wall is the entrance to the roof garden. This is approached up a couple of steps and through handsome wrought-iron gates. When necessary these gates have close-fitting, opaque glass screens behind them, which open out on either side on to the roof garden, being then out of sight, and thus making it possible to see the roof garden through the gates. In the left-hand wall is the only entrance to the room, through large double doors.

The roof garden can be treated in many ways, and can be as large or small as space permits. It should look out over a parapet on to an expanse of sky.

The furniture is arranged in this way: on the right, down stage, below the window, is a small table against the wall with a flower vase on it. On the other side of the window, up stage, is a radio-gramophone. By the window is an armchair.

Against the back wall, on the right-hand side of the gates, is an old embroidery frame with a stool in front of it. On the left-hand side of the roof garden is a small rostrum on which stands a grand piano placed at such an angle that when MR DULCIMER *sits at it he can survey the whole room. On the piano stands a bowl of flowers. The dais and piano fill up the left-hand corner. On the other side of the doors into the room, down stage, is the fireplace. Below this is a writing bureau with a telephone on top of it, and a small stool in front. The rest of the furniture consists of a couch at right angles to the fireplace, but as the piano is on a dais, the couch does not mask* MR DULCIMER, *when playing, from the audience.*

Behind the couch is a table useful as a side-table at dinner and for drinks. It should be as high as the back of the couch. In the middle of the room is a round dining-table with a chair on either side.

There are very few ornaments in the room, but it is suggested that the walls should be painted and not papered, and that over the mantelpiece should be a decorative painting by a modern artist.

When the curtain rises the room is empty and TRUMP, *an immaculate butler, enters with three evening papers in his hand. He places two on the bureau below the fireplace, and then opens the 'Evening Standard' and reads it for a moment. Hearing steps in the passage, he places it hurriedly on the other two. He then goes to the table in the centre which is laid for dinner for two people, and appears to be putting the finishing touches to the things on it.*

The doors open again, and MR DULCIMER *enters. He is a man of about forty-five, immaculately turned out, and wearing at present a double-breasted dinner jacket. He speaks exquisitely, in a clear voice, and with now and then a slight drawl. He has a habit of looking at you from under his eyes, and though a complete dilettante, he has an alert, vibrating personality. A man who could fascinate, repel and alarm. Instantly we know that he is the one thing missing in the room, and he seems to know it, too, for he stands a moment inside the doors, almost as if he were 'taking a call' for having created it. He walks to the end of the Knowle couch and stands looking round the room.*

TRUMP *is still busied with the table.*

DULCIMER: Trump!

TRUMP: Yes, sir!

DULCIMER: The room looks very naked!

TRUMP (*standing to attention*): I didn't get any fresh flowers, sir.

DULCIMER (*drawlingly*): And why didn't you get any fresh flowers?

TRUMP: You haven't used the ones from Silver Gates, sir. The gardener sent them up this morning.

DULCIMER: Why didn't you tell me sooner? I'm terribly overdressed for doing flowers.

TRUMP (*gravely, as he begins to move towards the door*): Shall I get you an apron, sir?

DULCIMER (*meditatingly, as he comes down to the hearth*): No. I don't think I'll have an apron.

TRUMP: Could you trust me to arrange them?

DULCIMER: What flowers has Paget sent?

TRUMP: Tulips, sir! . . . And irises and a rose or two.

DULCIMER: I don't think I could trust you with a tulip.

TRUMP: Perhaps not, sir . . .

DULCIMER (*decisively*): I'll do them. Get me that little table and my gloves.

TRUMP: Very good, sir.

TRUMP *goes to the small table, right, below the window, and moves it opposite the window seat.* DULCIMER *has moved to the bureau below the fireplace and has picked up the 'Evening Standard'. He holds it between his finger and thumb.*

DULCIMER: Someone's been tampering with the papers, Trump!

TRUMP (*innocently*): Really, sir? (*He fetches a vase from the piano.*)

DULCIMER: I hate sharing a newspaper. (*He drops the paper on the couch.* TRUMP *places the vase on the small table by the window.*) Is Mr Julian in yet? (*Coming to the centre of the room.*)

TRUMP: Not yet, sir!

DULCIMER: I do hope he's not going to be late again.

TRUMP: Perhaps he won't be in to dinner, sir?

DULCIMER (*with a drawl*): And why shouldn't he be in to dinner?

TRUMP (*with a slight suggestion that he knows more*): No reason, sir.

DULCIMER: Very well. Get me the flowers.

TRUMP: Yes, sir. (*He moves to the door.*)

DULCIMER: Trump!

TRUMP (*turning round*): Yes, sir?

DULCIMER (*taking a cigarette case out of his pocket*): You let me go out today without my cigarette case! I had to smoke Lady Pelham's. Unfiltered! I believe she smokes them for the coupons.

TRUMP: It shan't occur again, sir! (*Exits.*)

DULCIMER *walks across to the small table by the window and lights a cigarette.* TRUMP *returns with a tray of flowers, scissors and a pair of gloves. He places the tray on the table.*

DULCIMER (*as he puts on the gloves*): Thank you. I hope Paget has been careful this time about the stalks. (*He takes out an iris and examines it.*) That's better. (*He puts it in a vase.*) Get me an ashtray.

TRUMP *takes an ashtray from the centre table and puts it by him.*

We'll have the irises on the piano, and the tulips on the dinner table.

TRUMP: Very good, sir. (*Hearing the sound of a door slamming.*) I think that must be Mr Julian!

DULCIMER (*petulantly*): I've only just started these. I thought I had taught him how to time things properly.

Enter JULIAN, *a handsome boy in the early twenties, charming and well-made, but self-assured and self-indulged. Like* MR DULCIMER *he is dressed perfectly. He has just a suspicion of knowing that he is late for dinner. He is opening a couple of invitations.*

JULIAN: Hullo! Dulcie! I'm frightfully sorry I'm late!

Exit TRUMP. JULIAN *comes over to* DULCIMER's *side.*

DULCIMER: My dear boy. I'd almost given you up. What have you been doing with yourself?

JULIAN: I've been out all the afternoon. I've absolutely fallen in love with the new car.

DULCIMER: Have you? I'm so glad. I thought you'd like it.

JULIAN: I've been taking it for a run in Richmond Park. (*He moves over to the fireplace and puts the invitations on the bureau.*)

DULCIMER: How terribly healthy! I've been to a heartrending private view.

JULIAN: Did you buy anything? (*He picks up the paper off the couch.*)

DULCIMER: No. I missed you. You're always so instinctively right about modern art.

JULIAN *looks pleased.*

As a matter of fact, you promised to come.

JULIAN: Did I? I forgot all about it.

DULCIMER: You've been forgetting a good many things lately. Don't forget that we're going to the opera tomorrow night.

JULIAN (*not altogether pleased.*): Are we? (*He sits on the couch and looks at the paper.*)

DULCIMER: Yes. Edward Trammle has offered me his box. Fortunately I was out when he brought it in. I only hope he won't come too. I shall never forget how he fidgeted through the whole of *Götterdämmerung.*

JULIAN: What is it tomorrow?

DULCIMER: *Tristan.*

JULIAN: That means early dinner.

DULCIMER: Not at all. I never arrive at *Tristan* till the second act.

JULIAN (*with meaning*): I shall be in the mood for *Tristan* tomorrow.

DULCIMER (*carrying the bowl of tulips to the piano.*) It's the most exquisite love story ever imagined. Quite perfect. I'll go through the score again with you in the morning.

JULIAN (*moving to the window*): Aren't these first spring days marvellous?

DULCIMER (*from the piano*): Don't use that dreadful word! 'Marvellous' is the expletive of the ignorant and unimaginative. When you hear anyone describe an experience as 'marvellous', you can be sure that it has made no impression on them whatever. (*He comes back to the table and does the other vase.*)

JULIAN (*by the window*): I don't know how to describe what I felt this afternoon.

DULCIMER: Don't try then. Only poets can do justice to the spring, that cruel, terrifying time.

JULIAN: Terrifying?

DULCIMER: There is always something terrifying in the remorselessness of nature, something shattering in all this reassertion of the principle of life. Trump has got it badly. He rumpled the *Evening Standard.*

JULIAN (*laughing*): I believe I've got it too.

DULCIMER: There is a distinctly bucolic look in your eye. In another moment you'll tell me you've been to the Westminster Baths.

JULIAN (*moving round below the centre table and up to the roof garden gates*): I felt very like it.

DULCIMER: When the really warm days come, we'll go down to Silver Gates. You'll find the amber pool preferable to the sweaty transports of the Westminster Baths. (*Reflectively.*) I think I shall have amethyst cushions this year in the seats around the edge of the pool. Tomorrow we'll go and choose (*he makes a lot of the word*) the material together.

JULIAN: How you love the word 'choose'! (*He moves down below the couch.*)

DULCIMER: Choice is what separates the artist from the common herd. Nobody knows how to choose nowadays. I hope you will never forego your prerogative of choice. Never do anything that is unconsidered, or take what is second best.

JULIAN: But supposing one is carried away? There are moments when one just can't choose.

DULCIMER: Rise above those moments with a colossal assertion of your individuality. (*Pointing through the open window.*) Look at those colours down there in the Square. That is how I like to see nature, controlled and at my feet. Don't wallow in her.

JULIAN: I don't think I've quite got your detachment.

DULCIMER: It's the result of sensitiveness. But then, I think I've made you sensitive.

JULIAN: I'll rush into a dinner jacket. (*He goes out gaily.*)

DULCIMER (*as* TRUMP *enters*): Trump! Trump!

TRUMP: Yes, sir?

DULCIMER (*pointing to the table*): When on earth are you going to take all this away? I look like a wayside shrine! (TRUMP *puts the tulips on the table.*) I hate being lagered in with tables.

TRUMP *puts the table back by the window.* DULCIMER *takes off his gloves and puts them on the table. He then goes to the piano, sits down at it and plays softly.*

DULCIMER (*pointing to roof garden gates*): I think we'll have those closed.

TRUMP: These light evenings are deceptive, sir. (*He closes the doors.*) Shall I draw the curtains?

DULCIMER: Not yet. But we'll dine by candlelight.

TRUMP: Very good, sir. (*He goes to the bureau, takes a taper and a box of matches; lights the taper.*)

At that moment the sun goes in.

DULCIMER (*playing*): How obliging of the sun to go in! (*He watches* TRUMP *light the candles.*) That looks very attractive. The whole room looks attractive.

TRUMP: Shall I turn up the lights as well?

DULCIMER: No, thank you. I hate a glare.

TRUMP (*having collected the tray and gloves from the table below the window*): I've got the cocktails outside, sir!

DULCIMER: Very well; we'll drink cocktails till Mr Julian is ready. He deserves to miss them.

TRUMP: I've got a sidecar for Mr Julian.

Perhaps you would prefer sherry?

DULCIMER: Perhaps I should.

Exit TRUMP. MR DULCIMER *plays for a moment, then comes to the table and eats an olive meditatively.* TRUMP *returns with the drinks on a tray.*

TRUMP (*as* MR DULCIMER *takes his sherry from the tray*): Perhaps this is the moment to break a piece of bad news to you, sir.

DULCIMER: You mean that you've done the breaking already?

TRUMP (*behind the table*): Oh, no, sir, it's much worse than that.

DULCIMER (*a shadow crossing his face*): It's nothing about Mr Julian?

TRUMP: Oh dear, no, sir.

DULCIMER: Let me sit down first. (*He sits down on the couch. He sips his sherry.*)

TRUMP (*by the corner of the couch*): It's only this, sir. I'm afraid the drill is coming to the Square.

DULCIMER: The drill?

TRUMP: The pneumatic drill. They're going to have the road up.

DULCIMER (*deploringly*): Am I never to be left in peace?

TRUMP: I knew it would be a shock. I hardly knew how to tell you, sir.

DULCIMER: I shan't eat a thing at dinner.

TRUMP: It's a short dinner, sir.

DULCIMER: You've got an ice for Mr Julian?

TRUMP: Coupe 'Evelyn Laye'.

DULCIMER: Why?

TRUMP: It looks so beautiful, sir.

DULCIMER: I could have managed a plover's egg. How long are they to be kept away from me?

TRUMP: I'm afraid for ever, sir.

DULCIMER: Good God!

TRUMP: I had hoped the authorities would be satisfied with a year or two. But I'm afraid it's 'never again'! They're eating seagulls' eggs in some restaurants, sir.

DULCIMER: Where do they find them? On the Embankment?

Enter JULIAN, *also in a double-breasted dinner jacket. There is now a rather grotesque likeness between him and* MR DULCIMER.

JULIAN (*coming over to* TRUMP *behind the table, and taking his cocktail*): I'm ready, Trump.

Exit TRUMP.

DULCIMER: Julian, which would you rather, go to Silver Gates or to Margherita?

JULIAN: Must we go to either?

DULCIMER: I'm afraid we must. The road's coming up.

JULIAN: But I can't take Peter if we go to Italy.

DULCIMER: I suppose you can tear yourself away from your dog for a month or two?

JULIAN (*over by the window*): I don't much want to tear myself away from London. The nicest time of the year is just beginning.

DULCIMER: You know that they always mend the roads at the nicest time of the year.

JULIAN: Would that matter very much?

DULCIMER (*rising*): Would it matter? I refuse to stay here with the Square full of men frying bacon in tarpaulin huts. *He puts his glass on the table behind the couch, and moves back to the dining table and eats another olive.*

JULIAN: Well, I like the next couple of months in London. *He puts his glass on the table behind the couch and comes to the dining table and eats an olive.*

DULCIMER: Shall we sit down? This isn't a quick-lunch counter.

They sit on either side of the table.

JULIAN: It's going to be decent weather, too. We haven't had a fine season for ages.

DULCIMER: Supposing we go to Silver Gates? That's not far from London, and you can take your beloved Peter.

JULIAN *is silent.* TRUMP *comes in with the dinner on a trolley-waiter. The dinner can be made to seem natural and not too hurried if the first course is something easily disposed of, like tomato-juice cocktail, so that the second course follows at once, and if there are the pauses indicated by* JULIAN's *silence, in the dialogue that follows.*

I looked forward to dining with you tonight. I've been so bored all day. I had a most miserable lunch.

JULIAN (*curtly*): With whom?

DULCIMER: Millicent Armstrong. She would talk about the fourth dimension. All I got was a couple of quails. In the end I had to tell her that I was a very coarse feeder.

TRUMP *opens a bottle of champagne with a pop.*

What an exquisite noise! I didn't actually order it, Trump. Are you a thought reader?

TRUMP: I thought that everything pointed to it, sir. (*He fills* DULCIMER's *glass, then goes to* JULIAN.)

DULCIMER: Mr Julian will want a magnum if his melancholia continues. I hate people who eat in silence. It's so bestial. We shall end by having wireless during dinner.

JULIAN: The last thing I want to do is to spoil your dinner.

DULCIMER: I'm just devouring what's put in front of me simply because it's there. That's such a pity, because nobody else knows anything about food nowadays. It doesn't matter! Trump will stay and talk to me.

JULIAN: Don't be an ass!

DULCIMER: I knew it! You have been to the Westminster Baths and stayed in too long!

JULIAN: I'm sorry! I want to talk to you. I've got something to tell you. I daresay it will be rather a surprise.

DULCIMER (*to* TRUMP): Farewell! A long farewell!

Exit TRUMP *with the trolley-waiter, having cleared away the used crockery on to it.*

JULIAN: I've a very good reason for

wanting to stay in town.

DULCIMER (*conciliatory*): My dear boy, I'm sure you have!

JULIAN (*after a drink*): I've fallen in love!

DULCIMER: So you remarked just now. I think you said it was with your car.

JULIAN: I don't mean the car this time.

DULCIMER (*cautiously*): You mean?

JULIAN (*nodding his head*): I do.

DULCIMER: All I can say is that I'm sorry for the lady.

JULIAN: Thank you!

DULCIMER: Isn't a lover supposed to idle in 'the wanton summer air' and do something or other with gossamer? You look as if you'd formed an attachment for a police woman.

JULIAN: I'm depressed at having to go away and (*with a slight reluctance*) I thought you might be annoyed about it.

DULCIMER: My dear boy, you ought to know me better. After all the training I've given you in observation! Besides, it's quite . . . what shall I say? Quite an ordinary thing to do. You've played with the idea once or twice before.

JULIAN: I'm not playing this time. (*Firing up.*) I'm desperately in love. It wasn't the real thing before. I can't fight this. It's something outside myself. I can't find words to express it.

DULCIMER: Be as lyrical as you please! I shan't mind. The poorest lover has something of the poet about him.

JULIAN: It's no good my telling you about it unless you're going to be sensible.

DULCIMER: Of course I may have been half-witted all these years without knowing it. (*Conciliatory, as* JULIAN *rises.*) My dear Julian, I can see that you're in earnest. I've known for some time that something was absorbing you. Haven't I been discretion itself in asking no questions?

JULIAN: I suppose I have been a bit secretive.

DULCIMER: Never mind if you have. Tell me about it. I'm probably responsible for the good impression you have made. I take it that the lady returns your passion?

JULIAN: I think so, but you've had nothing to do with this!

DULCIMER (*humouring him*): Perhaps not. Every lover likes to think that he is original.

JULIAN (*rising and moving to the fireplace*): I mean you might not quite understand what I feel. I don't think you've ever been in love!

MR DULCIMER *winces, but* JULIAN *is not looking at him and so does not see him.*

Her name is Leonora Yale. Her people are retired Army and live somewhere in the country. She's a veterinary surgeon.

A moment's silence.

DULCIMER: I suppose that Peter introduced you?

JULIAN: I suppose he did in the first place.

DULCIMER: Another argument against dogs. They create unsubstantial intimacies.

JULIAN: Why unsubstantial?

DULCIMER: Everything seems durable while it lasts. May I put this crude question? How long will your passion for Miss Yale last?

JULIAN: You're certainly crude. I thought you'd be a little out of your depth over this.

DULCIMER: Out of my depth ! Because I ask the old question that has echoed down the ages! Very well then, I won't probe any further, but I must make my arrangements. You take your ecstasy to Silver Gates and I'll go to Margherita. That seems the best arrangement as you're both attached to animals.

JULIAN: I knew you wouldn't understand. (*Quietly.*) I want to *marry* Leo.

DULCIMER *lets his knife and fork fall on to his plate with a slight jarring sound.*

DULCIMER (*his face full of shadows but his voice controlled*): You never mentioned the word 'marry'. (*Leaning forward.*) My dear boy, are you serious?

JULIAN: Perfectly.

DULCIMER: How long have you known

her?

JULIAN: About three months.

DULCIMER: Why didn't you tell me before?

JULIAN: I kept quiet until I was sure.

DULCIMER: And when did you feel sure?

JULIAN: Last night.

DULCIMER (*after a drink*): Julian?

JULIAN: Yes.

DULCIMER: You don't think you'd like to give it another three months and then open the question again?

JULIAN: Ten years won't make any difference. I've made up my mind. I've seen Leo nearly every day. I've been to her surgery, I've met her under a variety of circumstances, and always felt the same.

DULCIMER: In another moment you'll tell me that you were made for each other.

JULIAN: Perhaps we were. But nothing you can say will laugh me out of it. This isn't just a matter of 'choosing'. It's got to be. That's the part I don't expect you to understand.

Enter TRUMP *with* JULIAN's *ice, coffee, and brandy.*

DULCIMER (*irritably*): Put the things on the table, Trump. We'll help ourselves.

TRUMP *does so.*

TRUMP: Will that be all, sir?

DULCIMER: That will be all for the moment.

Exit TRUMP.

(*Taking a cigarette.*) Really! Trump is very exasperating. He's forgotten the lighter!

JULIAN (*coming from the entrance to the roof garden*): I've got a match. (*He takes a box out of his pocket, lights* DULCIMER's *cigarette.*)

You see, Leo's got this Canine Infirmary at Notting Hill, and she's made a great success of it.

DULCIMER: Does she have to do this?

JULIAN (*sitting at the table again*): No, but she's got a flair for animals. So has Ranulf, her partner.

DULCIMER (*craftily*): So she's got a partner?

JULIAN: Yes. They've worked it up together.

DULCIMER (*dreamily*): I believe there was an Archbishop Ranulf in the Middle Ages. I think he got into trouble with the Pope.

JULIAN: She's a little older than I am.

DULCIMER: Is she beautiful?

JULIAN: I think so.

DULCIMER: And so you want to marry her? But of course you do. Lovers are always impulsive. That's why they make so many mistakes.

JULIAN: I know what I am doing. But I realise what this means to you . . . to us both. I shall hate leaving you, Dulcie. You've given me a wonderful life.

DULCIMER: You've been my son since you were eleven years old. Does Leonora know that I'm not your real father?

JULIAN: Yes, of course. I've told her I owe everything to you. My real father couldn't have done as much for me as you have.

DULCIMER (*grimly*): That's certainly true. He couldn't have done anything at all. You mean to get married quite soon?

JULIAN: If possible. (*A look at him.*) Then while Ranulf carries on at the surgery, I want to take Leo abroad. There are heaps of places I'd like to show her. She'd adore Italy.

DULCIMER: You might go to Italy for your honeymoon?

JULIAN: I'm quite keen to stay there for several months.

DULCIMER: Why not? There is scriptural warrant for it. Old Testament honeymoons lasted a year.

JULIAN (*hopefully*): You approve?

DULCIMER: Entirely. And then?

JULIAN: Then I suppose we must settle down somewhere. Leo wants to get on with her work and I'd like to be able to help her. She needs a better surgery in a more central place. I'd like to be able to give it to her.

DULCIMER (*quietly*): Have you told her

you will?

JULIAN: No. (*With a smile at him.*) Not exactly. We've naturally built a few castles. She's very keen on my getting a job.

DULCIMER: And what do you say to that?

JULIAN: I haven't encouraged it enormously. (*With another delightful smile.*)

DULCIMER (*rising and filling their glasses with brandy, then sitting down again. Craftily*): Well, I'm bound to say I think you've handled the whole situation with tact and imagination.

JULIAN: But I know quite well that everything does really depend on you. I can't move a step without you.

DULCIMER: I shall buy you a trousseau and give you away at St Paul's, Knightsbridge.

JULIAN: That's lovely of you! (*Feeling embarrassed.*) But I am just a little anxious to know what's going to happen after that!

DULCIMER: What do you imagine will happen?

JULIAN (*with charm*): I did rather hope that you'd increase my allowance.

DULCIMER: I've always loved your ingenuousness. It's one of your greatest charms. (*Then, like a steel trap, all his silkiness gone.*) I shouldn't dream of increasing it. In fact, if you leave me, I don't propose to make you any allowance whatever.

JULIAN (*laughingly*): Then you're just turning me adrift?

DULCIMER: That's hardly how I should describe a young man who proposes to support a wife.

JULIAN: Support a wife? That sounds rather dreary.

DULCIMER: It's an ugly middle-class term, but you force me to use it. After all, it will be a great novelty for you to earn your own living.

JULIAN (*grimly*): Yes, I suppose it will. (*He rises from the table and goes to the window.*)

DULCIMER: Aren't you going to finish your brandy?

JULIAN (*without looking round*): No thanks. (*Then turning round quickly.*) Do you mean that as soon as I marry Leo, I become penniless?

DULCIMER (*getting up from the table*): Come and sit over here (*pointing to the couch*) and let us try and understand one another.

He takes JULIAN's arm and they go towards the hearth.

Will you let me put the case from my point of view?

JULIAN (*by the fire*): Of course. I know that I haven't got any rights. As I'm not your own son I can't expect to have any.

DULCIMER (*standing at the left-hand corner of the couch*): What are rights? You've had privileges. You've been my constant companion. Have you ever appreciated the compliment?

JULIAN: Of course I have. You've given me everything I could possibly want.

DULCIMER: I did more than that. I created you. I've made you what you are because I rescued you from a life of squalor. I chose you instinctively, just as I have chosen everything else in my life. It was a bold experiment, but I didn't make a mistake. You have always been a very delightful son and companion to me. But life with me and life with Leo are two very different things. You can't expect them to overlap.

JULIAN (*sitting on the couch*): I suppose I can earn my own living like anyone else?

DULCIMER (*craftily*): What's to stop you? You're personable and accomplished. You've travelled. Above all, you've got my training and experience behind you. The blossoming time has come a little earlier than I expected. Never mind! All I ask is that in return for my careful nurture I may be allowed to watch you flower. That will interest me enormously, and I shall be very proud if you succeed. If you fail, I can always rescue you again.

JULIAN: I shan't fail.

DULCIMER (*craftily*): You'll be a poor advertisement for me if you do. (*He sits beside him.*) My dear boy, people will be only too glad to get you!

JULIAN (*eagerly*): Do you think they will?

DULCIMER: I'm sure of it. We must look out for an opening immediately.

JULIAN (*quite impressed by all this*): You didn't mind my – asking you?

DULCIMER: Of course I didn't.

JULIAN: I believe I can do anything I want to.

DULCIMER: Then I should be very wrong to smother your initiative with a few hundreds a year.

JULIAN: I shall have to put off marrying Leo for a bit. I'll explain that to her when she comes. She'll understand that. By the way – she'll be here in a few minutes.

DULCIMER (*springing up*): What?

JULIAN: We're going to the ballet. I asked her to pick me up.

DULCIMER: She's coming here tonight?

JULIAN: I want you to meet her.

DULCIMER (*in his usual ecstasy of protestation*): I do wish you wouldn't spring surprises on me. I'm as shy as an antelope when I'm surprised. (*He rings the bell.*)

The room is now in the imaginary confusion created by MR DULCIMER.

JULIAN (*coming to the table*): I may as well finish my ice. (*He carries it to the window seat.*)

DULCIMER (*ecstatically*): By all means, let us carry our food about the room. I dislike this Bohemian way of dining. I can see the end of all this. I shall sit on a cherry.

Enter TRUMP *with trolley-waiter.*

Clear away, Trump, as quickly as you can. We're expecting a lady here at any moment.

JULIAN: There's plenty of time. Here you are, Trump! I've had enough. (*He hands him the ice.*)

DULCIMER (*to* TRUMP): Needless to say, she's visiting Mr Julian.

The bell rings.

JULIAN: All right, Trump! I'll go. (*He exits.*)

DULCIMER: There! I knew that would happen! Caught in the middle of a vulgar shuffle! I feel as if I had been to the Aldershot Tattoo. Why doesn't he hurry up? If someone doesn't relieve the tension I shall snap!

JULIAN *returns with* LEONORA YALE.

Enter LEONORA YALE. *She is a beautiful girl, clean-cut, charming, strong-willed, decisive, quite free from pose, does not take other people's opinions or judge things on their face value. She is modern in the best sense of the word. She can wear clothes and knows how to wear them. As usual she makes an impression, and she makes it on* DULCIMER. *She is not quite what he expected. There is nothing middle-class about her. There is something about her of the thing well done, well turned out, that appeals to him. She speaks well and decisively. She comes into the room.* JULIAN *brings her to* DULCIMER.

JULIAN: Dulcie, this is Leo!

DULCIMER: I'm delighted to meet you. Julian has kept you dark for too long. I never even knew of your existence till dinner this evening.

LEONORA: I've known you for ages. I always watch you coming into the stalls on 'First Nights'.

DULCIMER: Are you a 'First Nighter'?

LEONORA: Not a real one, but whenever I go, I always enjoy your entrance.

DULCIMER: We'll make an entrance together at the Opera tomorrow. Won't you sit down? (*She sits in the left-hand corner of the couch.*)

JULIAN: That's a good idea! (*To* LEONORA.) It's *Tristan*.

LEONORA: Lovely! By the by, is my car safe in the square?

JULIAN (*sits on the left-hand chair of the centre table*): Perfectly. Trump will see to that. (*Exit* TRUMP *with the trolley-waiter.*)

LEONORA: Was that Trump? (*Nodding.*)

DULCIMER: Have you fallen for him as well?

LEONORA: He's nearly as intriguing as

you, isn't he? Quite the prelude to adventure.

DULCIMER: I'm dreading the day when my friends prefer to stay and talk to him instead of coming in here. One afternoon I shall find them all with him having kitchen tea.

They laugh. He sits beside her.

LEONORA: What a jolly window! I love looking down on to trees.

DULCIMER: I have to be high up. I can't stand noise.

LEONORA: You wouldn't like my waiting-room.

DULCIMER: Julian's been telling me about your work.

JULIAN: He wasn't interested. He hates dogs.

DULCIMER: He means that I won't let his terrier rampage about in here.

LEONORA: Well, of course not! This is much too exquisite a room for dogs, unless you had something that would keep very still on that rug over there. (*She points.*)

JULIAN: You mean a toy dog?

LEONORA: I was thinking of a Borzoi. They're so decorative.

DULCIMER: Well, perhaps! Have you a discarded Borzoi?

JULIAN: It's not a dog's home.

DULCIMER (*going over to the rug*): Yes. I think I can see something on that rug. Something graceful and slender! (*Seeing her look.*) That amuses you, doesn't it? But you professional people can never understand the artist.

LEONORA: I suppose it's all right if you've got the time. I wonder you've never gone in for decoration.

DULCIMER: I couldn't endure planning rooms for other people. My taste would have to be theirs.

LEONORA: I wish I could run my business that way.

DULCIMER: Do your clients interfere?

LEONORA: Not with the treatment, of course, but a lot of my time is taken up with humouring them. You should hear my bedside manner. (*Imitating herself.*)

'The little patient has passed a fairly good night!' Meaning some overfed Pekinese!

DULCIMER (*amused*): I shall consult you about the Borzoi!

LEONORA: I'll give you your money's worth.

DULCIMER: I hope you're very expensive? (*Coming and sitting beside her.*)

LEONORA: Very . . . To you!

DULCIMER: Are you very professional? Do you wear a white coat?

LEONORA: Oh, yes, always. A spotless one.

JULIAN: If we're going to the ballet, I must go and put on my coat and a spotless white tie. I shan't be long, darling. (*He throws her a kiss and exits.*)

LEONORA (*going over to the embroidery frame*): What a beautiful old frame!

DULCIMER (*from the couch*): It belonged to my grandmother.

LEONORA: And what lovely work!

DULCIMER (*pleased*): It's mine. Some of my happiest hours are spent there while Julian plays the piano.

LEONORA (*with a touch of sarcasm*): Is he good with his needle, too?

DULCIMER: No. I tried to teach him, but such gifts are not easily acquired. (*Sensing her thought.*) It doesn't quite meet with your approval, does it?

LEONORA: I'm bound to say that I'm glad he won't want to embroider. But then, I'm so poor at sewing myself.

DULCIMER (*indignantly*): Sewing? Is that all you see in my work? (*Rising and coming towards her.*) I don't believe it! There's nothing of the Philistine about you, even though you have this dreadful obsession for dumb animals. That's the Leo part of you. Leo's so fierce and hostile. I shall always call you Leonora.

LEONORA (*from the window*): Do. If you'll let me off calling you Dulcie!

DULCIMER: That's only Julian's pet name for me. (*As he walks back to the couch.*) Tell me, Leonora! If you hadn't known, you'd have taken us for father and son?

LEONORA: I think I should. I see now that Julian has many of your mannerisms. Is he at all like his real father?

DULCIMER: I hope not. I got him in time to prevent that.

LEONORA: I should rather like to meet Julian's father.

DULCIMER: There's nothing to stop you. He plies his trade in Camden Town.

LEONORA: What does he do?

DULCIMER: He has a dairy or a drapery or something dreadful.

LEONORA (*interested*): Really?

DULCIMER: That's enthralling, isn't it? Well, when you go, I hope he'll be sober. (*They are now seated again.*)

LEONORA: Is that the trouble?

DULCIMER: It used to be. I believe he's a reformed character now. Of course, I've never seen him since I adopted Julian.

LEONORA: It was very decent of you to rescue him.

DULCIMER: I shall never forget the day I first heard him sing at an Eisteddfod in Wales.

LEONORA (*quietly*): You fell in love with his voice?

DULCIMER (*after a tiny pause*): If you like to put it that way. He had the most exquisite treble voice I've ever heard. I had a record made of it. Some day I'll put it on when he isn't here.

LEONORA: Doesn't he like it?

DULCIMER: It's not that. I don't want to remind him of his beginnings. I pursued that voice to a back alley in some unpronounceable Welsh town, and there I found Julian with a drunken father and no mother. It would have been sacrilege to have left him there, but no one else had sensibility enough to see that.

LEONORA: Did you send him to school?

DULCIMER: I thought of doing so, but my interviews with headmasters were not encouraging.

LEONORA: I wish you had a record of

them.

DULCIMER: He may not have had a public school education, but Julian is as much at home in Paris or in Rome as he is in London.

LEONORA: That will be very useful. I love going abroad.

DULCIMER: He can paint. He knows something about music. He's cultured and charming, because I've taught him to be so.

LEONORA: Yes, I see you've taken a lot of pains with him. (*She realises what she's up against.*)

DULCIMER (*slowly*): He's my creation. I've succeeded where any ordinary 'father' would have failed. He's more than a son to me, and it will mean more to me to give him up. Perhaps that won't be necessary immediately?

LEONORA: Perhaps not quite immediately. (*She understands what he means.*)

Enter JULIAN. *He has changed into 'tails'.*

DULCIMER (*to* JULIAN): Leonora and I have been getting to know each other. (*Rising to go. To* LEONORA.) Do you think we're going to be friends?

LEONORA (*without enthusiasm*): I hope so.

DULCIMER: I hope so, too. Well, as it seems I'm going to spend the evening alone, I'll go and slip into something comfortable, if you'll excuse me. (*He exits.*)

JULIAN (*coming and sitting beside her*): Well, what have you been talking about? I hope you haven't been bored?

LEONORA: He'd never bore anybody.

JULIAN: No. He's pretty stimulating to live with.

LEONORA: He made me feel terribly wholesome and ordinary.

JULIAN: Did he talk about me?

LEONORA: He's been telling me what a wonderful education he's given you.

JULIAN: I've got something to tell you – something beastly.

LEONORA: Julian!

JULIAN: At dinner this evening, after I'd told him about you, he suddenly got all Victorian, and said that if I married anybody I must earn my own living. He cut me clean off without even a shilling. I never felt such a fool in my life.

LEONORA (*cheerfully*): Oh, well, we'll have to wait a bit, that's all.

JULIAN: It never entered my head that he wouldn't make me an allowance. It was quite natural to expect it. But he made it sound so unreasonable that I hadn't the nerve to argue about it.

LEONORA: Isn't it because your guardian doesn't want you to marry at all? He thinks you belong to him, and he knows you are under more of an obligation to him than if he was your real father.

JULIAN: I don't see that. I didn't ask him to adopt me. All the same, I'm glad he did.

LEONORA: Well, now, it's up to us to carry on without him. What do you think you'd like to do?

JULIAN: Let me see. I can drive a car. I can paint a bit, and play a bit, and I've got an eye for colour.

LEONORA: There isn't a sixpence in any of them.

JULIAN: I hate sixpences, anyway. They're no use except in cloakrooms.

LEONORA (*getting up under a sudden feeling that the situation is hopeless*): I wonder if we'd better call the whole thing off? (*She has her back to him.*)

JULIAN (*getting up*): Do you mean, not get married?

LEONORA (*facing him*): It seems so unfair to you. There's no earthly reason why you should suddenly have to become like everybody else and slave and grind out a living.

JULIAN: Look here, Leo! I haven't any illusions about myself. I know it's laughable at my age to be wondering what I'm going to be, like a boy in a fourth form, but I do know I'm going to be something so that I can marry you. And I will marry you, Leonora! I love . you more than anything in the world. You ask me what I want to do. Well, something that will make the time before we can get married as short as possible.

LEONORA (*with great sincerity and a touch of wistfulness*): Darling! That's the real you! Isn't it?

JULIAN: No more talk of calling the whole thing off!

LEONORA: I was only thinking of you when I said that, and if I'd seen the slightest flicker of relief in your face when I did say it . . .

JULIAN: Well?

LEONORA: Never mind!

JULIAN: Tell me!

LEONORA: I should have felt as if the end of everything had come. I love you so much that I don't mind how long I wait! I love you so!

A long kiss.

Now let's be sensible! (*Sitting on the chair left of the centre table.*) Julian, how would you like to be a vet?

JULIAN: Doesn't it mean passing exams, and things?

LEONORA: Well, why not? I could help you tremendously with your work, and when you were qualified, you could join us.

JULIAN: Is it a long business? Will it take a year?

LEONORA: More like three. Nearly as long as being a doctor.

JULIAN *groans.*

JULIAN: Oh, Leonora! Three years? It's a life time!

LEONORA: I don't see why we shouldn't get married after you've passed your first exam.

JULIAN (*coming to her side*): I'll pass *that* exam all right.

LEONORA: Of course you will.

JULIAN: When can I start?

LEONORA: You've got to break away from here first. I mean really break away.

JULIAN: Live on my own? How can I?

LEONORA: Haven't you got any money?

JULIAN: I've got some of this quarter's allowance. A good bit in fact. And I've got some things I can sell. That'll keep me going for a while. Why must I leave here?

LEONORA: Can you honestly see yourself doing any work here?

JULIAN: Dulcie wouldn't let me dissect cats, or keep anything of that kind. Otherwise I don't see what's to stop me.

LEONORA: He wouldn't let you do a stroke. He despises work and he'd never understand your wanting to be a vet. A man who doesn't like having a terrier in the sitting-room!

JULIAN: I wish he could hear you calling it a sitting-room! I'm afraid you don't like my guardian!

LEONORA: No. I don't like him. But I'm going to take him very seriously. We can't afford to trifle with him. Whatever you decide to do, he'll try to prevent it. Don't you feel that?

JULIAN (*gloomily*): Yes, I do.

LEONORA: I know what you'll be giving up and that you'll be giving it up for me. I adore you for it.

Kiss.

JULIAN: I shall clear out of here as soon as I can. I'll tackle Dulcie about it tonight.

LEONORA: You will choose the right moment, won't you?

JULIAN: Trump and I are geniuses at that. We can tell the wrong moment a mile off. It will give him a shock to see me working. Well, now that we've made this marvellous start, what about going to the ballet?

LEONORA: I should love it. (*They move.*) By the way, there's one question I haven't asked you. Who are you?

JULIAN: Who am I?

LEONORA: What's your real name?

JULIAN: Dulcie didn't tell you?

LEONORA: No, he brushed your father aside rather hurriedly.

JULIAN: My original name was Owen – David Owen.

LEONORA: You're not even Julian?

JULIAN: No. I'm plain David.

LEONORA: And very nice, too.

JULIAN: But I'm patented 'Julian Dulcimer,' or naturalised, or whatever it is.

LEONORA: When we're married, shall I be Mrs Owen or Mrs Dulcimer?

JULIAN: Which would you like to be?

LEONORA: Mrs Owen!

JULIAN: I knew you'd say that. We'll have to see about it. I suppose I can be 'rendered down' again or something.

LEONORA: I must meet my father-in-law.

JULIAN: You'll see him at the wedding. At least I suppose you will.

LEONORA: Suppose they both come?

They laugh.

At this moment the door opens. DULCIMER *sees them, and coughs a little ostentatiously.*

DULCIMER: Did I do that well? I've been practising coughing for the last ten minutes. What a lot you lovers have to say to each other.

JULIAN: We're just off.

DULCIMER: Julian can take you in his car and bring you back here for a drink. There's a wonderful atmosphere about this room in the small hours of the morning.

LEONORA: They mustn't be too small. I'm a working woman, Mr Dulcimer!

DULCIMER: When you come back, we'll think of a name for you to call me by. We'll all write things down on pieces of paper.

JULIAN (*at the door*): Come on, Leo!

They go out, closing the door behind them. DULCIMER *stands in the middle of the room, looking after them.*

Curtain.

Scene Two

The same. Some hours later. Nearly all the lights are turned out.

MR DULCIMER *is sitting in the armchair facing the window. A dance band is coming over the radio.*

TRUMP *enters with a plate of*

sandwiches.

DULCIMER (*without looking up*): What time is it, Trump?

TRUMP (*putting the sandwiches on the table.*) About a quarter to twelve, sir. (*He moves to turn on the lights.*)

DULCIMER: Leave the lights.

TRUMP: I've brought in a few sandwiches.

DULCIMER (*with his frequent habit of repeating remarks in the form of a question*): And why have you brought in a few sandwiches?

TRUMP: Mr Julian didn't have much dinner, sir, and as Miss Yale's car is still outside, I daresay she'll like one too.

The dance band stops, and there is heard the usual babel of voices and shuffling of feet.

DULCIMER (*pointing to the radio*): I expect Mr Julian and Miss Yale are in there by now!

TRUMP (*with a startled look at MR DULCIMER*): In there, sir? Oh, I see what you mean! At the Dorchester.

DULCIMER: Can you distinguish Mr Julian's voice?

TRUMP (*going up to the radio and listening*): No, sir! But then they never sound to me like voices.

The band begins again.

DULCIMER (*with a tinge of regret*): I expect Miss Yale dances well.

TRUMP: I'm sure she does, sir!

DULCIMER (*angrily*): Turn it off, Trump! (TRUMP *does so.*)

TRUMP: Is there anything more I can get you?

DULCIMER: No, thank you.

TRUMP: Goodnight, sir.

DULCIMER: Goodnight!

Exit TRUMP, meeting JULIAN in the doorway in top hat and dress overcoat.

JULIAN: Hullo, Dulcie! Had a dull evening? (*He puts his hat on the table and his overcoat and scarf on the left-hand chair. Then he turns up the other lights.*)

DULCIMER: Not at all. Where is Leonora?

JULIAN: She sent her apologies and wouldn't come in, after all! She's tired, and gets up earlier than we do. (*He is standing by the table and eating sandwiches.*)

DULCIMER (*regarding him curiously*): Did you have a good time?

JULIAN: Rather!

DULCIMER: I saw you both at the Dorchester.

JULIAN (*stopping in the middle of his sandwich, and looking at him in amazement*): However did you manage that?

DULCIMER (*moving across the room*): 'In my mind's eye, Horatio!' Dear me! I'm very full of quotations tonight. It's always a sign that something's disagreed with me when I'm full of quotations. I must find out what it is. (*He rings the bell.*)

JULIAN, *at the table, watches him, wondering what sort of a mood he is in. Enter TRUMP.*

TRUMP: Yes, sir?

DULCIMER: Something has disagreed with me, Trump. What is it?

TRUMP: I can't think of anything particular, sir. If I may say so, sir, we ate our dinner rather thoughtlessly.

DULCIMER: Did I gobble?

TRUMP: Oh, no sir! But the arrival of Miss Yale keyed us up a little beyond our usual concert pitch.

JULIAN (*amused*): Well done, Trump. Jolly good for this hour of the night. (*He goes to DULCIMER, takes him by the arm, and puts him on the couch.*) Sit down, Dulcie! I'll get some brandy! (*He goes back to the table.*)

DULCIMER (*surprised at his confident manner*): We're quite the assured lover, aren't we?

JULIAN (*ignoring this*): You don't want to keep Trump out of bed, do you?

DULCIMER: Do I want to keep you out of bed, Trump?

TRUMP: Probably, sir!

DULCIMER (*murmuring*): Go to your truckle-bed, Trump! I would willingly change places with you, but I feel like

King Henry IV in his nightgown. 'Get you to rest, cramm'd with distressful bread!' There I go again! (*Then, as* JULIAN *approaches him with brandy, he says icily.*) I'm not in need of brandy, thank you.

TRUMP *is trying to suppress a yawn.*

JULIAN (*shrugging his shoulders and putting the brandy on the table*): Very well! (*To* TRUMP.) Go on, Trump! Don't stand there swallowing yawns!

Exit TRUMP.

DULCIMER (*coldly*): Since when have you taken to ordering my servants about?

JULIAN: I only wanted to get rid of him. (*Taking the sandwiches and sitting by his side.*) I want to talk to you and you're generally at your best at this time. I haven't offended you, have I?

DULCIMER (*thawing*): No, my boy! Of course you haven't. But I don't know that I'm particularly sparkling tonight.

JULIAN: I don't want you to sparkle. I want you to be serious.

DULCIMER: What a dreadful request!

JULIAN: I mean I don't want you to be witty, just for a minute or two. You see, I've got a suggestion to make, and you may be a little surprised at it. To begin with, Leonora and I didn't go the ballet.

DULCIMER: Why not?

JULIAN: We did rather an extraordinary thing. (*Pause.*) We went to see my father instead.

DULCIMER: What?

JULIAN: We went to see my father instead. (DULCIMER *gets up in agitation and walks about the room.*) I liked him. So did Leo. I don't know why we went tonight. We had been talking about him before we left here.

DULCIMER: So you were impressed by your father?

JULIAN: I think I've had the wrong idea of him before.

DULCIMER: Do you mean that I've given you that wrong idea?

JULIAN: Perhaps he's changed. There's nothing disreputable about him. He was sitting quietly at home, reading the Bible.

DULCIMER: Good Heavens! Don't I read the Bible? Haven't I told you that you can't form your style without it?

JULIAN: He's a preacher in some local chapel. Well, Leo and I have been mapping out our future this evening. We can't be married till I've got a job, and I've decided to become a vet.

A tiny pause.

DULCIMER (*in hard, loud tones from the roof garden steps*): Go on! I've not the least desire to be witty.

JULIAN: It'll mean a lot of hard work and I've got to live somewhere while I'm doing it. I think it will be possible to live with my father. He rather liked the idea. Apparently he feels he's got something to make up to me.

DULCIMER: He's been a little slow at feeling that.

JULIAN: The college is close to where he lives. Everything just happens to fit. That's all.

DULCIMER: You asked me to be serious just now. I'm going to be. I think you're quite mad and rather uncouth.

JULIAN: I knew you wouldn't see it!

DULCIMER: I can see it quite clearly! (*Coming close to him.*) An impetuous boy, because he has fallen in love, wants to rush headlong out of my house at a moment's notice, without giving a thought to my wishes or plans!

JULIAN: That's not fair! I have thought about you.

DULCIMER: Then you certainly haven't thought about yourself. Do you really imagine that you'll find living with your father congenial?

JULIAN: I shall have too much to do to worry about that. I think we shall get on, and we shan't see very much of each other.

DULCIMER: Has he spacious apartments?

JULIAN: He can give me a room.

DULCIMER: I believe I was right. You *are* insane! I shall have you certified tomorrow.

JULIAN: You'll never see my point, but I

can see yours. To you I must be as mad as a hatter.

DULCIMER: Not only mad, Julian but rather cruel. A little vindictive perhaps.

JULIAN: Dulcie, I don't want to offend you, but surely you must see that I couldn't work here.

DULCIMER: Why not? You can pore over diagrams of dogs' intestines to your heart's content!

JULIAN: You'd loathe it if I did. (*Going to the bureau.*) Look at this! (*He picks up a large quill pen, exquisitely feathered in jade green.*) That's your idea of a pen! I couldn't work with that! (*He throws it down on the bureau.*) And that is typical of everything here! I don't want to be uncouth or ungrateful, but I know that the only sensible thing to do is to get away on my own.

DULCIMER (*with a penetrating voice*): On your own? Julian, are you hinting that I am the obstacle to your success?

JULIAN: We should get on each other's nerves a thousand times a day.

DULCIMER: Did Leonora make you think that?

JULIAN: No, not exactly. She agrees with me, though.

DULCIMER: You mean that you agree with her. (*As if thinking.*) I see. She's determined to get you away from me, and she's not wasting any time about it.

JULIAN: Well, I think I shall go to bed now. I've got a lot of things to arrange tomorrow. (*Coming up to* DULCIMER.) We're friends about this, aren't we?

DULCIMER *turns aside and refuses to take his hand.*

Oh, all right! But you're behaving very childishly!

DULCIMER (*turning round on him*): You fool! You little, self-confident fool!

JULIAN: I'm not going to quarrel with you. You'll see things differently in the morning. (*He exits.*)

For a moment or two MR DUCLIMER *paces the room like a tiger. Then he goes to the gramophone and puts on the 'Mars' record from Holst's 'Planets'. The music is a dramatisation of his mood. Then he goes to the window,* *opens it, and breathes in the air, afterwards turning off the lights turned on by* JULIAN.

Then, with his quick resolute stride, he walks back to the gramophone. He puts on a second record, and a boy's treble voice comes floating into the silent room.

He returns to the armchair and sits listening.

Curtain.

ACT TWO

Scene One

MR OWEN's *sitting-room in Camden Town. Three months later. August. A small, neat, simply furnished room. It can be set inside the Dulcimer flat. It is comfortable and contains good solid furniture, but the wallpaper is crude and the pictures and ornaments are chosen without taste.* MR OWEN *is proud of it.* JULIAN *detests it.*

The room has a fireplace on the right, the door is in the back wall towards the right and opens into a small hall with hat stand. On the other side of the door is a sash window looking out on to the street and giving a good view of some posters advertising Guinness. 'GUINNESS IS GOOD FOR YOU.'

The furniture of the room is arranged in this way. On either side of the fireplace is an armchair. Between the door and the window stands a small American organ, symbolic of a great deal of MR OWEN's *soul. It is open and a large volume of hymns rests on the music stand. In the window is a small table with a plant on it.*

In the left-hand corner, up stage, stands an open bureau, correspondence and business papers lying about on it. Above is a single shelf that now contains JULIAN's *scientific books. By the bureau is a waste-paper basket, and below it, down stage, a horsehair sofa. In the middle of the room is a solid square table with a coloured cloth and four chairs.*

It is suggested that there might be photographs of MR OWEN's *family, and perhaps one of* JULIAN *as a child, on the mantlepiece and elsewhere, but any decorations should be in keeping with the atmosphere of the room.*

JULIAN (*lolling in the armchair with a notebook in his hand*): I've got no brain this afternoon. I try to make it function but nothing happens. I've read that passage through three times and I haven't taken in a word.

LEONORA (*coming over from the window*): Darling, give me the book! I'll read it out to you. Put your legs straight. (*She sits on the arm of his chair.*) Now, where's the place?

JULIAN: Somewhere on that page. (*Pointing and giving her the book.*)

LEONORA: Boyle's law?

JULIAN: That's it.

LEONORA (*reading*): 'When the temperature of a gas ...

JULIAN (*interrupting*): Wait a minute! Let's get comfortable before we start. (*He draws her into the armchair beside him.*) There! That's better! (*Kissing her.*) This is the perfect way to coach for any exam.

LEONORA (*trying to be serious*): Now, listen!

JULIAN: Angel, I could listen for ever. (*He looks at her adoringly.*)

LEONORA: This is Boyle's law.

JULIAN: Who was Boyle?

LEONORA: Never mind who he was. He formulated this law, which you've got to remember.

JULIAN: I believe he formulated that wallpaper, too, which I'm very anxious to forget.

LEONORA: Darling, it's miraculous of you to stand it. I do know what it means to you. I shouldn't mind myself, but then I'm not so desperately sensitive.

JULIAN: Don't tell me you'd ever live in a room like this!

LEONORA: Of course not! Our flat's going to be lovely – I've got all sorts of ideas.

JULIAN: Tell me about them.

LEONORA: Well, they'll include a refrigerator. (*She moves a little in the chair as if hot.*)

JULIAN (*surprised*): Of course they will.

LEONORA (*amused at him*): Every flat hasn't got one.

JULIAN: Good God! Hasn't it?

LEONORA: Certainly not. They're still considered luxuries.

JULIAN: 'Luxury' is a word invented by people with no imagination. It's only another word for decency. Baths were luxuries once.

LEONORA: At any rate, you've got a bathroom.

JULIAN: Only just. I wouldn't keep a goldfish in it. The whole scheme of things is preposterous. It's natural to be clean, it's natural to be cool. They ought either to be free or subsidised.

LEONORA: Darling, I'm afraid you've left your perfect world for a very imperfect one.

JULIAN: Which I gladly accept because you're in it, but it shan't hold us a second longer than is absolutely necessary, shall it?

LEONORA: Not one second, darling, I promise you that.

JULIAN: Good. Let us Boyle!

LEONORA: This is the law. (*She reads.*) 'When the temperature of a gas does not alter, the product of its volume and pressure is constant.'

JULIAN: Isn't that nonsense? I love your voice, Leo. It rises and falls over those ridiculous words and the whole room is full of music.

LEONORA: Yes, but have you taken in what it's about?

JULIAN: Not a syllable, darling! Anyone who wants to 'take in' Boyle's law with you sitting there, looking so adorable, is a frosty-minded wretch.

LEONORA: Then there's 'Dalton's Law of Partial Pressures'.

JULIAN: 'Partial Pressures!' Parcel Post!

LEONORA (*reading*): 'By partial pressure is meant the pressure that any one gas would exert if it alone were present, filling the whole space.'

JULIAN: It sounds like a word picture of father!

LEONORA (*laughing and getting up and putting the book down on the table*): Well, I don't think we'll do any more this afternoon.

JULIAN (*gravely*): I think it is that I'm a little 'off' physics. Let's have a look at anatomy. (*He rises and goes to the bookcase above the writing-table, from which he takes a book. As he passes the window, he pauses and looks at the poster on the opposite wall.*) Guinness is good for you! (*Coming to* LEONORA's *side.*) I've rather taken to anatomy.

LEONORA (*encouragingly*): You ought to know a lot about it already. You couldn't draw unless you did.

JULIAN: Anatomy's got pictures. Look at that dear little rabbit all pinned out with A's and B's and C's. (*Showing her.*)

LEONORA: Isn't he a pet?

JULIAN: Go ahead. Ask me some questions. I do know something about bones.

LEONORA (*taking the book*): Let me see. What's the sacrum.

JULIAN (*putting his arm round her waist*): The sacrum, my angel, is the triangular bone at the back of the pelvis.

LEONORA: Splendid!

JULIAN: Though I can't conceive how one earns a living by knowing that. (*She sits in the armchair again.*)

LEONORA (*eagerly*): And what is the carpus? (*She is in the armchair opposite him.*)

JULIAN (*frowning*): The carcase?

LEONORA: Carpus! C-A-R-P-U-S!

JULIAN: Well, that's funny now! That seems to have slipped away. Have I got a carpus?

LEONORA: Yes.

JULIAN: Has everybody?

LEONORA: Certainly.

JULIAN: I've missed it, somehow. (*He sings to the tune of 'Today I feel so Happy.'*)
You say I've got a carpus!
   A carpus! A carpus!
I know I've got a carpus!
   I don't know where it is!

LEONORA (*pointing to her hand*): It's that part of the skeleton which unites the hand to the forearm.

JULIAN (*with deep interest*): Is it? Let me see. (*He goes on his knees in front of her and takes her hand.*) Just there! (*Pointing to the spot.*)

LEONORA (*showing him*): A little higher up.

JULIAN (*kissing her wrist*): That's the exact spot. (*Naïvely.*) I don't think I should ever get bored by anatomy. It's the only red letter in my alphabet.

(*Counting off wearily.*) Anatomy, Botany, Biology, Chemistry. Then there's a ghastly leap and we land on physics.

LEONORA: It's only about Heat, Light, and Sound.

JULIAN: Why learn about them? Heat, a thing I detest; light, which ought to be shaded always; sound! Well, there's too much in the streets already. No, darling, I wish to go no further into the matter!

LEONORA (*taking the book from him*): All right, we won't do any more today. You'll pass it on your head. (*She puts it back in the shelf.*)

JULIAN (*standing by the centre table*): I suppose I shall! It's all so new to me not to be certain of myself. Anything I've done before I've done, and there's an end of it. I don't take to this competing business. (LEONORA *comes to him.*)

LEONORA (*seriously*): Don't you think, darling, that that's the difference between being an amateur and a professional? It doesn't really matter whether the amateur gets there or not.

JULIAN: I don't know so much about that. Amateurs take themselves very seriously.

LEONORA: Well, at any rate, you can't live an amateur life.

JULIAN: I think that's just what I've been doing, and I've got a deuce of a lot of fun out of it.

LEONORA: Yes, but I know that you're worth ever so much more than that. (*A long kiss.*)

JULIAN: D'you think I'm an amateur lover?

LEONORA: No!

JULIAN (*going back to the fireplace*): Even Isaiah would admit that I've had a hell of a day. I've had three hours with a crammer, taken down his blasted notes, and read Boyle at home.

LEONORA: You're beginning to feel that this is home?

JULIAN: No. I can't quite say that. I haven't been trained to live with a minor prophet.

LEONORA: I admire him for having the courage of his convictions.

JULIAN: Yes, but I do wish he'd stop calling me Davy!

LEONORA: David's a good name!

JULIAN: Yes, but 'Davy'! It doesn't go with me at all. What's he up to this afternoon?

LEONORA: (*with a 'cold' Welsh accent*): It's Thursday. Early closing!

JULIAN: And sermon night!

LEONORA: Let's try and keep off the chapel for once. It always leads to trouble.

JULIAN: Not a hope! The chapel's like drink to him.

LEONORA: Not a very fortunate remark!

JULIAN: It was quite unconscious. Sometimes I wish he would drink a bit! It might cheer him up!

The door bangs.

LEONORA: There he is! Now be careful what you say!

JULIAN: Woe unto the ungodly!

Enter WILLIAM OWEN. *He is a wiry man with a beard, a determined face and uncompromising eyes. His hair is grey and his clothes workaday clothes. He is a man who has suffered a good deal and who might have gone to the bad altogether had it not been for religion. Through religion he has pulled himself together and is proud of the fact. Through the chapel he finds an outlet for his poetry, his fanaticism, and capacity to preach. He is not a hard man, but he has not much understanding of or tolerance for* JULIAN DULCIMER. *To him he is just 'Davy', his extravagant son, who ought to think only of passing his exams.*
He comes in with a file of bills in his hand.

OWEN (*as he hangs his hat and coat up on the stand outside*): Hullo, Leo! Hullo, Davy my boy! How are your studies? Have you done well today? (*He sits in the armchair.*)

JULIAN (*teasing him*): Top in everything. The teachers were awfully pleased. I mean this one is.

LEONORA: What have you been doing, Isaiah?

JULIAN (*teasing him*): Been to the pictures?

OWEN (*putting his bills on the bureau*): I flatter myself that I've a higher idea of recreation than that.

JULIAN: Wait a minute! You don't know what the stage show is this week.

OWEN: What should I be doing with stage shows?

JULIAN: You'd enjoy this one. It's not the Rhumba Girls. It's grand opera. The whole of *Cavalleria Rusticana*. Will you go to hell for an hour for the sake of grand opera?

LEONORA: Do, Isaiah! It would do you a world of good.

OWEN (*sitting in the armchair above the fireplace*): I don't like jokes about hell, Leo. It's a very real place.

LEONORA: I didn't mean to shock you, but I'm sure you don't have half enough pleasure in your life.

OWEN: Principle before pleasure, I should have said.

LEONORA (*regretfully*): Always?

OWEN: Goodness gracious, yes! (*Getting out his pipe.*)

LEONORA: You lead such a model life with that dear little dairy downstairs, full of fresh eggs and glasses of milk.

JULIAN: Watered.

OWEN: Don't you dare say that to me, Davy!

JULIAN: Anyhow, Leo's quite right. You ought to unbend sometimes.

OWEN: And supposing I couldn't straighten up again? Besides, do you know what the picture is? Rosalind Turner in *Outraged*. What would the chapel say if they saw me going to see that?

LEONORA: You could preach a wonderful sermon next Sunday on the Evils of Hollywood.

OWEN: I did that last Sunday, so it would fall rather flat. I preached for an hour on the 'lure of the screen'. I should like to have heard the music, though! Never mind. At Christmas the chapel is doing the '*Messiah.*' That will be grand.

He moves to the bureau to get his tobacco.

LEONORA: Have you had some tea?

OWEN: Yes, thank you. I've been over to Brixton to see my sister-in-law. (*To JULIAN.*) Your Aunt Lily is very anxious to see you.

JULIAN: What, again? (OWEN *goes back to the armchair and fills his pipe.*)

OWEN: She asks about you every time I go there.

LEONORA *sits in the armchair below the fireplace.* JULIAN *is at the table reading the 'Methodist Times'.*

JULIAN: What an awful thought.

OWEN (*a little annoyed*): I'm sorry you find your family uncongenial.

JULIAN: I've come to it rather late in life. I'm afraid of it. Honestly I am. Aunt Lily's got a laugh like a double bass.

OWEN: You be thankful she wants to make you welcome.

JULIAN: And as for my cousin Trevor!

OWEN: You needn't patronise Trevor, either. He's doing very well for himself.

JULIAN: He let me know that all right.

OWEN: You didn't like him because he said you looked like something out of Hope Brothers.

JULIAN (*turning to* LEO): Now I ask you, Leo! Could I have been more grossly insulted?

LEONORA: I think it is rather a libel.

OWEN: I thought it hit the nail on the head.

JULIAN: My 'family' as you call it, may be doing very well for itself, but it does not know anything about clothes.

OWEN: Whenever I see Trevor, he is always tidily turned out.

JULIAN: Yes, that's just about it. (*He moves to the sofa.*)

OWEN: You could learn a lot from him! He'd smarten you up no end!

JULIAN (*aghast*): Smarten me up?

OWEN: Make a man of you instead of a tailor's dummy!

LEONORA (*seeing the look on* JULIAN's *face*): Now you two, it's a waste of time arguing about clothes. We can't all look alike.

OWEN: Julian can dress up as much as he pleases, but he's got to be more affable all round. It's not my sister only. It's anybody who comes here. (*To* JULIAN.) It's no use being uppish when you've nothing to be uppish about. This isn't the Hotel Camden, you know. If you're not satisfied, you can go to the Ritz!

LEONORA: Julian's perfectly satisfied, Isaiah. You mustn't imagine things.

OWEN: I've a pretty good ear for undertones. However, he'll soon have a chance of turning over a new leaf. Lily and Trevor are coming here this evening. (*To* JULIAN.) Now, mind you don't call me Isaiah in front of them!

JULIAN: There's no fear of that! We shan't be here! Leo and I are going out! (*Coming back to the table.*)

OWEN (*shaking his finger at* LEONORA): More pleasure, I suppose?

LEONORA (*charmingly*): Lots more, I hope!

OWEN: I'm afraid, Leo, you're like all the rest. Pleasure, pleasure, pleasure!

A knock at the front door.

LEONORA: I'll go.

She exits.

OWEN (*coming to the table and sitting opposite him. In a conciliatory mood*): Davy, my boy, I don't want to seem inquisitive, but when you've spent your money, where will you get any more from?

JULIAN: I'll settle that when the day comes.

OWEN: But you can't go over the abyss with your eyes open. Save your money. You've got nothing to spend it on. Your home isn't so bad, is it?

JULIAN: No, of course it isn't.

OWEN: I didn't mean what I said about the Hotel Camden, but I can't bear to see you wasting you money on rubbish. How much did that tie cost? Nearly five shillings, I suppose?

JULIAN: Nearly fifteen.

OWEN (*awed in spite of his convictions*): Did it now? It's wicked. I'd rather wear a bootlace than pay so much. I want you to take life more seriously. It doesn't take much to lead you away from the right path. Do you know what will keep you on it?

JULIAN: A good balance at the bank.

OWEN (*gravely*): No, Davy, it's not that. Prayer and Purpose, my boy! That's what you want. Prayer and Purpose! They've been the backbone of my life for the last fifteen years.

JULIAN: I'm afraid they haven't exactly come my way.

Enter LEONORA.

LEONORA: Telegram for you, darling! (*She hands it to* JULIAN. *He opens it.*)

JULIAN: Splendid! Dulcie's back! (LEONORA *and* OWEN *look at each other.*) He arrived this afternoon! There's no answer! Why ever didn't he tell me? I'd have met him.

LEONORA *goes off and dismisses the telegraph boy, returning at once.*

OWEN: He'll keep all right till tomorrow.

JULIAN: I expect he's had a marvellous time at Silver Gates. I can see it all stretched out there in the sun!

OWEN (*getting up*): I must begin to collect my thoughts for Sunday. Where did I leave my Bible? I know, it's by my bedside. (*He exits.*)

JULIAN: That sounds rather ominous.

LEONORA (*who has been watching him.*): Darling, you're not too terribly pleased at Dulcie's coming back, are you?

JULIAN: I can't help being glad, but (*taking her hands*) you've got nothing to be afraid of.

LEONORA: You won't let the old life come between us and spoil our plans?

JULIAN: Of course not. I'm glad he's back, though. I'll tell you why presently. (*He crosses over to the fireplace. Enter* OWEN *with a large Bible under his arm.*)

OWEN: I've got something this week that'll make them sit up! (*He puts the Bible on the table and opens it. He stands in front of the Bible.*) Now listen to this!

LEONORA: That's right, Isaiah! You try it on us first!

OWEN (*a little taken aback*): I'm not sure that I was including you, Leo. It's about the ungodly.

JULIAN: I thought it would be.

OWEN: Listen! (*Declaiming.*) 'I myself have seen the wicked in great power and spreading himself like a green bay tree.'

JULIAN (*regretfully*): Happy days!

OWEN (*getting worked up and turning on him quite fiercely*): Do you think so? (*With uplifted hand.*) Wait! Listen to the Psalmist's conclusion! 'Yet he passed away, and lo, he was not: yea, I sought him, but he could not be found.'

JULIAN: Come now, Isaiah, I'm not quite ripe for passing away yet!

OWEN: Perhaps not. But you're on the way if you don't look out. Remember, it's watching you that has sent me to that text. 'He passed away, and lo, he was not!' (*With a sweep of his hand.*) Wiped out completely!

LEONORA: Do you believe, Isaiah, that that actually happens?

OWEN: It's true enough! It's happening every day! Look at those earthquakes! God moves in a mysterious way to bring about His will.

JULIAN: Isaiah, you're a barbarian! You belong to the Old Testament! I believe you'd enjoy being an instrument of destruction.

OWEN: If it was the Lord's will, He would not find me wanting! I've seen the day of reckoning come time and time again.

LEONORA: But Julian doesn't deserve a reckoning!

OWEN: Not if he comes to chapel!

JULIAN: I'll come next Sunday. I wouldn't miss hearing you expound that for worlds. It's a new sensation being preached at by one's own father.

OWEN: It will be hot, I promise you. I've only given you a taste of what is to come! I'm no light-weight in the pulpit.

JULIAN: You must give us a gala show on Sunday. Something more terrific than you've ever done before.

OWEN: You may humbug now. You won't feel like humbugging when you come out of chapel!

JULIAN: All right. I must have a last ungodly fling! I'm going out to buy twenty Player's.

He exits. OWEN *turns after him with an exasperated 'Davy!'*

LEONORA (*reassuringly*): He's just being naughty, Isaiah!

OWEN (*sitting at the table while she sits at the other side, confidentially*): I want him to take a pull at himself in time. That's why I'm trying to put the fear of God into him. He won't stick to his books. I can't make him see the importance of it.

LEONORA: He's made a very good start.

OWEN: He's not done so badly, but he doesn't put enough will power into it. He doesn't concentrate.

LEONORA: I hope Dulcimer won't make it more difficult for him. I wish he'd stayed at Silver Gates. Julian has had nothing to distract him whilst his guardian was away.

OWEN: You've a great respect for Dulcimer, haven't you?

LEONORA: I've no illusions about his attraction for Julian. I can see that by the way Julian likes getting his letters. Dulcimer's got a huge personality, and he's rotten to the core.

OWEN: I remember all you told me about him.

LEONORA (*rising*): We'll get the better of him.

OWEN: We'll fight him together! (*Wistfully.*) You don't blame me for handing Davy over?

LEONORA (*having moved over to the window*): Of course I don't.

OWEN: I blame myself sometimes. It wasn't a very creditable transaction. There was more in it than I've told you. (*With shame.*) I got £500 for David, on condition that I had no more to do with him, but I didn't know so much about Mr Dulcimer then as I do now. I was an awful drunkard at that time. I've wondered over and over again how I could have brought myself to sign that document. I must have been blind drunk at the time. I had come back from the war and my wife had died, and everything had gone to pot. (*Naïvely.*) And yet, do you know, from the moment I got that £500, everything flourished.

LEONORA (*with a smile*): Like a green bay tree!

OWEN (*ruefully*): Perhaps the cap fits me after all. I tell you, Leo, I get in an awful muddle sometimes as to who are the ungodly and who aren't! Anyhow, I can't get away from it. I should never have got on and ended up by buying this business in London, if I hadn't had that start twelve years ago!

LEONORA: Don't worry over it. Julian will be all right. (*More to herself than to him.*)

OWEN: At any rate, I've set him an example. I've pulled myself together. (*He sees what she is looking at out of the window and joins her.*) Do you see that old poster there? Fifteen years ago I would rather have sat in a charnel-house than sat opposite that! Now it's the symbol of my triumph! I could gaze at it unmoved for ever!

LEONORA: Have you told Julian all about yourself?

OWEN: No. I can't talk to him like I can talk to you, Leo.

LEONORA: I think he'd like to know, and I think it would help him to understand.

OWEN: I'm afraid not. He doesn't want to join up with me in any way. You see, Dulcimer has made him think himself a gentleman. That's where we are poles apart. I've no use for that sort of gentleman.

LEONORA: But you're very proud of him, all the same, aren't you?

OWEN: He's my son! My home is his as long as he cares to stay. He doesn't know how often I've wanted him, but that old Dulcimer kept him so close. Directly he was twenty-one I asked for him back, but it was no good.

LEONORA: We're allies over Dulcimer.

OWEN: No doubt he told Davy the tale about me. Still, I'm not a great catch.

LEONORA: You love him as I do.

OWEN: There's nothing I wouldn't do to help him, but a father's love hasn't much of a look in after twelve years of luxury. The best thing that ever happened to him was to fall in love with you.

LEONORA (*with great sincerity*): I'm terribly fond of him, Isaiah. (*He kisses her lightly on the forehead.*)

OWEN: Let's have some music. (*He sits at the organ.*) This old organ has been my solace many a time.

LEONORA: Play one of your old Welsh airs.

OWEN: I'll play you *Tone Botel.* It's an old tune that was found in a bottle washed up out of the sea. (*He plays that fine but sombre air.*)

LEONORA (*after the first bars are over*): There's a wonderful roll in it, isn't there?

OWEN (*playing*): You want to hear a thousand people singing it up at Mountain Ash on Sunday evening. There's the strength of the mountains in it.

While he is playing, JULIAN *comes back and stands listening on the right.* OWEN *sees him in a minute and stops.*

OWEN: I didn't see you, Davy!

JULIAN: Don't stop! Something prehistoric in me stirs at that!

OWEN (*playing*): It's the music of your country, Davy! You can't help being stirred.

JULIAN: I've left all that that stands for a long way behind. I think it is like you, Isaiah! Rugged and rather sad!

A knock at the front door.

Who on earth can that be?

OWEN: Run and see, my boy. It can't be your Aunt Lily yet.

JULIAN (*confidentially to* LEONORA): If it is, remember, we're going out!

Exit JULIAN. *When he is gone,* OWEN *plays again.*

LEONORA (*going to the table*): I think we'll get off soon. I don't want to be caught!

OWEN: What are you going to see?

LEONORA (*looking down the advertisements in the paper*): Some show or other. Something gay. I think Julian wants to see *Spangles on Europe*.

OWEN: What does that mean?

LEONORA: God knows! I don't.

Voices are heard on the stairs. Enter JULIAN followed by TRUMP, looking neat and rather sinister, with his hat in his hand. OWEN stops playing.

JULIAN: Leo! Here's Trump with a message from Dulcie!

TRUMP: Mr Dulcimer presents his compliments, miss, and hopes that you and Mr Julian will dine with him this evening?

LEONORA (*wanting to get out of it*): Haven't we an engagement already, Julian?

JULIAN: No. We can easily go to a show another evening.

TRUMP: He's looking forward to seeing you both, sir.

JULIAN: How is he?

TRUMP: Very fit, sir. A little bored with the country, I fancy. Shall I tell him you're coming, sir?

JULIAN (*to* LEONORA): We are coming, aren't we?

LEONORA: I suppose so.

TRUMP: The car will be round here at a quarter-to-eight, sir.

JULIAN: Make it seven-thirty, and then I can go and call for Miss Yale.

TRUMP: Very good, sir.

JULIAN: Seven-thirty. (*Exit* TRUMP.)

OWEN (*who has been taking in* TRUMP *during this conversation*): How does that fellow justify his existence?

JULIAN: By knowing what Dulcie wants almost before he knows it himself.

OWEN: He's Mr Dulcimer's keeper, is he?

JULIAN (*smiling*): Not exactly. Look here, Isaiah, would you mind frightfully letting me have a word with Leo?

OWEN: Not at all, my boy. I'll take my Bible into the other room. (*He gets it.*) But do you know what I should do this evening, if I were you? I'd go to *Spangles on Europe*. (*He exits.*)

JULIAN (*to* LEONORA): Darling, you look as if you'd seen the Devil!

LEONORA: Why on earth couldn't he have left us alone a little bit longer?

JULIAN (*coming to join her on the left-hand side of the table*): It's only natural he should want to see us.

LEONORA: He doesn't want to see me. That's quite certain.

JULIAN (*coaxingly*): Yes, he does.

LEONORA: No, Julian, And you know that perfectly well. He has no use for me whatever. (*Firmly.*)

JULIAN (*a little irritably*): Well, do you want me to ring him up and get out of it?

LEONORA: I should love you to.

JULIAN: Don't you think it would be rather rude?

LEONORA: I shouldn't care how rude it was. It would be so good for him to see that he can't just send for you whenever he pleases.

JULIAN: Are you jealous of Dulcie?

LEONORA (*protesting, but without conviction*): No! Of course I'm not!

JULIAN: It would be rather a ridiculous situation if you were!

LEONORA (*again with that unhappy note in her voice*): Wouldn't it? (*She sits on a chair.*)

JULIAN: I'll tell you why I particularly want to go tonight. He hasn't seen me for nearly three months, and he's sure to be amiable. It's an excellent moment for reopening the subject of an allowance.

LEONORA: Darling, he'll never change his mind about that.

JULIAN: I'll make him change it. (*Moving round to the other side of the table.*) There's no earthly reason why I shouldn't have an allowance. From every point of view, I'm entitled to it. I think he was just testing me. He'll be quite different when he sees I've had a shot at working.

LEONORA: You mean to give up the idea of being a vet if he consents?

JULIAN (*leans across the table*): If he consents I've got all sorts of schemes.

LEONORA: And if he refuses?

JULIAN: Then I stay here and go on with what I am doing. But if he consents it means that we can get married tomorrow!

LEONORA: That's worth risking anything for. (*He doesn't see what is behind her words.*)

JULIAN: Darling Leo! Happier now?

LEONORA: I'll go with you, Julian.

JULIAN: It won't be a very pleasant evening for me because I shall have this on my mind. After dinner, I want you to invent some engagement, and leave me to tackle him. I couldn't do it with you there.

LEONORA: No, of course you couldn't. All right. I'll clear out early.

JULIAN: Splendid! Now you must go home and dress, and put on your prettiest frock. This is my idea if tonight comes off . . .

They go out together, talking.

Curtain.

Scene Two

At MR DULCIMER's *flat. The same evening. The gates into the roof garden are without their screens.*

The dinner, which has been unusual in its arrangement, is drawing to a close. The centre table has gone and MR DULCIMER *sits at a small table in the middle of the room separated from* JULIAN *and* LEONORA, *who are at a similar small table near the window, but so placed that* MR DULCIMER *can see both their faces. There is yet a third table, up stage left, with a chair on each side but without diners. Each table is identical, with lace cloth, flowers, and shaded candle lamp.*

This arrangement is one of MR DULCIMER's *jokes, but it serves to isolate* JULIAN *and* LEONORA. *The dinner has been excellent. Throughout it* MR DULCIMER *has communicated with them through* TRUMP, *who acts up to* MR DULCIMER's *whim by posing as a magnificent Maître d'hôtel.*

The joke has amused JULIAN, *who has entered into the game and has ordered*

every item of the dinner with the utmost gravity from TRUMP's *menu card.* LEONORA *has also entered into the spirit of it, but she has been a little embarrassed for she knows that all through the meal* MR DULCIMER *has been watching her.*

When the curtain rises TRUMP *is obsequiously attending to the imaginary diners at the third table.* MR DULCIMER *is scribbling a note in pencil.*

LEONORA (*attracting his attention*): Julian! Have you enjoyed your dinner? (*She unconciously lowers her voice.*)

DULCIMER: Trump! (TRUMP *leaves the imaginary diners and comes to him.*) Will you give this to the gentleman at the other table?

TRUMP: Certainly, sir. (*He takes the note to* JULIAN.)

JULIAN: Thank you. (*He reads the note, laughs, and scribbles a reply.* TRUMP *takes it to* DULCIMER.) I haven't had a dinner like this since . . . well, not since I left home.

He casts half an eye on DULCIMER *who is sipping brandy meditatively.* DULCIMER *reads the note. Exit* TRUMP.

LEONORA: But I mean, have you enjoyed having it this way?

JULIAN: I haven't minded. In fact, it's been rather fun. As if I really had been taking you out to dinner. We'll have lots of these later on.

LEONORA: Shall we have to go on playing this game all the evening?

JULIAN: Good Lord, no! Dulcie will suddenly call it off, especially as we've played up to him so well. He can't bear anyone not to enter into a joke or to seem stupid and awkward over it.

LEONORA: I'm beginning to feel self-conscious now. It's gone on too long, and I know he's watching me. He's been watching me all the time.

JULIAN: Don't give in! You've been splendid! It hasn't spoiled your dinner, has it?

LEONORA: Not a bit. (*Enter* TRUMP.) As long as I don't think he's done it just to annoy me and make me look a fool.

JULIAN: Rather not. He used to spring all

sorts of surprises on me when I was a boy, and see how I reacted to them. It was his idea of education. Whatever the occasion, never be gauche or nonplussed! It did smarten one up. Here comes the ice pudding!

TRUMP *is entering with a large and very exquisitely designed ice pudding shaped like a small rose tree in bloom. The roses are made of strawberry ice. He carries it round the room showing it to the diners at the imaginary table as well.* MR DULCIMER *comes out of his apparent reverie and gazes at it languidly.*

TRUMP (*coming up to* LEONORA): Will madame take ice pudding?

LEONORA (*who has already exclaimed as the pudding came into the room*): Yes, please, if you can bear cutting it.

TRUMP: We like our guests to pick the flowers. I will give madame a little of this one. (*He helps her.*)

JULIAN (*to* LEONORA): Have a liqueur, darling?

LEONORA: No, thanks.

JULIAN (*to* TRUMP, *as he helps him*): I seem to remember a very fine old brandy when I was here in the old days.

TRUMP: The 1796, sir?

JULIAN: That must be it.

TRUMP: Certainly, sir.

JULIAN: Your face seems familiar, too.

TRUMP: Thank you, sir. (*He moves away with the pudding to* DULCIMER.)

DULCIMER: Not for me, thank you. (*Taking a couple of roses from the bowl in front of him.*) Do you think I dare interrupt that charming couple once more?

TRUMP: I'm sure they'll only be too delighted, sir.

DULCIMER: You really think so? Then give the lady these roses with my compliments. Tell her that they will add to the illusion.

TRUMP *puts the pudding on* DULCIMER's *table and takes the roses to* LEONORA.

TRUMP: With the compliments of the gentleman at the centre table, madame.

LEONORA (*taking the roses*): Aren't they exquisite? Thank him very much.

DULCIMER: Maître d'hôtel!

TRUMP: Yes, sir?

DULCIMER: Remove the rose bush and bring me some more brandy.

TRUMP *takes the pudding to the side table behind the couch and gets the brandy from there.*

LEONORA: We can't keep it up much longer. I shall laugh in a minute.

JULIAN: I've known him pretend to be someone else for a whole day. Have some more pudding to keep you going?

LEONORA: No, thanks. (*Then , after a moment.*) Do you think we can play it out to the very end? I mean, pretend to pay for the dinner and then go off somewhere together?

JULIAN: I'm afraid we can't do quite that, but it'll help to bring matters to a head. (*To* TRUMP, *who has given* MR DULCIMER *his brandy.*) Waiter!

TRUMP (*turning to* JULIAN *and feigning indignation of an exquisite kind*): Maître d'hôtel, sir.

JULIAN (*with a smile*): I beg your pardon! Anyhow, let me have my bill!

TRUMP: Certainly, sir! (*He pretends to go and fetch the bill.*)

JULIAN: Bring me a cheque form will you?

TRUMP (*nonplussed for a moment*): A cheque form, sir?

JULIAN: Good heavens, you know me well enough for that, don't you?

TRUMP: We should do, sir! (*Under his breath.*) That's torn it!

JULIAN: Well, look sharp, we're going to the Paramount to see *The Man About Town*. We're late as it is.

TRUMP: I believe it's a good second act, sir! (*To himself*) Oh well, here goes! (*He walks over to the bureau and looks for* MR DULCIMER's *cheque book.*)

LEONORA: Is he going to let him get it?

JULIAN (*watching* DULCIMER *out of the corner of his eye*): Wait a minute!

DULCIMER (*speaking over his shoulder to* TRUMP):When you've quite finished rummaging among my papers, Trump, will you please bring coffee?

TRUMP (*relieved that the game is over*): Yes, sir! (*He exits.*)

JULIAN (*smiling*): I think we win, Dulcie?

DULCIMER (*getting up*): Your game, my boy. Very neatly played.

JULIAN: Now say 'How do you do? to Leo, and stop acting.

DULCIMER (*coming over to them*): I shan't say anything so banal after admiring you both for the last half-hour. A delightful couple! (*To* LEONORA *in explanation.*) It's so refreshing to see people sometimes from an unusual angle.

LEONORA: I think it's a marvellous game. I can imagine all kinds of possibilities.

DULCIMER: It's a relief from the obvious and monotonous. They are the ghosts that haunt modern civilisation. Nowadays everybody does everything and nobody does it well. I can't join in the great display of uninspired competence, so I contrive little originalities of my own.

JULIAN: You're a 'bright' old thing, aren't you?

DULCIMER: Let's sit and smoke! (*He sits at their table, taking the spare chair from his own table.*) So the course of love runs smoothly even though it runs through Camden Town.

LEONORA (*emphatically*): It runs beautifully, Mr Dulcimer.

DULCIMER (*after a tiny pause*): I left my cigarette holder in the roof garden, Julian. I wish you'd get if for me.

JULIAN (*getting up after a quick look at* LEONORA): Right you are! (*He exits.* DULCIMER *gets up and shuts the gates of the roof garden.*)

LEONORA (*getting up and continuing her remark*): I shall win.

DULCIMER (*turning round and smiling innocently*): What a fierce little thing it is! Of course you'll win as you call it, if by that you mean that you'll marry Julian. (*Coming to her.*)

LEONORA (*firmly*): I do mean that!

DULCIMER: Well, then, that's all right. (*He pats her hand. She withdraws it.*) Still determined to see me as an enemy just because I didn't fling you at each other's heads like any ordinary parent would have done. (*He sits again at her table on the same chair. She takes the chair* JULIAN *sat in before.*) By the way, how is the official parent?

LEONORA: He's very fit. He's awfully pleased to have Julian back.

DULCIMER: He wants to resume parenthood you know. He wrote to me about it.

LEONORA: He's very anxious to be a real father to Julian.

DULCIMER: Perhaps the moment has come for that too.

LEONORA: Do you really mean that? Would you let him go?

DULCIMER: Let him go! You really must disabuse yourself of this notion that I wish to detain him. It's simply that I don't suddenly expose sensitive hot-house plants to harsh winds, not even when you're the Lady of the Garden. I took a certain amount of risk in doing what I did.

LEONORA: But he's survived all right.

DULCIMER: I can see that. I was watching you both carefully just now.

LEONORA: I knew you were.

DULCIMER: Again that note of suspicion! Just because I go out of my way to test things to make quite sure. You both had a theory that you were in love . . .

LEONORA: It was never a theory with me!

DULCIMER (*protestingly*): I know! But it might have been! Isn't that true?

LEONORA: I suppose it is.

DULCIMER: The last time you were here you were both very impetuous. You wanted me to cover you with large allowances . . .

LEONORA: No. I never wanted that. I knew that Julian could do without it!

DULCIMER: And that part of the experiment is working, too?

LEONORA: He's made a splendid start!

DULCIMER: And knows all about Foot and Mouth Disease?

LEONORA: Very nearly all.

DULCIMER: I can see the change in him. He's got a purpose in his life.

LEONORA (*enigmatically*): I'm glad you see that.

DULCIMER: And don't you think that an allowance two months ago might have undermined him? Now, of course . . .

LEONORA (*almost afraid to put her thoughts into words*): You mean that you feel differently about it now?

DULCIMER: I mean that at every crisis in Julian's life, I want to be behind him with just that bias in the right direction that a real father never seems able to give. You can't believe that, can you?

LEONORA: I should like to believe it very much.

DULCIMER: I remember the moment so well, when you suddenly took it into your head to dislike me. You were standing over there. (*Pointing.*)

LEONORA: I couldn't help myself then. I can't help myself now.

DULCIMER: And yet, quite a number of people have liked me! Some have even said that I was fascinating! (*With that disarming drawl of his.*) Do I fascinate you, Leonora?

LEONORA: Yes. Shall I tell you how? I'm afraid it won't sound very complimentary. (*Rising.*) You fascinate me like a snake fascinates.

DULCIMER (*seemingly horrified*): You mean that you're afraid of me?

LEONORA (*firmly*): Not for a second. You see, I'm not under the spell. I mean that I like watching you, just as much as you like watching me.

DULCIMER (*rising and walking about the room*): Oh, dear! Why wasn't I born ordinary? Ordinary people aren't accused of casting spells, or turned into things at the zoo. (*Indignantly.*) I know what it is. You'd have liked a nice suburban wooing! High tea and then the Upper Circle at *Cavalcade*. I'm sorry! I don't know how to set about it. I just don't.

Enter JULIAN from the roof garden.

JULIAN: I can't find your cigarette holder anywhere on the roof.

DULCIMER (*moving to the fireplace*): It doesn't matter. I must have dropped it down a chimney.

JULIAN: What are you standing on your hind legs for?

DULCIMER: Begging, my dear boy! Begging for a little of the milk of human kindness.

LEONORA: Mr Dulcimer has started another game now. This time he's the great misunderstood, and he's annoyed with me because I won't play.

JULIAN: I've no misunderstandings about anything. I'm just happy and comfortable.

DULCIMER: You mustn't be happy or comfortable! You must sit up to the table and have a nice cup of cocoa! (*He sits on the couch.*)

JULIAN: That's not a bad idea! (*He goes to the table behind the couch and helps himself to another glass of brandy.*) Here's to comfort!

DULCIMER *and* LEONORA *are both watching him.*

LEONORA: As a matter of fact, Mr Dulcimer and I understand each other perfectly. Whatever we say, we both see into each other's minds quite a long way.

JULIAN (*languidly*): How simple!

LEONORA (*firmly*): I think it is, too! (*She rises.*) At any rate I'm going to leave it to you now.

DULCIMER (*surprised, not understanding*): You're not going?

LEONORA (*chaffing him*): My suburban habits again! Bed early!

JULIAN: Don't go yet!

LEONORA: You know that I've got to. I only hope that Mr Dulcimer won't think me rude. I've got a couple of sick dogs to look after. (DULCIMER *winces.*)

JULIAN (*earnestly*): Don't go, Leo! Not quite yet! (*He is struggling mentally between her and his old life.*)

LEONORA: All right! I'll stay a little longer!

Enter TRUMP with coffee.

JULIAN (*pushing brandy bottle away*): I'm as firm as a rock.

LEONORA: Darling, don't be absurd.

JULIAN: I mean that and all it symbolises. I can't actually push the whole room away, but I do!

LEONORA (*in whisper*): Darling, I love you!

TRUMP *pours coffee.*

DULCIMER (*turning round*): You must stay till you've had your coffee.

TRUMP *hands it round.*

LEONORA: I'll be delighted to.

DULCIMER (*to* TRUMP, *as he hands him coffee*): Clear away the Monseigneur! (*Pointing to the two tables.*)

TRUMP: Yes, sir. (*He moves the centre table bodily from the room after having turned out the light. Then he returns with the trolley-waiter, and during the following dialogue puts the other two tables out of the way, and clears the things from them.*)

DULCIMER: I'm afraid we must be obvious for once and turn on that dreadful wireless. (JULIAN *does so.*) You see, Leonora, I'm much more ordinary than you think, I've just this single room. Here I am and here I have to stay.

LEONORA (*coming over to him and sitting by his side. Amused*): Poor dear! So hampered and hemmed in!

DULCIMER: So few rooms mean anything, and I could just do something with this one, and then of course there was the roof garden. That counted for something.

JULIAN (*coming near them. Joking*): It's not a bad little common room.

DULCIMER: It has its drawbacks of course. One can never 'join the ladies'.

LEONORA: Well, you asked me to stay!

DULCIMER (*kindly*): I want you to stay! I always remember your appreciation of this room the first time you saw it.

LEONORA: You don't forget things, do you?

DULCIMER: I make vivid mental notes of anything I like or dislike. (*To* TRUMP who is clearing away.*) What's that tune?

TRUMP: I think it's a new fox trot, sir. 'I like her for liking her baby.'

DULCIMER: Don't you think you ought to dance?

LEONORA: I don't feel like it, do you, Julian?

JULIAN: Come on! Let's try!

They dance.

DULCIMER (*tormenting himself with the sight*): You were right, Trump!

TRUMP (*stopping in his work*): Was I, sir?

DULCIMER: You said that Miss Yale danced well.

They are now on the other side of the room. MR DULCIMER *gets up.*

TRUMP: Is anything wrong, sir?

DULCIMER: Yes. (*He puts his coffee cup on the mantelpiece.*)

TRUMP: I'm sorry, sir!

DULCIMER: I've lost my cigarette holder. It's on the roof somewhere.

TRUMP: Let me look, sir!

DULCIMER (*harshly*): No, you get on with your work. I shall call down every chimney. (*He exits quickly on to the roof garden.*)

TRUMP *watches him and smiles. He knows.*

JULIAN (*stopping dancing*): Has he gone? (*He speaks over* LEONORA's *shoulder.*)

TRUMP (*pointing to the roof garden*): Out there, sir! (*He exits with the trolley-waiter.*)

JULIAN: You really think he's come round?

LEONORA: I couldn't tell. He never quite came to the point.

JULIAN: I'll bring him to the point.

LEONORA: But if nothing comes of it, you won't let him undermine us, will you? Even if these two months have meant a huge amount of work, they've brought us still closer together, haven't they?

JULIAN: Closer than ever, darling!

LEONORA (*moving to the roof garden*): Is he watching us?

JULIAN (*following her*): He's out there in the darkness.

LEONORA: I know. Watching!

JULIAN: Darling, what a bogey you make of him!

LEONORA: It's not only himself. It's everything he stands for! It's this room, and luxury, and comfort . . . and idleness . . .

JULIAN: And everything that's mine by right. Why shouldn't I have it? I shall work then, with security behind me, instead of this void stretching out for centuries.

LEONORA: Yes, but supposing he won't.

JULIAN: Then we just go on as we are.

LEONORA: Promise?

JULIAN: Promise!

LEONORA: We'll think of something.

JULIAN: Of course, darling Leo! (*He puts his arm round her.*)

LEONORA (*seeing that DULCIMER is coming back*): Take care!

JULIAN: Let him see that we mean business.

A long embrace.
DULCIMER returns from the roof. He switches off the radio. They break.

JULIAN: Well, Dulcie, is it a starry night?

DULCIMER: The Coliseum appears to be in the ascendant at the moment.

LEONORA: Now, I really must be off. Can I ring you up before I go to bed?

JULIAN: Rather!

LEONORA: Here? You won't be going at once?

JULIAN: Not for ages.

LEONORA: I don't want to bring your father down to answer it.

JULIAN: Ring me here.

LEONORA: Just to say 'goodnight'. (*And to hear the result of his talk.*)

JULIAN: I'll get your wrap. (*He goes out of the room.*)

DULCIMER (*to LEONORA*): Don't forget your roses. (*He gets them from the table.*) Would you hate me to pin them into your dress?

LEONORA: I've nothing to fasten them with.

DULCIMER (*looking at her earnestly*): Will you carry them? Wait a minute. (*He gets a silver penknife from the bureau and strips the thorns from the stalks.*) There! Now they are as harmless as I am.

LEONORA *takes them, looking at him steadily.*

LEONORA: They're delicious. (*She smells them.*)

JULIAN *returns with her cloak.*

JULIAN (*putting it round her*): Same time as usual, tomorrow?

DULCIMER *rings the bell.*

LEONORA: Yes, darling. Don't come down. (*To DULCIMER.*) Goodnight!

JULIAN: I'll see you to the lift. (*He goes out with her.*)

DULCIMER *watches them go, then turns down some of the lights, and going to the piano, plays softly. JULIAN comes back, wanders round the room, and leans on the piano.*

Have you ever played the harmonium, Dulcie? (*Dreamily.*) It's not an instrument you can stroke like you're stroking that piano. Is that Chopin?

DULCIMER: Sonata in B Minor.

JULIAN: It seems to call out all the peacefulness of the room, but you make it seem magical. (*Coming to the couch and sitting down.*) Who was the person who heard 'sounds and sweet airs' and 'cried to sleep again'?

DULCIMER (*quoting*): 'Sounds and sweet airs, that give delight, and hurt not . . .

JULIAN: Yes! That's it!

DULCIMER: 'and then in dreaming,
The clouds, methought would open, and show riches,
Ready to drop upon me; that, when I waked,
I cried to dream again.'

JULIAN: You read it to me once. 'Riches

ready to drop upon me,' and Leo . . .
(*Then he suddenly springs to his feet.*)

MR DULCIMER *stops playing.*

I was nearly passing out. (*He braces himself up.*) I expect the room's hot.

DULCIMER: Go on to the roof and get some air. (*He comes towards him.*)

JULIAN: I'm all right. I haven't been used to anything soft for such a long time. I felt as if I was drowning.

DULCIMER: You were always very imaginative. Sit down again. I won't play any more if my playing makes you swoon.

JULIAN *sits on the couch again, this time a little apprehensively.*
DULCIMER *stands behind him.*

Perhaps you need a restorative? (*He takes up the brandy from the table behind.*)

JULIAN: No thanks.

DULCIMER: It is rather too good to take medicinally. (*He sits beside* JULIAN.) So things haven't lost their glamour?

JULIAN: I've missed everything horribly, and it's marvellous to be back. Why did you have that freak dinner tonight?

DULCIMER: I was just thinking of you and Leonora. You might have hated the thought of this place and of me and of everything to do with it. Then the formality, the removal to a distance, would have reassured you. You would have eaten your dinner, perhaps we should have smiled at each other once or twice, like one does, you'd have paid your bill and departed.

JULIAN: That's just what Leo wanted to do!

DULCIMER: And by now you'd have been peacefully enjoying Continuous Variety. (*Springing up.*) What a fool I've been! An ill-mannered fool! To start a game and then refuse to play it out! You wanted to go! But then you found that the prison door wasn't really open! Like the captives in the Bastille you reached the last corridor only to rush into your gaoler's arms! (*He has worked himself up into a fine passion.*)

JULIAN (*half-amused and half-alarmed*): You know quite well that I didn't think

anything of the kind! I was thankful to get back here, and hated not being able to talk to you all through dinner. Now sit down, and as I said before, stop acting!

DULCIMER (*sitting down beside him*): At least you can never say that I kept you against your will, even though I have no respect for natural ties!

JULIAN: I've had an eye-opener over them, I can assure you. Do let me enjoy myself a little bit! I'm going back to 'natural ties' soon enough!

DULCIMER (*interested and inwardly anxious*): Do you find they count for much?

JULIAN: More than I expected. I suppose that's because he is my father. I suppose he got a footing inside me during those first eleven years.

DULCIMER (*indignantly*): He never bothered about you at all.

JULIAN: Well, there it is! He's utterly impossible, but he exists. I don't suppose you can understand. You never knew your father, did you?

DULCIMER: No.

JULIAN: But you adored your mother.

DULCIMER: She was the only woman who ever meant a thing to me.

JULIAN: And then of course I have some strange affinity with him over the past. He plays those ghastly Welsh hymns, and I listen to them, and something happens to me. I don't know what it is.

DULCIMER: Some of those melodies are extraordinarily fine.

JULIAN: It isn't anything aesthetic. It isn't even pleasure. It calls from somewhere very far off and makes me feel I belong to something very old. I thought what a contrast it was just now. You at the piano and father at the harmonium. But they both speak . . . Now let's forget Camden Town.

DULCIMER: I should like you to have been at Silver Gates this time. I took your advice about the music room. It now faces the swimming pool.

JULIAN: I always told you it ought to.

DULCIMER: You were perfectly right. I've had the pool floodlighted. Now at night the box hedges enclose a lagoon of deep Mediterranean blue. Ruinously expensive!

JULIAN: Marvellous! I mean – how exquisite! (*They laugh.*)

DULCIMER: We must give a fancy dress bathing party. Venetian and very slippery. (*All the time he is watching* JULIAN *closely.*)

JULIAN: My God! So while you're splashing in the moonlight, I shall be sweating in Camden Town!

DULCIMER (*realising that the spell is working, and getting up*): Now, won't you change your mind? (*He goes to the table behind and holds up the brandy bottle.*)

JULIAN: Well, I don't see why I shouldn't.

DULCIMER *gives him some brandy and takes some himself.*

Yes! That's not for invalids!

DULCIMER (*standing*): Leonora tells me that you've settled down to work wonderfully!

JULIAN: Did she say that? But I don't think I've taken her in! Not really! She knows that I'm not getting on, but she's a fine encourager.

DULCIMER: She certainly made me think you'd made a good start.

JULIAN: I've tried. I genuinely have. But I can't get up any interest in the stuff. What's the point in reading up a lot of flapdoodle in order to give some filthy little Pekinese an emetic?

DULCIMER: I should hate to give anyone an emetic. I could never get into the right frame of mind. But then, I haven't the call! (*He moves right.*)

JULIAN: Nor have I. Dulcie, it is no good shirking the fact any longer. I'm no good at it.

DULCIMER (*coming back to him*): We won't despair after two months.

JULIAN (*firmly*): I despaired after a fortnight. I knew then.

DULCIMER (*with assumed surprise*): You give it up?

JULIAN: I'm afraid so. As far as exams are concerned.

DULCIMER (*sitting beside him after showing relief*): Shall I make a suggestion?

JULIAN (*earnestly and hopefully*): I wish you would.

DULCIMER: Take a rest and then come back to it. Come for a holiday.

JULIAN: I could do with a holiday.

DULCIMER: Come to the Villa at Margherita.

JULIAN: Can I bring Leo?

DULCIMER: Of course.

JULIAN: I know she won't though. (DULCIMER *shows relief in his face.*) She'll never leave her work just now, especially after giving up so much time to me.

DULCIMER: Can't you tear yourself away from her for a week or two?

JULIAN: I suppose I could. (*He gets up and moves a little away to the right.*)

DULCIMER: You're so adhesive, Julian. First it was Peter. Now it's Leonora.

JULIAN: They're not quite the same thing.

DULCIMER: For heaven's sake don't you begin to misunderstand me. I was merely admiring your loyalty, but I don't want to drag you there.

JULIAN: You know I'd adore to come! (*The struggle in him is now definitely beginning.*)

DULCIMER (*sprawling on the couch*): I daresay I was only going to make a convenience of you. The ceiling wants touching up badly. The Cupids on it look like very old charwomen. It's delicate work, but no doubt I can get it done.

JULIAN (*coming and standing at the head of the couch*): Dulcie! You know perfectly well that I'd give my head to come to Italy. The point is, I've got to earn a living. (DULCIMER *sits straight and* JULIAN *beside him.*) Dulcie, I've never asked you for anything much before. I've never had to ask you. Now I must put it into words, though I hate doing it. Can't you reconsider your decision?

DULCIMER: What decision?

JULIAN: I've been screwing up my

courage all the evening to ask you for an allowance. The fact is I simply cannot earn.

DULCIMER (*suavely*): Supposing I do reconsider my decision?

JULIAN (*eagerly*): Then that would make everything all right. I don't want to be idle. I never have been idle. I like having something to do all the time. You see, my idea is to live in the country, away from all this that I can't afford.

DULCIMER: You think you could endure the country – always?

JULIAN: I'd like to run kennels or something of the kind. I haven't the slighest intention of vegetating ... we've got all sorts of schemes. We thought it might be possible to run polo ponies.

DULCIMER: What sum of money do you think would make it possible?

JULIAN: Well, we'd have to make a start. That costs a good bit, I know.

DULCIMER: It's no good underestimating that. By the time you'd bought your house and equipped it with livestock, you'd have spent the best part of four or five thousand pounds.

JULIAN (*on tenterhooks*): I'm afraid I should. But then we could live on very little. I think that five hundred a year would do us well. That would mean a home and security, and I should be delivered for ever from this nightmare of daily bread.

DULCIMER: It almost seems a pity I didn't make you a plumber.

JULIAN (*smiling ruefully*): I rather wish I had been taught something.

DULCIMER *sighs and is silent.*

What are you thinking?

DULCIMER: I was thinking that six months hence, or a year hence, you'll find that your allowance isn't enough and that your menagerie doesn't pay, and you'll come and ask for more.

JULIAN: I promise you I'll never ask you for a penny again!

DULCIMER: Like the tiger, you'll have tasted blood and you'll be greedy to taste more!

JULIAN: Then you mean that you won't help me?

DULCIMER (*looking at him gravely*): I won't give you any money, Julian. (*He gets up and walks away to the window as JULIAN did in Act One.*) JULIAN *watches him.*

JULIAN (*after a moment*): Dulcie?

DULCIMER: Well?

JULIAN: You want me to be happy, don't you?

DULCIMER (*turning round fiercely*): Want you to be happy? You've always been happy. I've made you happy!

JULIAN: Yes, but I must go on. I can't just stand still.

DULCIMER: You must be as you are. You must develop naturally. (*Standing by the couch.*) Listen, Julian! There is nothing to be ashamed of or disappointed over in not being able to earn a living. You aren't made that way, that's all. I delivered you for ever from what you call 'the nightmare of daily bread'. You have a home and security that nothing can take from you, and you won't recognise it.

JULIAN (*emphatically*): I want to get married, I tell you!

DULCIMER: For goodness' sake, don't be strident!

JULIAN: I can't always pick and choose my words, just to please you!

DULCIMER: I'm not complaining of your language yet. I only ask you not to shout!

JULIAN: You seem to think that what is soft and expensive and luxurious is everything!

DULCIMER (*quickly*): And, don't you? Haven't you proved it tonight? Haven't the last two months proved it? What matters to you most is to be comfortable, to have pleasant rooms and pleasant meals, and money in your pocket. You have tried the other thing, and hated it, haven't you? (*He sits in the armchair near the window.*) Very well, then. Be honest with yourself. Don't try to be some other person. Be Julian Dulcimer.

JULIAN: But I'm not Julian Dulcimer!

DULCIMER: Do you want me to believe that you're David Owen just because you were stirred a little at some crude revivalist hymn?

JULIAN (*getting up*): You can't understand what I am or what I want!

DULCIMER (*also getting up*): By all means let us talk this out standing up. It's very fatiguing, but I can see that you mean to be emphatic!

JULIAN (*coming over to him*): Dulcie, do for one moment be human! Can't you try to understand what I'm struggling against?

DULCIMER: I do, perfectly. But why struggle with no chance of succeeding?

JULIAN: Why shouldn't I succeed?

DULCIMER: Because you can't be two people at the same time. You cannot be Julian Dulcimer and a married man. They have been fighting with each other from the first moment they met. My dear boy, it's quite natural that you should want to include Leonora in your scheme, but unfortunately there isn't room for her.

JULIAN (*surprised*): Why?

DULCIMER: Well, you don't want her to have to keep you, do you?

JULIAN (*moving away*): I haven't the slightest intention of her doing so! (*He sits on the couch.*)

DULCIMER: Yet, that is what it will come to! You want me to let you pretend for a while that you are what is known as a breadwinner, but in the end you'll depend on your wife. All these dreams of dogs and polo ponies and other country nonsense will crumble into dust the first morning you don't feel like getting up, or fancy a day in town. You couldn't stand up to your inclination for a second, and why should you?

JULIAN (*turning round*): You think you know me, but you're wrong!

DULCIMER: Very well, then! Go and get married! (*Vehemently.*) Disregard your temperament, your disposition, your everything that cries out against it! Beat out a living from the world and fashion a home for your wife, and live in it, and be happy ever after! Can you do it?

JULIAN: Why do you torment me like this?

DULCIMER: Can you say, 'Leonora comes before everything else? I don't care what I do and where I live so long as she is with me!' Of course you can't. But you haven't the courage to admit it, and it's only a fool who won't recognise his own limitations.

A silence.

However, I suppose that your silence means that you do recognise them, so we won't use any more harsh names. You're not really the fool you're trying so hard to be. (*Passing in front of him to the hearth.*)

JULIAN (*turning on him fiercely*): By God, I'm not! I'm not fool enough to be one thing, and that is your slave!

DULCIMER: Don't be ridiculous!

JULIAN (*trembling*): You think my life is yours to arrange as you please, but you're wrong again. I'm damned well going to do what I like with it! I think I detest you and your luxurious ways, and your beastly superior air about everything. I shall live where I like and how I like, and you can go to hell! (*The telephone rings.*)

DULCIMER: Prove it, then! Now's your chance! (*Holding the receiver towards him.*) Tell her! You little canting fool! You know that luxury is the breath of your life. You couldn't do without it for a second. What you are feeling is a childish revulsion against yourself. You wanted to be noble and romantic, and you're disappointed because you can't be! Self-loathing is always painful, but fortunately one outgrows it. Tell her that I won't help you, and that you'll fight your way to her through poverty and struggle and self-denial! Don't keep her waiting! (*He holds the receiver nearer to him.*)

JULIAN *takes the receiver and tries hard to answer* LEONORA, *then with an exclamation of despair drops the receiver on the floor and falls on the couch in a fit of weeping.* DULCIMER *picks up the receiver and replaces it, then goes to the bell and rings it. He then walks quickly to the piano, seats himself at it and plays the Chopin Sonata. Enter* TRUMP.

DULCIMER (*playing as the 'phone rings again*): Get Mr Julian's room ready, please!

TRUMP: Very good, sir! (*He glances at the 'phone, then at* DULCIMER, *then goes.*)

The phone continues to ring.

Curtain.

ACT THREE

Scene One

At MR DULCIMER's *flat. Next morning.*

The arrangement of the room is as in Act One. The centre table is now back in its place; on it stands an open attaché case, but the audience cannot see the contents. The table behind the couch is gone.

MR DULCIMER *is seated at the bureau.* TRUMP *enters carrying a brown paper parcel which he puts on the table near the case.*

DULCIMER (*looking up*): Oh, there you are Trump! I want you to send off this wire. We're going abroad. Do you like the idea? (*He hands him the wire.*)

TRUMP: Shall we be away long, sir? (*He seems a little perturbed at the news.*)

DULCIMER: About six months, I think.

TRUMP: Really, sir?

DULCIMER: Yes. Mr Julian and I both want a change. He's been overworking. I'm anxious about him. (*Seeing his face.*) You look a little dashed at my news. *You've* not been forming any attachments, have you?

TRUMP: No, sir. I'm quite heart-whole.

DULCIMER: Good. For a moment I thought that you'd been tainted.

TRUMP: No, sir. Quite immune, as yet.

DULCIMER: That's right. We shall be passing into a more temperate zone in a day or two, beyond the ravages of this terrible disease. We'll take sanctuary first at Margherita. That's why I want Michele to get that wire as soon as possible. So that he may get the villa ready. Later on, I dare say, we shall be moving about. (*He moves across the room, picking up the parcel from the table. He takes off the paper, throws it on to the window seat and puts the book on the centre table.*)

TRUMP: When are we starting, sir?

DULCIMER: Tonight.

TRUMP: Shall I make the usual travelling arrangements?

DULCIMER: Please. And tell Mortimer I'm taking the car. We need movement and distraction.

TRUMP: Very good, sir.

Exit TRUMP. DULCIMER *goes to the bureau, gets his passport, etc., unlocks the drawer, takes out a revolver and puts them all in the attaché case. Enter* JULIAN *a moment later, in a very elaborate dressing-gown.* DULCIMER *is now by the roof garden and is carolling 'O, Sole Mio'.*

JULIAN: You sound very gay this morning.

DULCIMER: My dear boy, I've gone all holiday. The Blue Train is in my blood. Tomorrow evening we shall be by the Mediterranean. Don't you think that a little of Italy will be rather fun?

JULIAN (*sitting down by the window in the armchair*): I shall be glad to get away anywhere. (*Not with very great enthusiasm.*)

DULCIMER (*handing him the book*): This came for you, just now.

JULIAN: What is it? (*Taking it.*)

DULCIMER: It's Deller's *Impressions of the Umbrian Towns*. There's a picture of Perugia in the early morning that's rather lovely.

JULIAN (*opening the book*): Are we going to the Umbrian towns?

DULCIMER: Would you like to?

JULIAN: I don't care where we go as long as it's somewhere new, something I haven't seen before.

DULCIMER: We'll take the car and break new ground.

JULIAN (*looking at the pictures*): That's refreshing.

DULCIMER: I thought you knew Deller's work? I've been meaning to give you this for a long time. I sent down for it directly after breakfast this morning. I wanted something to blot out yesterday evening.

JULIAN: It's awfully kind of you, Dulcie.

DULCIMER: Let me have it for a moment. (*He takes the book and writes in it with his pen.*) There! (*He hands it back.*)

JULIAN (*reading*): 'Addio to all misunderstandings.' (*He smiles, but just a little sadly.*)

DULCIMER (*lightly*): It will do to read in the train. (*He goes back to the roof garden.*)

JULIAN: Yes. For God's sake, let's be off!

DULCIMER: Trump's fixed everything up.

JULIAN: I should like to get into the car and go at once.

DULCIMER: I think everything points today to a very good lunch somewhere and then a little shopping. You'll want to get some things, won't you.

JULIAN: One or two, I suppose.

DULCIMER: A super-lunch and then a little agreeable spending in Bond Street or thereabouts. We won't get back till it's time to start.

JULIAN: I've got to see Leo some time for a minute.

DULCIMER (*cautiously*): Perhaps you'll write?

JULIAN: No. I must see her.

DULCIMER: I can drop you at the surgery for five minutes.

JULIAN: Yes. That will do.

DULCIMER (*ingratiatingly and coming to him*): Don't be too hard on yourself. Six months' probation before you finally make up your mind is a most reasonable request.

JULIAN: I shall be glad to get it over, all the same.

Enter TRUMP.

DULCIMER: What is it?

TRUMP: Miss Yale would like to see Mr Julian.

JULIAN (*getting up*): Where is she?

TRUMP: In the hall, sir. I didn't know whether you had time to see people.

JULIAN (*crossing to the couch*): Show her in.

TRUMP: Very good, sir.

Exit TRUMP.

DULCIMER: Would you like me to tackle this?

JULIAN (*very pale*): No thanks, Dulcie.

DULCIMER: All right. I'll clear out and

leave you together. (*Putting his hand on his shoulder.*) I'm sure she'll understand.

JULIAN (*simply*): I hope she will.

DULCIMER *goes to the door. As he gets to it,* TRUMP *opens it and shows in* LEONORA.

TRUMP: Miss Yale.

DULCIMER (*unpleasantly agreeable*): Good morning, Leonora! (*As she ejaculates 'Julian!'*) Now you mustn't scold him. We got very late last night and hadn't the heart to disturb you.

LEONORA: But I rang you quite early and couldn't get any reply.

DULCIMER: We were here all the evening. However, Julian will tell you all about it. (*He exits.*)

LEONORA (*coming to* JULIAN): Good morning, darling! (*They kiss uncomfortably.*) What did happen? I rang up Isaiah this morning and found that you hadn't been home last night.

JULIAN: No. I stayed here.

LEONORA (*seeing that there is something different about him*): I see. Isaiah is rather worried. He came along with me. He's waiting outside in the square. (*Taking hold of his hand and drawing him down on to the couch.*) Julian, darling, don't mind! What's it matter if he won't give you any money? That's why you didn't answer the phone, wasn't it?

JULIAN: I couldn't get a penny out of him, Leo.

LEONORA: I knew that was it. Well, we're not going to let money stand between us and our happiness, are we? I expect we've worried too much about it. Last night when I didn't hear from you, I made up my mind what we'd do. We'll get married at once and damn the money. I've got enough for two, with a squeeze.

JULIAN (*in misery*): I can't let you do that, Leo. It's lovely of you to suggest it, but I can't.

LEONORA: You wouldn't mind skimping a little with me, would you? Until something turned up. I think we'd better put the idea of exams out of our heads, don't you?

JULIAN (*almost amused, in spite of himself*): Darling, I do.

LEONORA: Everybody who's got a job hasn't passed an exam. Something will come along.

JULIAN: One can always tout note-paper round to people's front doors.

LEONORA: We've not come to that yet. We'll get uncertainty out of our life first and then set to work to build it up. You'll feel far more confident of yourself when you're married to me.

JULIAN: Leo, I can't marry you!

LEONORA: Julian!

JULIAN: Not yet. I couldn't come and live on you. I should be miserable every minute of the time.

LEONORA (*lightly*): Darling, you're not turning me down, are you? It's a firm offer.

JULIAN: Of course I'm not turning you down. It was marvellous of you to have thought of it. It's just unthinkable to me, that's all. You can't imagine what a drag I should be.

LEONORA: Darling, don't go on apologising, for yourself. I can see all the drawbacks perfectly well.

JULIAN (*nerving himself*): I'm not apologising, but I won't pretend any more. It's like this. I've been accustomed to living in one way too long to give it up. I must have comfort. I must have pleasure. I must have money to spend. I must. (*Moving to the centre table.*) I tried to do without them, but it's been hell all the time. When I came back here last night, I knew what hell it had been.

LEONORA: So that was why you didn't go to your father's?

JULIAN: That was it. The moment I came back here, everything began to get hold of me again. I tried to fight it, but it was too strong. I suppose one must be as one is made. You don't know what it means to me to sleep in a comfortable bed again, with decent sheets.

LEONORA (*kindly*): Don't you think you've rather got the idea that you're the only person who's ever been comfortable? (*Coming to him.*) I have quite a fair amount of comfort, but I don't make it my God.

JULIAN: I hate and detest everything that's cheap and ugly and second-best.

LEONORA: That I can understand, but it's a terrible thought to me that you don't mind how you get your luxury or who gives it to you so long as you get it.

JULIAN: I don't think I do mind. Not much. (*He moves to the window and stands with his back to her.*)

LEONORA: You don't realise what you're saying. If you think that, it means that you're just a taker, a parasite. You're not really worth keeping alive.

JULIAN (*turning round*): I'm sorry you think so poorly of me!

LEONORA: I'm only taking you at your own valuation. Do you think it's pleasant for me to find out that the man I love isn't a man at all, but only a bundle of sensations?

JULIAN (*coming back to the table*): I've done my best to control circumstances. If I'm so worthless, you'll soon be able to forget me.

LEONORA: My God, I hope so! I'll do my best, I promise you. To think of all that I've been offering you and you haven't even begun to understand what I was saying.

JULIAN: Can't you see that it's the thought of you that's been making me so desperately miserable?

LEONORA: Desperately miserable! You don't know what the words mean! You haven't any feelings, not real feelings. If you cared anything for me, if you'd ever cared, you'd have chucked all this to the winds, really chucked it. Not just gone a little way off and hankered after it all the time. I've been fool enough to imagine that there was something more in you, something that hadn't a chance to get out, and that my love would set it free. I ought to have known last night when you didn't answer the phone that you'd succumbed to all this again . . . and to him.

JULIAN: I can't help it. He's been the biggest thing in my life.

LEONORA: Anyone can see that. I wonder how much you really care about him? I hope I shan't meet you one day in Piccadilly with a painted face, just because you must have linen sheets!

JULIAN: You needn't be blatant just because I've been honest with you. I'm sick to death of being talked at. (*He moves to the hearth.*)

LEONORA: Poor Julian, I won't talk any more or plan or scheme or try to put energy and self respect in you. But if ever you can come to me and prove that what I've loved exists, I'll marry you.

JULIAN: If you haven't married someone else.

LEONORA: Quite. But you don't realise that you chose a faithful one. God! That makes me angry and bitter. What a pitiful waste!

JULIAN (*turning to her*): I'll prove to you yet that I'm not as rotten as you think.

LEONORA: I hope so!

JULIAN (*sitting on the couch*): I'm going away for six months just to get a breather, and I'm going to do some hard thinking about myself.

LEONORA: I wonder why you like to go on playing with the idea of me? That's the part I can't understand. You know you don't want me. You've said so, and yet you can't quite cut yourself off.

JULIAN: I do want you.

At this moment the door opens and MR DULCIMER *enters. He is very conscious that everything has turned out as he expected. He comes between them, standing at the corner of the couch with his hand on* JULIAN's *shoulder.*

DULCIMER (*to* LEONORA): Well, has Julian explained everything to you?

LEONORA: Oh, yes. (*Moving away.*) He's made it all perfectly clear.

DULCIMER: I don't want to break in on any intimacies, but (*To* JULIAN) I do think that you ought to finish your toilet. (*Meaning the dressing-gown.*) That's a dressy little garment, Julian, but they are still very conservative at the Ritz, especially about lunch-time. (*He moves to the roof garden.*)

JULIAN: I shall be ready in a few minutes.

DULCIMER: Don't rush into your

clothes. There's plenty of time. I've told the car to be here in half an hour. Will that do?

JULIAN: Yes.

DULCIMER: Tell Trump to bring a glass of champagne to your dressing-room. There's nothing like a glass of champagne for giving a fillip to the tie. (*He goes into the roof garden.*)

JULIAN (*coming to* LEONORA): Goodbye, Leo.

LEONORA: Goodbye, Julian.

JULIAN: I suppose there's nothing more to be said.

LEONORA: No. I suppose there isn't.

He goes out quickly. When he has gone, she makes a move to go.

DULCIMER (*returning and standing on the top step into the roof garden.*) Must you go for a minute?

LEONORA (*turning round*): I can't think of anything to say to you, Mr Dulcimer. At least, nothing adequate. I know you're pleased with the way things have gone.

DULCIMER: Can one be pleased at the inevitable? I knew what would happen. I foresaw it from the start. My comment is merely *La commèdia è finita.* I'm glad you take it philosophically. I should have been sorry if you had been really hurt.

LEONORA: And I should have loathed your pity!

DULCIMER: And yet I do pity you. There is something definitely pathetic in the way you have set yourself up against me. You really thought that you could succeed! Even now that you've failed I feel that you would like to have a real tilt at me. We have carried on a subconscious warfare. We've never come to the surface and fought in the open.

LEONORA: I've made no secret of what I've thought of you, how utterly I've loathed and despised you. I knew from the first that you were a deadly enemy. Yet, even now, I'm wondering how you dare to destroy Julian as you have done. Why couldn't you have let him go?

DULCIMER: Because he is to me youth and charm and companionship. I admit the claims of these indefinable things. I must have them.

LEONORA: And yet, I doubt if he really cares any more for you than he does for me. He stays with you for the sake of what you can give him. If we were both penniless, he'd come to me.

DULCIMER (*stepping down to her*): You're welcome to think so. We can't put it to the proof. But I can see what brought you together. You're both dreamers, idealists. There's not much of it in Julian. But I shall quite probably have a lot of trouble still with you, with the idealised picture of you as his wife. It will only be a faint stirring of course, but I shall have to quiet him.

LEONORA: Haven't you any conscience at all about keeping him from what is normal and healthy, what is best for him?

DULCIMER: I didn't adopt him to please my conscience, if I have one, or to give him what was best for him. My aim was to make him like, and to be unable to do without, what was best for me. That makes you open your eyes wide, doesn't it? You see I'm not like you good people, with one eye on an ideal and the other on reality, a feverish urge towards goodness and then a degraded relapse towards what your natures clamour for insistently. I am a materialist and I glory in it. But I never have to struggle to maintain my position. I know exactly what I want out of life and I get it.

LEONORA: You get what you want out of life simply because you can pay for it. Your foundations are entirely in the sand. Another convulsion in the world and you might vanish tomorrow.

DULCIMER: Certainly. I admit that money isn't the rock it used to be. But I like to have it to use. I like the power of money. I have created comfort and beauty and constant change of scene out of money, and a cage for Julian's soul in which he sings to me as sweetly as in that stuffy Welsh schoolroom all those years ago. And if the convulsion comes, which you no doubt are praying for, there is always this.

He puts his hand into the attaché case and takes out an exquisitely jewelled revolver, replacing it at once.

LEONORA: You wouldn't have the pluck to face things, then! Not even with Julian!

DULCIMER: He wouldn't stay with me then, why should he? I should have nothing to offer him. As you admit, he's coming back to me because I've made him a better offer. You can only offer him your love, and the so-called 'demands' made by love, another foolish, futile little marriage . . .

LEONORA (*fiercely*): I offer him life and everything that makes life worth having and worth living. You can talk and make your words seem very plausible. On your own confession you've no real hold on life!

DULCIMER: Life is bearable so long as I have Julian. You made me very angry when you first came into our lives. I thought for one moment that you might succeed and then I saw myself alone and demanding human sympathy. That made me feel very degraded.

LEONORA: Degraded?

DULCIMER: Yes. You see, I don't think I've ever asked for anything for years. But I must have a focussing point for all my activities and interests and self-expression. That focussing point is Julian. If you take him away, I'm lost. I admit that. Like you, I have feelings, but with Julian in my life I am never troubled by them. He keeps them constant and satisfied. (*He moves as he says this to the window.*)

LEONORA: And so he's just to minister to your emptiness and vanity and self-esteem. His mission is to make you think that you are really alive. You shan't keep him! Even if he doesn't come to me, he shall know what you've done to him!

She is making for the door when he intercepts her.

DULCIMER (*with a voice that cuts like a whip*): Come back! (*He walks quickly to her.*) I can assure you that the repulsion you feel is mutual. You have forced your way into my life and into my house and I won't have vulgar scenes in either! I have gone to the trouble of explaining myself to you because you will insist that you have a foothold in my affairs. You haven't!

Understand that once and for all! This discussion has taken place partly because it amuses me, but more to make certain that it shall never take place again. From now on you will cease interfering with me and with Julian! I gave you an opportunity of making good and you have failed. I knew you would fail and I have told you why. (*Moving away to the table and speaking calmly.*) There is nothing more to be said, and I hope you will now have the good taste to leave my house as quietly as you came.

LEONORA: I'm not going! Not like this! If I went now, I should be just surrendering. I don't care if it's your house or what your wretched susceptibilities are! I'm not beaten yet! I won't be beaten! What I'm fighting for is worth a scene and I'm not afraid of making one!

Voices are heard outside. Enter TRUMP.

TRUMP: There's a gentleman, sir, in the hall. He wants to know if Miss Yale's ready.

LEONORA (*running to the door before TRUMP has finished speaking*): Isaiah! Come in! I want you to help me! Isaiah!

She returns, almost dragging MR OWEN. Exit TRUMP.

OWEN: What are you doing, Leo? I thought you were never coming!

LEONORA: Listen, Isaiah! This man has got hold of Julian body and soul! He's going to take him abroad, and if we let him go we'll never see him again.

DULCIMER (*coming up to them*): How do you do, Mr Owen! We seem destined to meet under very peculiar circumstances. (*He holds out his hand. OWEN does not take it.*) I hear that you've gone up the world since I saw you last. (*He goes and sits at the writing-table.*)

OWEN: Wait a minute, Leo! I haven't got my bearings yet! I'm taking it all in as fast as I can! (*Horrified.*) Is it all over between you and David? (DULCIMER *is addressing labels.*)

LEONORA: Yes. That's all been a mistake. Don't think about me. What we've got to do is save him from

Dulcimer.

OWEN: Very well, then, all I've got to say to him is this. (*Going to him.*) I want my son!

DULCIMER (*turning round*): I'm grateful to you for being concise, Mr Owen! Leonora has positively battered me with words. You at any rate have a point and come to it quickly! 'I want my son!' How admirably put!

OWEN: Perhaps you'll be as brief in your answer!

DULCIMER: I will, with pleasure. You can't have him!

OWEN: Why not?

DULCIMER: Because I don't wish it! Now that must really do! I've got a lot of letters to finish and arrangements to make. (*He turns back to the bureau.*)

OWEN: And you think that will satisfy me!

DULCIMER (*writing and not looking round*): I'm afraid it will have to!

OWEN: Well, it won't! (*Coming closer.*)

DULCIMER (*turning round again*): Mr Owen, I think that you're a businessman first and a prophet second. Let's stick to business! Twelve years ago we made a contract, and you did very well under it. That contract still holds good.

OWEN: No, it doesn't, then! Julian's of age now, and if he wasn't, there was nothing in our agreement to say that you might corrupt him altogether!

DULCIMER: Ah! I was afraid I'd overestimated your common sense. The prophet is stronger than the milkman, I see! (*He turns back to the table.*)

OWEN: You won't impress me with your nasty insults!

DULCIMER: Mr Owen! I've really been very tolerant and extremely courteous, but your time is up. Please leave me in peace.

OWEN (*to* LEONORA): What am I to do, Leo?

LEONORA (*coming to him*): Don't give in yet! We've got to get Julian away, somehow!

OWEN (*to* LEONORA): I must see him

before I go!

Enter TRUMP.

TRUMP: The car is at the door, sir! (LEONORA *runs to the window and looks down at the car.*)

DULCIMER (*getting up, and giving the labels to* TRUMP, *who goes out*): At last! Now that really must be the end. I've got to go out, and I can't leave you two in possession. (*He moves to the centre.*)

OWEN: Before I go, I'm going to see my son!

JULIAN *is heard calling,* 'Dulcie!'

LEONORA: He's coming now! (*She comes to the centre*)

DULCIMER: You're a remarkable man, Mr Owen! You've only to utter a wish and it is instantly gratified!

JULIAN *hurries in and stands at the end of the couch.*

JULIAN: Dulcie! Where on earth have you been? I've been sitting in the car for nearly five minutes. Aren't you . . . (*He sees* LEONORA *and* OWEN.) What on earth is going on now?

DULCIMER: Another crisis, my boy! But I'm afraid we've reached a deadlock!

JULIAN (*irritably to* LEONORA *and* OWEN): What do you want?

OWEN (*coming to* JULIAN): I want to speak to you, David! Just a word!

LEONORA (*to* JULIAN): Do listen to him!

JULIAN: Well, what is it?

OWEN: David, I'm not making up grand sentences now! I'm speaking to you from my heart. I want you to believe me when I say that this man is wicked. He's evil. You don't realise how evil he is! I want you to get away before he destroys your soul altogether!

JULIAN: I don't know anything about my soul, but I'll be thankful to get away! I'm wearied to death of being ordered about by each one of you in turn! (*To* OWEN.) You want me to be one thing, and Leo another, and Dulcie a third. Well, I'm sick of it! What I should like to do would be to go off by myself away from all of you, and find out who I really am and what I really want to do.

LEONORA (*eagerly*): Julian, why don't you? What a splendid idea! We'll help him to do it, won't we Isaiah?

OWEN: Yes. Come on, my boy! It's the best possible thing you can do! Be quick, now!

JULIAN: By God! I will! (*He turns to the door, and begins to go.*)

DULCIMER (*with all the will power he can command*): Julian! (*Going quickly to him.*) Come back! (JULIAN *turns and during the speech comes slowly towards him.*) You can't choose! You haven't any choice! You know perfectly well what you want and where your happiness lies!

LEONORA (*pleadingly*): Darling! Please!

DULCIMER: Don't let them torment you with their miserable misgivings! They're a relic of your race and your early upbringing.

OWEN (*pleadingly*): Davy!

DULCIMER: I delivered you from all that, long ago! (*Gripping his arms.*) Stay here, Julian! (JULIAN *struggles in agony for a moment, then half collapses across the back of the couch.*)

JULIAN: I can't! (MR OWEN's *eye lights on the revolver in the attaché case.*)

DULCIMER (*turning round in triumph and facing the others*): There! Now, are you satisfied? Perhaps you'll . . . (*But before he can say any more,* MR OWEN *has picked up the revolver and fired.* MR DULCIMER *drops dead, clutching at the couch as he falls.* LEONORA *and* JULIAN *drop on to their knees beside him.*)

OWEN (*with deep emotion*): There! Davy! You're free at last!

Curtain.

Scene Two

The same. Six months later, about five o'clock in the afternoon.

The gates to the roof garden are closed and the glass screens are in position. A fire is burning, and on the wall over the piano facing the audience is a death mask of MR DULCIMER.

LEONORA *is standing by the armchair near the window.*

JULIAN *hurries in. He wears an overcoat and scarf. He puts his hat on the piano as he passes.*

JULIAN: Hullo! Leo! It's lovely of you to come! I hope I haven't kept you waiting a frightful time. I've been tearing along from the lawyer's as hard as I could. (*He has thrown his coat and scarf over the armchair.*)

LEONORA (*quietly*): I've only been here about five minutes.

JULIAN: Oh! Good! I know I ought to have come to you, but I couldn't face the surgery today. I wanted to see you alone. (*Smiling.*) Well, Leo?

LEONORA (*looking at him steadily*): Well, Julian?

JULIAN (*confidently*): It's all right, now. (*With childish pride.*) I'm a very rich man. We can get married tomorrow.

LEONORA (*still looking at him steadily*): Are you going to keep this money?

JULIAN (*surprised*): Keep it? What else should I do?

LEONORA: Do? Get a hundred miles away from all that it stands for, from all it has meant in your life, from all it has done to me!

JULIAN: Are you serious? Dulcie wanted me to have it. He left me everything.

LEONORA (*quietly*): I know.

JULIAN: He looked on me as his son. Why shouldn't I keep it? You're not going to be peculiar now? Surely at last we're going to be happy?

LEONORA: Happy? With your father in prison?

JULIAN: Poor old Isaiah! He'd always got a bee in his bonnet.

LEONORA: You really think that he killed Dulcimer because he was mad?

JULIAN: Didn't everybody think so? Judge and jury and all the rest of them. I don't see how you can get away from it. Religious mania.

LEONORA: He knew exactly what he was doing. You know perfectly well that he killed him because he thought he could save you.

JULIAN: Really, Leo, I don't know what you do want! We couldn't be married unless I had money, and now you're being difficult because I've got it. I only wanted the money to give to you.

LEONORA: I couldn't touch it! Not after all the unhappiness it has brought! Don't have anything to do with it! Give it up!

JULIAN: Leonora! Don't be a fool.

LEONORA: Are you going to let Isaiah's sacrifice be wasted?

JULIAN: Don't be fantastic!

LEONORA (*turning to go*): Then I've nothing to stay for. In a day or two you'll be thankful I've gone!

JULIAN: Now you're just being brutal!

LEONORA: I'd rather be brutal than so utterly callous as you! You've got rid of your guardian, your father's at Broadmoor, and now you're getting rid of me!

JULIAN *turns round and tries to speak.*

No! don't say anything! I expect I'm well out of it! (*As she moves to the door, her eye falls on DULCIMER's death mask over the piano.*) What's that?

JULIAN: That's his death mask. He wanted it done. He left instructions in his will.

LEONORA (*after another look*): I don't wonder he's smiling! (*She exits.*)

JULIAN *goes over to the piano and leans on it looking at the mask. He is ruffled and irritated.* TRUMP *comes in with tea on a tray.*

TRUMP: Are you alone for tea, sir?

JULIAN: Yes, Trump. Miss Yale has gone. (*A second's pause.*) We're not going to be married, after all.

TRUMP (*looking up at the mask*): Mr Dulcimer always said, sir, that a man could never settle down until he'd got women out of his life.

JULIAN: I expect he was right. (*He moves to the couch.*) He nearly always was.

TRUMP (*putting tea on the centre table*): If you're not going to be married, sir, perhaps you will reconsider my notice. I should be proud to serve you as a bachelor, sir, but a married establishment means women servants. And that . . . (*He makes an eloquent pause.*)

JULIAN: I hope I shall keep you for life, Trump. You understand my ways.

TRUMP: Thank you, sir. (*He moves to the door.*)

JULIAN: I don't think I want any tea. I'll just have a cocktail.

TRUMP (*coming back to the table and removing the tray*): A sidecar, sir? Very good. By the way, the flowers have come from Silver Gates.

JULIAN (*with a DULCIMER drawl*): Do you think I ought to do them now, Trump.

TRUMP: Just as you please, sir.

JULIAN (*rises*): Perhaps I ought. The room does look rather naked.

TRUMP: I'll fetch you the flowers, sir.

Exit TRUMP.

JULIAN *lights a cigarette and goes to the window.*

TRUMP *returns with the tray of flowers, scissors, and gloves. Then he gets the small table, as in Act One, and places it in front of JULIAN. JULIAN picks up the gloves.*

TRUMP *gets a vase from the piano and puts it on the small table.*

JULIAN: Not the green vase, Trump!

TRUMP: Mr Dulcimer always preferred the green vase for iris, sir.

JULIAN (*putting on the gloves*): I like to make my own choice. Choice, Trump, is what distinguishes the artist from the common herd. I prefer the amber vase. (*This is already on the table in front of him.*)

TRUMP: Very good, sir. (*He replaces the green vase on the piano.*)

JULIAN (*examining the flowers*): Some of these irises are rather poor, Trump. Badly chosen.

TRUMP: I'm sorry, sir. I'll fetch you some water. (*He exits.*)

JULIAN (*with a flower in his hand*): I must tell Paget to be more careful about the stalks.

He begins to arrange the flowers. The death mask continues to smile.

Slow curtain.

PASSING BY

Passing By was first presented by Gay Sweatshop and Inter Action Productions at the Almost Free Theatre, London, on 9 June 1975, with the following cast:

TOBY   Simon Callow
SIMON   Michael Dickinson

Directed by Drew Griffiths
Designed by Norman Coates

Passing By

I wrote *Passing By* in New York in the autumn of 1972. Lifetimes ago. I hoped to create a gentle, romantic and loving encounter between two men, in which their gayness was simply a fact – completely easy and open and never a problem.

The play was first presented in a small workshop production in New York in 1974. The result was well meaning but inadequate; the problem – the reluctance of interesting young American actors to play 'happy' homosexuals. They were quite willing to limp their wrists onstage, indeed even to cut them – that constituted 'character' playing. Anything free and natural was thought to be a threat to future employment. (That *was* 1974; within a few years the situation had radically improved for the better.)

The first full production of *Passing By* was given in London in the summer of 1975 by the Gay Sweatshop at the Almost Free Theatre. The Gay Sweatshop had just been formed under the leadership of Drew Griffiths and Gerald Chapman and their work, at that time, was on a particularly high level. The director was Drew Griffiths and the actors Simon Callow (Toby) and Michael Dickinson (Simon).

This production was a revelation and a turning point for me. Writing for the theatre had, until then, filled me with despair; I was penniless, I was usually unproduced, and when I *was* produced, it was improperly so. For the first time my work came truly alive on a stage. The director and actors were strong, tender, humane and technically accomplished, and the producing company had a guiding vision. And *on stage* it all made sense. It no longer seemed quite as foolhardy to go on writing. (The original Gay Sweatshop has had, I think, enormous influence; in my case it was quite direct; for others, perhaps more subtle and subliminal, but its impact was far stronger than can be measured on paper.)

Passing By has been infrequently revived. A particularly fine production was given by The Hartford Stage Company in 1979, directed by Ron Logamarsino. A New York gay magazine reviewed it and criticised it for its lack of leather bars. The changing times have sometimes been in conflict with the play's sense of innocence. It was to have received its first full-scale production in New York this past summer (1983). It was an event I greatly anticipated, but I cancelled it for fear that the tragic AIDS epidemic raging through New York would throw the story of two men who happen to contract hepatitis into a completely misleading light and fan some of the misconceived and prejudiced linkage of homosexuality and physical illness that was then popular in the American press.

My hopes for future productions of *Passing By* are thus based not only on my fondness for the play but the desire for a healthier atmosphere in which it can be properly perceived.

Martin Sherman
November 1983

ACT ONE

Scene One

A small movie theatre in Manhattan. A summer evening. 1972.

We see only an excerpt of the theatre – one row; it occupies a side of the stage. Flickering lights are reflected from the screen and dialogue is heard – in French.

TOBY sits alone in the row. He is thirty, but looks slightly younger. He has wild, gentle, wandering eyes. He watches the film with a great sense of love and familiarity.

SIMON enters and sits in the row, on the aisle, a few seats away from TOBY. He is strongly built; twenty-six, but looks slightly older. TOBY looks at SIMON as he sits down, then turns away. The movie dialogue continues.

SIMON glances at TOBY; TOBY turns, they catch each other's eye. They both turn away, embarrassed. The movie dialogue continues.

A woman on the screen has started to sing; the song is warm, romantic, bittersweet, very Gallic. Both men relax.

TOBY smiles; he turns and looks at SIMON. SIMON feels his stare. SIMON finally turns and looks at TOBY. TOBY laughs and shrugs his shoulders. SIMON smiles.

The song continues, as

blackout.

Scene Two

TOBY's apartment. The next morning.

TOBY has a large one room apartment. It is in considerable disarray. There is a small kitchenette; and a hallway, leading past the front door, to a bathroom door. The room is filled with packed cartons and crates; a lot of the bookcases and drawers are empty or half-empty. A guitar lies near the bed; a television set is nearby. There are several large pieces of canvas covered with sheets, and artist's equipment around the room. The apartment occupies the major portion of the stage.

TOBY and SIMON are asleep in bed. TOBY wakes up. He looks around him. He looks at SIMON. He watches SIMON sleep. He smiles.

TOBY gets out of bed. He walks to the largest canvas, He uncovers it, and stares at the painting. Finally, he replaces the cover. He starts across the room toward the stove. Suddenly, he grabs his foot.

TOBY: Ouch! Damn it!

SIMON opens his eyes and sits up.

SIMON: What is it?

TOBY: Nothing.

SIMON: Someone screamed.

TOBY: Go back to sleep. It's nothing. (*He starts for the bathroom.*)

SIMON (*watching* TOBY): You're limping.

TOBY: No.

SIMON: That's a limp.

TOBY: OK.

SIMON: What is it?

TOBY: A splinter.

SIMON: Let me see. (TOBY *hesitates.*) Come on.

TOBY (*hops over to the bed*): I didn't want to wake you.

SIMON: Let me see. (*He takes* TOBY's *foot, examines it.*)

TOBY: It's bad, huh?

SIMON: It's large.

TOBY: I knew it! (*He hops up, goes to the telephone, dials a number.*)

SIMON: What are you doing?

TOBY: Calling the doctor.

SIMON: For a splinter? (*He gets out of bed.*)

TOBY: You can get lockjaw from a splinter.

SIMON takes the phone away from him and hangs it up.

Hey!

SIMON: You have a knife?

TOBY: Sure.

SIMON: OK. *I'll* take it out. Where is it?

TOBY: With a *knife*?

SIMON: Yes.

TOBY: A knife is big.

SIMON: All right. A scissors.

TOBY: How about a straight pin?

SIMON: Do you have a scissors?

TOBY: On the desk. (*He starts for the desk;* SIMON *stops him.*)

SIMON: I'll get it. (*He goes to the desk.*)

TOBY (*returns to bed*): Hey, I'm sorry. I really didn't want to wake you. We didn't get much sleep. What are you doing?

SIMON (*at the sink*): Washing the scissors.

TOBY: Shouldn't it be sterile?

SIMON: I'm washing it in hot water.

TOBY: A pin is safer.

SIMON (*returning to the bed*): Shut up. I'm very good at this.

TOBY: You are?

SIMON: Yeah. I do it all the time.

TOBY: Hey, are *you* a doctor?

SIMON: No. (*He takes* TOBY's *foot, starts poking.*) A diver.

SIMON: A *diver*?

SIMON: Yes.

TOBY: You mean – off of boards into water?

SIMON: Yes.

TOBY: I want my foot back.

TOBY: Shut up. (*He washes the area with a towel.*)

TOBY: I asked you what you did last night. You wouldn't tell me.

SIMON: I didn't know you then. Hold still. We get splinters all the time. From the diving boards.

TOBY: Oh. I never thought of that. Ouch!

SIMON: Quiet. (*He removes a tiny piece of wood with the scissors.*) There.

TOBY: There what?

SIMON: It's out.

TOBY: The whole thing?

SIMON: Sure.

TOBY: That was fast.

SIMON: I'm good. (*He puts the scissors away.*)

TOBY: You are. (*He takes* SIMON's *hand.*) Thanks.

SIMON: Sure.

TOBY (*kisses* SIMON): Good morning.

SIMON (*kisses* TOBY *back*): You better put a band-aid on it.

TOBY: Right.

TOBY *hops into the bathroom.* SIMON *looks around the apartment, examines it for a moment, then calls out.*)

SIMON: Where are my clothes?

TOBY (*from the bathroom*): In the closet.

SIMON: Where's the closet?

TOBY (*from the bathroom*): In the hallway.

SIMON *goes to the hall closet, and looks through it.* TOBY *comes into the hallway.*

TOBY: Are you leaving?

SIMON: It's nine o'clock.

TOBY: So?

SIMON: I have a lot to do. (*He finds his clothes.*)

TOBY: Oh. Me too.

SIMON: Yeah? You're an artist. You can sleep late.

TOBY: I have a job. I have to be there in three hours.

SIMON (*dressing*): What kind of job?

TOBY: In a wine store. Taylor-McLean.

SIMON: Where are you going?

TOBY: What?

SIMON (*points to boxes*): Everything's packed up.

TOBY: Oh. France. (*He gets a robe from the closet, puts it on.*) I have a grant. I leave in two weeks. Do you want some coffee? (*He goes to the sink.*)

SIMON: No thanks.

TOBY: Good. I don't know how to make coffee. I drink tea. How about some tea?

SIMON: No thanks.

TOBY (*puts a kettle on the stove*): I only

have one tea bag. But it's good for two. Honest!

SIMON: No. I gotta go. (*He finishes dressing, starts to speak, hesitates . . .*) You know, I haven't done this for a long time.

TOBY: What? Fuck?

SIMON: No . . . Just . . .

TOBY: I know. I don't usually do it either. I just wanted to see a movie. (*He goes to* SIMON.) It was nice.

SIMON: Yes. It was.

TOBY: Come on, have some tea.

SIMON: No. I really have a lot to do. (*He goes to the door.*)

TOBY: OK.

SIMON: Thank you for . . . (*He laughs.*) A nice time.

TOBY: You're welcome. Hey, come here . . .

TOBY *embraces* SIMON; *they kiss.*

SIMON: Goodbye.

TOBY: Goodbye.

SIMON *starts to leave.*

Hey!

SIMON *turns round.*

Thanks for the splinter.

SIMON (*smiles*): It was easy.

SIMON *leaves.*

TOBY *locks the door. The kettle whistles.* TOBY *goes to get it. He steps on another piece of wood.*

TOBY: Ouch!

TOBY *hops to the stove, turns the gas off under the kettle, then hops to a chair and examines his foot.*

He picks up the phone and dials a number.

TOBY: Hello. Doctor Bronstein? Yeah, it's Toby. Doctor, I have a splinter . . .

Blackout.

Scene Three

A wine store. One week later.

A very small section of the store occupies a side of the stage. There is a counter, with some wine bottles on display, and a cash-register. The floor in front of the counter is filled with broken glass.

SIMON *enters. He looks around, examines the wine bottles, avoids the broken glass. He is searching for someone.*

TOBY *enters with a broom and dustpan. He is harried. He sees* SIMON.

TOBY: Be careful. There's glass on the floor. Oh. Hi.

SIMON: Hi. How are you?

TOBY: OK. (*He stares at* SIMON.) What are you doing here?

SIMON: I just happened to be passing by. I remembered the name of the store.

TOBY: Oh. That's nice. In fact – it's perfect. You couldn't have picked a better time. Do you see that man over there? I don't know if you can tell, he has one leg shorter than the other. He's the manager. They always have defects, don't they – managers? Can you stand . . . (*He moves* SIMON *to the side.*) like over here? (*He pushes* SIMON *a bit more to the side.*) Right . . . a little this way, great . . . now I don't think he can see me.

SIMON: *What* are you doing?

TOBY: I dropped a bottle of wine. OK. Just stand there. (*He goes behind the counter.*) He knows I broke it, but he hasn't seen the label yet. It's Chateau Lafite Rothschild. Rothschild, are you ready! Do you know how much that costs? Eighty dollars. They take it out of your salary. That's *more* than my salary. (*He takes a wine bottle from behind the counter.*) So just stand there. Right. (*He goes to the spot where the broken glass is.*) Now!

SIMON: What's that?

TOBY: Torres De La Riviera. Spanish chablis. Cheapest wine in the store. Tastes like feet. Here goes . . . (*He drops the wine bottle onto the floor; it breaks.*)

SIMON: You're crazy.

TOBY: Nope. I'll show him *this* broken bottle and he'll dock me ninety cents. No problem. (*He starts to sweep the floor.*) I keep dropping these things. It's not a good job for me. Boy, am I glad you stopped in.

SIMON: Yeah, well I was just passing by . . .

TOBY: Bullshit.

SIMON: What?

TOBY: Forget it. I'm a little crazed today. You were just passing by.

SIMON: OK. It isn't true.

TOBY: You've been to twenty wine stores looking for me.

SIMON: Six.

TOBY (*pleased*): You have? Really?

SIMON: Yes.

TOBY: Wow.

SIMON: I thought maybe . . . we could go out for dinner or something.

TOBY: Oh. A *date!*

SIMON (*looks at* TOBY *strangely, turns to leave*): I'm sorry. I shouldn't have come in.

TOBY (*sweeping the glass into his pan*): No. Look, *I'm* sorry. I don't know what I'm saying. *I hate this job.* Move your feet. Thanks. I can't go out. I'm tired; I mean *really* tired.

SIMON: How about tomorrow?

TOBY: Well, I'm flattered, but Jesus, I'm leaving in a week. Do you know what I mean, there's no room in my life to see *anybody*.

SIMON: Oh. Sure.

TOBY: You look so sad. I don't understand. You're very humpy. You've gotta know a lot of people.

SIMON: Not here.

TOBY (*puts the broom and dustpan away*): You don't live here?

SIMON: No. Miami Beach.

TOBY: Feh! Where you staying?

SIMON: In a hotel. I'm waiting to hear about a job.

TOBY: A job. You're going to dive in New York?

SIMON: No, it's for a radio station.

TOBY: You're going to dive on radio?

SIMON: No. A reporting job, sportscaster.

TOBY: Oh. Yeah. You have a good voice.

SIMON: Look, I'm going crazy. Oh, forget it . . .

TOBY: You were in such a hurry to leave my place last week. Haven't met anyone else, huh?

SIMON: No. Well, I met a kid. A nineteen-year-old kid. Wounded eyes. I took him to my hotel room. He put on the television set. He watched television while we made love. Reruns of *I Love Lucy*. They were older than he was. He didn't talk, except for 'far out' which he said once every twenty minutes. That was it. I'm going crazy. Well, it's not your problem . . . (*He starts to leave.*)

TOBY: Wait. I'm so tired there's nothing I can do *except* talk. How's that?

SIMON: That's great.

TOBY: OK. I'm off in fifteen minutes. Give me a dollar and a half.

SIMON: You charge? For talk?

TOBY: No. You're gonna buy some wine. I'll pay you back, don't worry.

SIMON: I can afford it.

TOBY: No. There's a reason. A little rip-off. We need some wine, right? Come on . . . I'll show you. Give me the money.

SIMON: Here. (*He hands him a dollar and a half.*)

TOBY: Good. (*He rings it up on the cash register.*) Now, here's your slip – so it's all legal – and here's a shopping bag and here's a dollar and a half bottle of Côte du Rhone. It's a wonderful *vin ordinaire* . . . (*He gives him a shopping bag from behind the counter, and a wine bottle, then reaches under the counter, takes out another wine bottle, puts it into the shopping bag.*) *and* here's a bottle of Puilly Fuisse, it's one step above Chablis, incredible, six dollars . . . (*He takes out another wine bottle.*) *and* a bottle of Chateau Deauville, very dry Bordeaux, *magnifique*, ten dollars . . . OK. I'll meet you in front of Woolworths.

SIMON: I can't do this. It's illegal.

TOBY: So what?

SIMON: If I'm arrested, I can't practice law in New York.

TOBY: You're a diver!

SIMON: Yes, but I have a law degree.

TOBY: You have a *law degree*?

SIMON: Sure. I'll probably never use it, but just suppose . . .

TOBY: I promise you you won't be arrested.

SIMON: How do you know?

TOBY: Look, I'm too tired for this. I'll scream, I'll yell. Then you *will* get arrested, right here in the store. It's better to take your chances outside.

SIMON: You *are* crazy.

TOBY: Nope.

SIMON: Take it back. (*He hands him the shopping bag.*)

TOBY: Fine. Have fun in your hotel room.

SIMON: Unfair.

TOBY: That's life.

SIMON: Bastard. (*He takes the shopping bag back.*) Where the hell is Woolworths?

TOBY: Across the street.

SIMON: You better show up.

TOBY: Don't worry. You have *my* wine.

SIMON *leaves, as*

blackout.

Scene Four

Fifteen minutes later.

A bench outside the park. TOBY *and* SIMON *enter.* SIMON *is carrying the shopping bag.* TOBY *is walking with considerable difficulty.*

TOBY: Thank God! A bench! (*He sits.*)

SIMON: Are you all right?

TOBY: Oy! Don't ask.

SIMON (*laughs*): You sound like one of those old ladies in Florida. (*He sits next to him.*)

TOBY: I can't help it. I have to sit.

SIMON: The subway's just down the block.

TOBY: I know. I just can't walk another step. I've never been so tired in my life.

SIMON: Makes me nervous.

TOBY: What?

SIMON: Sitting here.

TOBY: Why?

SIMON: We have stolen goods.

TOBY: Baby, no one's after us. I have to rest.

SIMON: You don't exercise enough.

TOBY: Huh?

SIMON: That's why you're falling apart.

TOBY: I'm not falling apart.

SIMON: Why did your legs give out?

TOBY: I don't know. It's been happening all week. Nerves.

SIMON: It's not nerves. (*He feels* TOBY's *leg.*) I can feel what it is.

TOBY: Don't do that.

SIMON: Do you have any idea how important your body is?

TOBY: I realise. Believe me. It's nerves.

SIMON: You should go to a gym.

TOBY: I went to a gym once. I ruptured myself.

SIMON: Then join a pool.

TOBY: I can't swim.

SIMON: Ah! If you could swim, you wouldn't collapse in the street.

TOBY: *I'm collapsing because I'm tired.*

SIMON: You can't be that tired if you can shout.

TOBY: Why are you *arguing* with me? It's not that kind of tired. It's different. I can't explain it. It's the strangest thing I've ever felt.

SIMON: Come to the subway.

TOBY: In a minute. I have to explain. It's tension. That's all.

SIMON: It's not tension.

TOBY: How do you know? I have a gas bubble in my stomach. Feel it. It's beating like my heart. I'm all nerve ends. Everything's catching up with me.

This whole lousy year. I had two one-man shows scheduled last season, you know that? Two shows! Finally! So one gallery burnt down, and the other – the owner was arrested for smuggling. Smuggling, for God's sake! No one *smuggles* anymore. No shows. It's like I'm painting for myself. That's not good. You can't make plans. That's the big lesson. You can't count on *anything*. My lover left me. He was into suicide. I changed all that. I made him *hunger* for life. He got too hungry; life had more to offer than me. I taught him how to sketch; *he* had a one-man show last month. *His* galleries don't burn down. And I was proud of him, that's what's fucking awful. I wasn't even angry. Oh what the hell, I have to get out of this city. I have this grant, it's fine, it will keep me alive for a few months. Except maybe I can't paint anymore. My mind is tired. Whatever it is that makes you paint, that's tired. And it never stops. Everyday something happens, and it's awful. Last time I made love – I mean, before you – I whiplashed my neck. You know how my day began? A can of shaving cream exploded in my hand. And last week an egg dropped on my head. I'm not kidding. In the middle of the street, out of nowhere. Where'd it come from? God is dropping eggs on me. He's run out of plagues. And the people I've loved – oh man, my luck rubs off. Such a casualty list. Sweet, good people, swallowed by this town; eggs dropping on *everybody's* head, and I'm tired of it all; why shouldn't I be? Why shouldn't my legs give out?

Silence.

SIMON: I don't know. It isn't good to feel sorry for yourself.

TOBY: Yeah. I know. It's very selfish. I'm sure you have as many problems as I do.

SIMON: No.

TOBY: Well, not *as* many. But some.

SIMON: The only problem I have is getting you into the subway.

TOBY: You don't want to talk about them.

SIMON: There isn't anything to talk about.

TOBY: *Nothing's* wrong with you?

SIMON: Nothing.

TOBY: Impossible.

SIMON: Little things.

TOBY: I don't mean *little* things.

SIMON: OK. Nothing's wrong.

TOBY: Something has to be. Suppose you don't get your job?

SIMON: I go home.

TOBY: Yeah. *And* . . .

SIMON: I get my *old* job back. I'm a great diving instructor. There's no one in the world who can teach or do a better inward two and a half somersault in a pike position.

TOBY: I see.

SIMON: I won a bronze medal in the 1968 Olympics.

TOBY: Figures. I guess there aren't any lovers walking out on *you*.

Silence.

Are there?

SIMON: The opposite.

TOBY: Naturally.

SIMON: A wonderful person too. A judge. I left him.

TOBY: A judge yet!

SIMON (*absently*): He'd like me back.

TOBY: And your body?

SIMON: What about it?

TOBY: No aches or pains?

SIMON: I'm in perfect shape.

TOBY: That's *disgusting!* You don't exist! Wait a minute – you hate being alone in the hotel.

SIMON: Right.

TOBY: Aha! You said you were going crazy.

SIMON: A figure of speech. You're not getting me on that.

TOBY: But you're *not happy* alone in that hotel.

SIMON: I'm not, but . . .

TOBY: No buts.

SIMON: But it will only last another week. That's not a tragedy.

TOBY: It's enough. For me, it's enough. I

can deal with that. You're not happy alone in your hotel. Thank God! I can't tell you how that's picked me up.

SIMON: Good. Now can we make it to the subway?

TOBY: I could make it to Spain. (*He rises, touches* SIMON's *shoulder, and looks into his eyes.*) I could kiss you too. But we'd be arrested. Why are you staring at me.

SIMON: Your eyes.

TOBY: What about them?

SIMON: I never noticed their colour before.

TOBY: Brown.

SIMON: No. Yellow.

TOBY: Let's go to the subway.

SIMON: They're yellow.

TOBY: My eyes are brown.

SIMON: You're crazy. They're bright yellow. I've never seen yellow eyes before.

TOBY: My eyes are brown!

SIMON: Why would I lie to you?

TOBY: I don't know. Why would *I* lie?

SIMON: You wouldn't, but you're a little eccentric. You probably don't even know the colour of your hair.

TOBY: Look, I'm no fool. My eyes are brown.

SIMON: We're standing in the sunlight. I can't make a mistake. Yellow!

TOBY: Where's a mirror? Do you have a mirror?

SIMON: Of course I don't have a mirror.

TOBY: Why would you lie to me?

SIMON: That's what *I* asked.

TOBY: You're not lying.

SIMON: Come on. The subway has a mirror.

TOBY: Yellow?

SIMON: Yes.

TOBY: Just the pupils?

SIMON: Yes. Well . . . a little around the edges.

TOBY: The edges? Yellow?

SIMON: Yes, yellow. I'm going into the subway . . .

TOBY: Oh God!

SIMON: . . . and you can follow if you want.

TOBY: Forget the subway. Call a cab.

SIMON: Why?

TOBY: Don't ask. Just call a cab. And take me to a hospital!

Blackout.

Scene Five

TOBY's *apartment. One week later.*

TOBY *is lying in bed, his head propped up on many pillows. He looks tired and drawn. There are more boxes in the room now; the canvasses have been packed in crates. The telephone rings. It lies next to* TOBY's *bed. He reaches for it.*

TOBY: Hello. No, the apartment is *not* available; I told the agent to take it off the list. I haven't sublet it to anyone; I have hepatitis. Well, that means I'll be in town for at least eight weeks. No, I should *not* be in a hospital, it's too expensive, my doctor's letting me stay home, the store sends me food, and I'm OK, and if I *were* in a hospital, the apartment would still not be available. No, I don't expect to be better in a month; I don't think that's possible. How do you know if I sound all right? How do you know how I normally sound? Full of *pep*? Listen, these are my few minutes of energy; I'll be drifting off before you know it . . . and why the hell am I wasting my few minutes on you; the apartment is *not* available. No, don't check on me every week. I gotta hang, I'm fading . . .

TOBY *hangs the receiver up. He closes his eyes. His doorbell rings.*

TOBY (*shouts*): The door's open.

SIMON *enters. He holds a paper bag.*

TOBY: Oh.

SIMON: Hi.

TOBY: Hi

SIMON: I'm sorry for barging in.

TOBY: That's all right.

SIMON: I know you must be mad at me.

TOBY: I'm not mad.

SIMON: You should be. I haven't called. I didn't send a card. Nothing.

TOBY: I'm not mad.

SIMON: I'm a real shit.

TOBY: Come in and sit down.

SIMON: I'm really sorry.

TOBY: Stop saying that.

SIMON: No . . . I'm sorry for being like this now . . .

TOBY: Like what?

SIMON: Drunk.

TOBY: Drunk?

SIMON: Yes. I'm sorry.

TOBY: You could never tell.

SIMON: On *your* wine. The Puilly Fuissé and Chateau Deauville and Côte du Rhone; I have some of that left . . .

He takes a wine bottle out of his paperbag; offers it to TOBY.

TOBY: I can't drink.

SIMON: Oh, that's right. Do you mind? (*He drinks some wine.*) I never do this. You mustn't tell anyone. (*He spills some of the wine on the floor, behind* TOBY's *area of vision.*) I spilled some. I spilled some on your floor. I'm sorry. I didn't mean to spill it. I never spill things. I didn't get my job. No one knows that yet. Don't tell anyone.

TOBY: You didn't ask how I was . . .

SIMON: I'll wipe it up with my handkerchief. I don't have a handkerchief. I'm sorry; I'll use one of your towels. I'm really sorry I left the hospital after the doctor came. I don't like hospitals, I don't like disease. Of course, I realised later I've been so exposed to your germs, it doesn't matter anymore. But that was later. This doesn't get the wine off. I'm sorry; I'll pay for a throw-rug. They said they'd rather have a hockey star report the sports news. More people care about hockey than water sports. But no one knows yet. So don't tell anyone.

TOBY: Don't you care how I am?

SIMON: I'm sorry. I guess I'm not a good visitor. I haven't even asked you how you are. You see, I can't get my job back in Florida. That's the problem. Oh – I lied to you last week, I don't like to talk about myself to strangers. I'm sorry I lied. I mean, I had only seen you two times. In Florida, you'd be a stranger. In New York, you're my best friend. They gave my job to a kid from *this* year's Olympics. I'm twenty-six. I'm growing old.

TOBY: I don't understand a word you're saying.

SIMON: Age is a problem for a diver. I mean, some people I know worry about age because of their looks, but I don't care about that; I care about the perfection of an inward two and a half somersault in a pike position, and it gets less perfect as your body ages. You see, people think I'm insane, they do, because I care so much about diving; I mean, my father wanted me to care about law, but it doesn't interest me. I got my degree so I'd have something to fall back on, but I don't want to *fall back*. I spilled some more wine. I'm sorry. It's a pretty colour. It won't really help but I'll wipe it up. I never spill things. I'm always in control.

TOBY: You spilled something? I can't see you.

SIMON: I'm sorry. I know you don't want to hear all of this when you're so sick, but I have no one else to talk to. You see, I thought I could grow old on radio, talking about sports and more than that – competition, good health, strong bodies, things I know about, things I care about. But they wanted a hockey player. I told my friends in Florida I was getting the job; I'm ashamed to go back; but that's foolish anyhow, since they're really not friends. I mean, I'm a wonderful body, with a medal on it, and I have a perfect tan on my wonderful body, and you can eat out on that for years in Florida, and no one cares that *I* care about diving. I like being in water because when I'm out of water, I don't think I'm real. All that time alone in the hotel room, all I could do was think, and I didn't know who I was, because, like I say, I'm not real. You're real. Lots of people are real. But I'm not, and I don't understand how you become real. I can't wipe this anymore. And you can't drink, right? I have some peanuts.

He takes a small bag of peanuts from his pocket.

Would you like some peanuts? No – they've gotta be bad for you when you're sick. I'm sorry I didn't bring any flowers. I never eat peanuts. I got them from this vendor near the 59th Street Bridge. I walked to the 59th Street Bridge. I decided to kill myself. I mean, there's no point being alive if you're not real, so I walked to the 59th Street Bridge, because that seemed the best way, and I had a lot of wine, and I walked to the centre of the bridge and I stood there, staring way down at the water, ready to dive off, and you know what? I found myself preparing for an inward two and a half somersault in a pike position. And that seemed silly, and I started to cry, and I wanted to talk, so I came here because I didn't know anyone else and someone *has* to listen to me, but I don't know if I do want to talk, maybe it's better to die, except I never drink wine and you can't tell if that makes you strange or not and I knew you'd listen.

A long silence.

Do you see what I mean?

A long silence.

Tell me what you think.

A long silence.

SIMON *goes to* TOBY. TOBY *is asleep.*

SIMON: You're asleep. You didn't hear anything.

SIMON *starts banging on* TOBY's *chest.* TOBY *wakes up.*

TOBY: Ouch! Hey!

SIMON: Why didn't you listen?

TOBY: What is this? Stop hitting me. I'm sick.

SIMON *stops, controls himself.*

Jesus!

SIMON: I'm sorry.

TOBY: Don't be sorry again. *Why* were you hitting me?

SIMON: I'm drunk.

TOBY: You certainly are. I'm a hepatitic. You don't hit a hepatitic.

SIMON: You missed everything I said.

TOBY: So say it again.

SIMON: I don't remember any of it. I just don't want to die.

TOBY: What is this? You're not going to die.

SIMON: You can't promise that.

TOBY: Take my word. (*He takes* SIMON's *hand.*)

SIMON: I have to leave. I'm going to cry again and I don't cry. I don't do any of the things I've just done.

TOBY: I see a tear. (*He traces it down* SIMON's *cheek.*)

SIMON: Don't tell anyone.

TOBY: Who would I tell? Oh God!

SIMON: I gotta leave you alone.

TOBY (*stares at him*): Poor baby.

SIMON: I gotta leave you alone.

TOBY: No. There's something else you got to do. Go into the bathroom.

SIMON: What?

TOBY: Don't ask questions. Just go.

SIMON: Into the bathroom?

TOBY: Yes.

SIMON: Are you sure?

TOBY: I'm sure.

SIMON: OK. (*He gets up, goes into the bathroom.*)

TOBY: Poor baby.

SIMON (*calling from the bathroom*): I'm in the bathroom.

TOBY: Good. Look into the mirror.

SIMON (*from the bathroom*): I can't hear you.

TOBY: *Look into the mirror!*

SIMON (*from the bathroom*): OK. I'm looking.

TOBY: Good. Now tell me – *what colour are your eyes?*

Blackout.

ACT TWO

Scene One

TOBY's *apartment. Three days later. Afternoon.*

TOBY's *studio bed has opened into two separate beds.* TOBY *and* SIMON *are lying in the beds.*

TOBY *is reading a book.* SIMON *is tossing in his bed, muttering.*

SIMON: Damn it . . .

> TOBY *continues reading.*

> Damn it . . .

> TOBY *continues reading.*

> Shit . . .

TOBY: You're certainly taking it like a sport.

SIMON: Bastard . . . goddamn . . .

TOBY: Look, it's been three days. Isn't there something else you can say?

SIMON: Fuck off.

TOBY: You better get used to it.

SIMON: I am never sick.

TOBY: Past tense.

SIMON: I have complete control over my body.

TOBY: You had.

SIMON: I'll never dive again.

TOBY: Oh for Christ's sake! I thought you hated self-pity. You'll dive again, you'll dive again. Believe me. You'll swim again too; you'll even walk again. It's just gonna take time. We're going to have to stay in bed for a while, so face it.

SIMON: Fuck off.

TOBY: You're a pill.

SIMON: There should be a medicine for this.

TOBY: Well, there isn't. Just bed rest.

SIMON: I should have gone to a hospital. I'd be better off in a hospital.

TOBY: So go. I'm not stopping you. Spend the money. I don't care.

SIMON: You *offered* me your place. It's the least you can do.

TOBY: So stop complaining.

SIMON: You gave me this disease.

TOBY: I'm sorry, I'm sorry.

SIMON: I want some juice.

TOBY: You had juice with dinner.

SIMON: I need more.

TOBY (*reading again*): That's nice.

SIMON: My throat is parched.

TOBY: No wonder – you've been cursing all day.

SIMON: I have to have juice.

TOBY (*puts the book down*): Well what do you want me to do?

SIMON: You're ten days stronger than I am. Can't you get me some?

TOBY: I was up an hour ago to go the bathroom. I can't get up again.

SIMON: You only think of yourself.

> TOBY *starts to read again.*

> My throat is *so* dry.

TOBY (*slams the book shut*): If I get some juice . . . will you shut up?

SIMON: Yes.

TOBY: All right. (*He gets up.*) I should have insisted you go to a hospital. (*He starts to walk very slowly, then stops.*) Oh God! It's awful up here. You know, when I'm lying down, I really feel like I have energy. But standing up . . . it's like moving under water.

SIMON: It is?

TOBY: Yeah. Probably be *perfect* for you. (*He walks again, at a snail's pace.*)

SIMON: Where's the juice?

TOBY: *I'm getting it!*

SIMON: I can't tell you how dry my mouth is.

TOBY (*reaches the refrigerator*): You're worse than I am. You're really worse than I am. (*Exhausted, he sits on the floor, by the refrigerator.*)

SIMON: What kind of juice are you getting?

TOBY: I don't know. I'm sitting.

SIMON: Why are you sitting?

TOBY: *Because I have to.*

SIMON: My mouth has never been dry like this.

TOBY: I'll get it in a minute.

SIMON: I think I'm dying.

TOBY: Dear God, thank you, in your wisdom, for giving me a debilitating disease. Or else I'd kill him. (*He stands up, opens the refrigerator door, looks inside.*) What kind of juice do you want?

SIMON: What is there?

TOBY: Apple and orange.

SIMON: Apple.

TOBY: Apple. (*He pours juice into a glass.*)

SIMON: I have stomach pains too. I'm used to muscles aching. That's healthy pain. But my liver is hurting. My liver never hurt me.

TOBY: I don't blame it. If I were your liver, I'd hurt you. (*He starts back with the juice, walking very slowly.*)

SIMON: Coach Harris prided himself on his team's strength; we never got sick.

TOBY: You're no longer in college.

SIMON: He'd have a heart attack if he knew I was ill.

TOBY: So much for *his* strength.

SIMON: Where's the juice?

TOBY: IT'S COMING!

SIMON: My mouth can't stand it . . . I think I have a fever . . . My body temperature is irregular . . .

TOBY *has reached* SIMON's *bed.*

What are you doing?

TOBY: Standing over you.

Silence.

SIMON: You're going to throw that juice at me, aren't you?

TOBY: I'm thinking of it.

SIMON: That would be cruel.

TOBY: Yes. It would.

SIMON: Don't do it.

TOBY: Here. (*He hands him the juice.*) I'm not cruel.

SIMON: Thank you.

TOBY: You're welcome.

SIMON: There are chemicals in this.

TOBY (*getting back into bed*): That's nice.

SIMON: Preservatives. That's why I'm sick. Bad food in this city. I can't drink it.

TOBY: *You can't drink it?*

SIMON: I'd rather have orange juice.

TOBY: Drink the apple juice.

SIMON: I can't. I'm too tired.

Pause.

TOBY: You are?

SIMON (*turns over in bed*): So tired . . .

TOBY: Oh God, please let him fall asleep.

SIMON: So tired . . .

TOBY: Please God, a little something for Toby. Let the yenta fall asleep.

SIMON: So tired . . . (*He falls asleep.*)

TOBY (*to God*): I'd thank you, but you owe me.

Blackout.

Scene Two

Two weeks later. Afternoon.

TOBY *and* SIMON *are in their beds.*

A bit of organ music from the television set. TOBY *sits up and turns the television set off. He looks over to* SIMON.

TOBY: Well?

SIMON: Well?

TOBY: Who do you think knocked Rita up?

SIMON: Her father.

TOBY: That nice doctor. You really think so?

SIMON: I don't trust him.

TOBY: I thought it was the guy with curly hair, the cute one.

SIMON: The junkie?

TOBY: Yeah.

SIMON: Impossible.

TOBY: Why?

SIMON: He's paralysed from the waist down.

TOBY: But didn't someone say the motorcycle accident only happened two months ago?

SIMON: He wasn't in *that* accident. That's the blonde kid. The curly one fell through his office window.

TOBY: Why'd he do that?

SIMON: How do I know?

TOBY: Rita's very neurotic. Have you noticed? I'll bet it's a false pregnancy.

SIMON: Toby . . .

TOBY: She probably wants curly-hair to marry her.

SIMON: Toby . . .

TOBY: Although I can't imagine why if he's paralysed.

SIMON: Toby!

TOBY: What?

SIMON: We're talking about it.

TOBY: So?

SIMON: We're *discussing* a *soap opera*!

TOBY: Well it's silly to watch without discussing.

SIMON: Our minds will turn to jelly.

TOBY: What else do you suggest? How many books can you read a day?

SIMON: But we can get hooked on these things. That's not good for you.

TOBY: What's good? They've helped the last two weeks fly by, haven't they? *I'm so bored*!

SIMON: Me too.

TOBY: I know.

SIMON: More than you.

TOBY: Oh, really?

SIMON: You're used to lying about; I'm used to activity.

TOBY: That does it. Why don't you leave?

SIMON: Stop telling me to leave. Let me talk.

TOBY: Sure. Talk. I am bored out of my mind! Let's play Monopoly. I have a French set.

SIMON: I'd rather talk.

TOBY: The Monopoly board is Paris instead of Atlantic City.

SIMON: I want to talk to you.

TOBY: So talk! I'm not stopping you.

Silence.

You're not talking.

SIMON: I want to say thank you.

TOBY: What?

SIMON: Thank you. That's what I wanted to say.

TOBY: What for?

SIMON (*mumbles*): I don't know.

TOBY: Some thanks.

SIMON: Because I'm a lousy patient. That's what for.

TOBY: It's all right.

SIMON: I'm not used to this, that's the problem. I've made my body, I mean – yeah, I mean my body – into my own work of art, like one of your paintings . . .

TOBY: Oh come on!

SIMON: It's true.

TOBY: You've never seen my paintings.

SIMON: Because they're covered up.

TOBY: Because they're going into storage, where they belong.

SIMON: Anyhow, my body was so disciplined . . .

TOBY: What makes you think my paintings are art?

SIMON: I'm guessing.

TOBY: Don't guess. I just splash colours on, that's all.

SIMON: I don't believe that.

TOBY: Works of art sell. Why are you depressing me?

SIMON: I'm not depressing you. Forget I said anything. I'm trying to talk about *me,* anyhow.

TOBY: So talk.

SIMON: I forgot where I was.

TOBY: Your body. Where else?

SIMON: It's never been weak before. It's like a stranger.

TOBY: It will pass.

SIMON: How do I know?

TOBY: Everything passes.

SIMON: Nonsense.

TOBY: Believe me, it's true. You've led a sheltered life.

SIMON: That's not true.

TOBY: It sure is. You've always been pampered.

SIMON: I have not.

TOBY: I'll bet your judge pampered you.

SIMON: No.

TOBY: No?

SIMON: A little.

TOBY: That's all?

SIMON: OK. A lot. So what? I never liked it.

TOBY: You loved it.

SIMON: Don't start on me. Christ, I was trying to *thank* you. You're very hard to thank.

TOBY: No, I'm not.

SIMON: You won't let me do it.

TOBY: You go off on tangents.

SIMON: You *create* them.

TOBY: So thank me.

SIMON: I already did.

TOBY: Then you're welcome.

SIMON: I mean it. You probably don't believe I mean it. But I appreciate it. You've been very nice.

TOBY: 'Nice'?

SIMON: Yes.

TOBY: Everyone tells me I'm 'nice'. Then they walk all over me. I don't want to be 'nice'.

SIMON: I'm sorry I said it.

TOBY: It's such a colourless word, 'nice' . . .

SIMON: I'm sorry I said anything.

Silence.

TOBY: Simon?

SIMON: What?

TOBY: I'm happy you're here.

SIMON: You're happy I'm sick?

TOBY: No, I didn't mean that. You know what I mean. I'm happy you're here. I'm happy I'm nice.

TOBY *reaches his hand out;* SIMON *does also; their hands clasp between the beds.*

Silence.

SIMON: I'm happy you don't pamper me.

Silence.

TOBY: Simon?

SIMON: What?

TOBY: We're very happy.

They laugh.

Blackout.

Scene Three

Ten days later. Evening.

SIMON *is asleep.* TOBY *is sitting on the floor, leaning against his own bed, with a sketch pad and pencil. He is sketching* SIMON.

SIMON *opens his eyes. He turns and sees* TOBY.

SIMON: What are you doing?

TOBY: Nothing.

SIMON: Let me see.

TOBY: Go back to sleep.

SIMON: Come on.

TOBY: It's just a sketch.

SIMON: Can't I look at it?

TOBY: No. Go to sleep.

SIMON: Not unless you show me.

TOBY (*gets up, hands* SIMON *the pad*): There. Big deal.

SIMON: It's good.

TOBY: Of course it's good. What did you think it would be? (*He reaches for the pad;* SIMON *pulls it away.*)

SIMON: I was *complimenting* you.

TOBY: It's just a sketch.

SIMON: Looks just like me.

TOBY (*hands the pad back*): Lay off, will you! It wasn't anything.

SIMON: Come here . . .

TOBY *sits on the floor in front of* SIMON's *bed.*

Don't be so sensitive.

TOBY: Don't tell me what to be.

SIMON (*examines* TOBY's *skin*): Let me look at you. You're not yellow anymore.

TOBY (*examines* SIMON): Neither are you.

SIMON: How about my eyes?

TOBY: They're clear.

SIMON: So are yours. We're getting better.

TOBY: I know.

SIMON (*caresses* TOBY's *body with his hand*): I like your skin.

TOBY: I like your hand.

SIMON: Toby?

TOBY: Yeah?

SIMON: What colour was your urine today?

TOBY: Oh come on, do we have to go through this again?

SIMON: Just tell me what colour your urine was.

TOBY: It's embarrassing.

SIMON: Tell me.

TOBY: Orange.

SIMON: Just orange?

TOBY: Simon!

SIMON: I want to know.

TOBY: There was a tinge of yellow.

SIMON: Just a tinge?

TOBY: Yes.

SIMON: Mine was *half* orange and *half* yellow.

TOBY: Yippee.

SIMON: I'm ahead!

TOBY: It's not a game.

SIMON: I know. But I'm still ahead. And I came from behind.

TOBY: You're gonna win a gold medal.

SIMON: When we're both better, I'm going to teach you how to take care of yourself.

TOBY: Impossible.

SIMON: It's easy. You'll see. Simple exercises. And I'll have you swimming in a week. I'm serious.

TOBY: Are you *really*?

SIMON: Come here.

TOBY *gets into bed with* SIMON.

We're going to buy bicycles.

TOBY: We are?

SIMON: Sure. Saves subway money. And it's good for your legs.

TOBY: I don't know how to use a hand brake.

SIMON: I'll teach you. We'll ride all over the city.

TOBY: You don't know anything about this city.

SIMON: I'll learn. You'll teach me.

TOBY: OK.

SIMON: Will you take me to the park?

TOBY: If you want.

SIMON: On a Sunday afternoon?

TOBY: Sure.

SIMON: To the fountain?

TOBY: Why?

SIMON: I heard about it. Is it nice?

TOBY: I guess. All it is is people. If you want to go to the fountain, we'll go to the fountain.

SIMON: Can we ride there on our bikes?

TOBY: Yes.

SIMON: Good. I like simple things.

TOBY: Obviously.

SIMON: Don't you?

TOBY: Yeah.

SIMON: Smart ass. Now go to sleep.

TOBY: Simon . . .

SIMON: Shh! Go to sleep.

SIMON *closes his eyes.* TOBY *also does and snuggles close to* SIMON.

TOBY: I can't wait until we're well.

Blackout.

Scene Four

Ten days later. Afternoon.

SIMON *is at the desk, writing letters.*
TOBY *is sitting on his bed, strumming his guitar. They are both tense.*

The telephone rings. They stare at it for a moment. No one moves. Finally, TOBY *rises.*

TOBY: I'll get it. (*He picks up the receiver.*) Hello. Oh, it's you. We're fine. We feel much better. The apartment is *still* not available. Look, I can't have our weekly chat right now; we're waiting for the doctor to call with the results of our blood tests. I can't talk! Goodbye. (*He hangs up.*) He never gives up. (*He returns to the guitar.*)

Silence.

SIMON: I wish the doctor would call.

TOBY: He will.

SIMON: Change your mind.

TOBY: No, you change yours.

SIMON: Let's not talk about it.

TOBY: Maybe we're still sick.

SIMON: Maybe.

Silence.

You can paint anywhere.

TOBY: I can't paint here.

SIMON: You were sketching last week.

TOBY: There's a difference.

Silence.

It was a good sketch. It made me want to work again.

SIMON: Then change your mind.

TOBY: I can't. What's important is to do the work. That's all that's important. When I'm here, I want to be famous. It's part of the oxygen in New York; you can't escape it. And you spend so much time trying to be famous, you don't do the work. (*He looks up.*) That's a warning too.

SIMON: I don't want to be famous.

TOBY: Sure you do. Change *your* mind. Oh look, I'm older than you. You're a baby. You don't know yet.

SIMON: That's the point. What happens when I'm twenty-eight?

TOBY: Nothing much.

SIMON: A lot. I have to change my life. Stay here with me.

TOBY: I can't. I went to an astrologer once. He told me I'd be successful when I'm forty-five. Forty-five! That's fifteeen years yet. Until then, pure shit. Well, who knows if I'm going to last until forty-five? What's important is to do your work. That's all.

SIMON: Do it here.

TOBY: I can't

Silence.

Think of the oceans you've never swum in. Clear, blue water you can see through. Wonderful rocks to dive off of. High in the mountains. Like in the movies. Come with me.

SIMON: That's silly.

TOBY: I know. Come with me.

SIMON: I can't. I'm finishing these letters and I'm mailing them to every station manager in New York. I'm mentioning my law degree. I don't think there's ever been a sportscaster with a law degree.

TOBY: Do you know how long it's been since anyone's wanted to be on *radio*?

SIMON: Don't make fun of me.

TOBY: I'm not. It just doesn't make sense.

SIMON: It makes as much sense as drawing pictures. Don't laugh at me.

Silence.

Someday you'll push a button and hear my voice.

TOBY: You *do* want to be famous.

SIMON: Just wait.

TOBY: I won't be here.

Silence.

SIMON: I was going to teach you to ride a bike. And swim.

TOBY: There are bicycles in Paris. Teach me there.

SIMON: I can't.

TOBY: We can swim in the Mediterranean, in the Adriatic . . .

SIMON: Toby, cut the nonsense. Change

your mind. Please.

TOBY: Why do I have to change *my* mind?

Silence.

TOBY (*goes to* SIMON, *takes* SIMON's *hand*): Look, we don't even know each other. We've just been sick together. I told you a long time ago, you can't plan on anything. We didn't have any energy. We forgot. Simon, I want you to come with me so badly . . . But you're right. You can't. If I stopped you from doing what you wanted, I'd kill you. If you kept me in this awful city, you'd kill me. You know something – if you're true to yourself, whatever that is, you're immortal. Someone said that, some poet type. I guess that's better than being famous. And what's funny is that it's because of you I think I'll be able to paint. I mean, nothing you said. Nothing special you did. No lightning flashes. It's just that a little loving can do an awful lot. You bank it, you draw on it later. It helps you get to forty-five.

SIMON: But it's unfair. You're the reason I want to stay in New York. You made me feel real. You treated me real. That's all I needed.

TOBY: Of course it's unfair. You think God's slipping or something?

SIMON: I don't want to talk about this. Maybe we're still sick.

TOBY: Maybe.

SIMON: Then we'll have some time. I'm still very weak.

TOBY: So am I.

SIMON: It's hard for me to walk.

TOBY: Or stand.

SIMON: I get dizzy.

TOBY: My liver still hurts.

SIMON: Not as much mine. I'm in much worse shape than you.

The telephone rings. They stare at it.

You get it.

TOBY (*picks up the receiver*): Hello. Yes, doctor. What were they? Oh. Are you sure? I see. I'll tell him. Yes, I understand. Thank you. (*He hangs up, looks at* SIMON, *a long silence.*) We're better.

Blackout.

Scene Five

Two weeks later. Afternoon.

The front door is open. No one is in the room. A suitcase lies on the floor.

TOBY *enters, followed by* SIMON.

TOBY: I forgot something. I know I forgot something.

SIMON: Everything's in the cab . . .

TOBY: There! (*He points to the suitcase.*)

SIMON: Except for that. I've got it. Relax.

SIMON *takes the suitcase out.* TOBY *looks around the room.* SIMON *returns.*

TOBY: That's it?

SIMON: That's it.

TOBY: You'll send the crates into storage?

SIMON: Tuesday.

TOBY: I'm sorry to leave you with it. The charter flight was so cheap; I couldn't pass it up.

SIMON: It's no problem. I'm lucky to have the apartment.

A car-horn honks off stage.

TOBY (*shouts out the door*): In a minute.

SIMON: Let me come to the airport.

TOBY: No. I won't know what to say. Anyhow, they won't let us kiss or hug or anything. Stay here. My guitar! I forgot my guitar.

SIMON: It's right here. (*He points to the guitar, next to the bed.*)

TOBY: I know I forgot *something* . . .

SIMON: Send me a list.

TOBY: I'm so nervous. I get so nervous when I travel. Well. (*He shrugs his shoulders.*) That's everything, huh?

SIMON: Remember, don't do too much or you'll have a relapse.

TOBY: I'll stay in bed half a day. I promise. You're the one who has to be careful. You're going to run around and do inward somersaults and things.

SIMON: I'll be careful. I promise.

TOBY: Well, I guess I have everything. Do I?

SIMON: Yes.

TOBY: I'm ready.

SIMON: Is that what you're wearing? (*He points to* TOBY's *shirt.*)

TOBY: Sure. It's hot outside.

SIMON: But it's cool in London, and that's where you land.

TOBY: And I'll catch cold!

SIMON: Right.

TOBY: I can't go.

SIMON: Take my sweater. (*He takes a sweater from a drawer.*)

The horn honks.

TOBY (*shouts out the door*): In a *minute*. (*He takes the sweater from* SIMON.) Thanks.

SIMON: Don't put it on now.

TOBY (*putting the sweater on*): I have to or I'll lose it. Listen, did I tell you about the rent . . . don't pay until the fourteenth because that's when the girls upstairs pay theirs and you screw it for them if you . . . *I'M STUCK!*

SIMON: What?

TOBY: *I'm stuck!* I put my head through the arm part.

TOBY's *head is stuck in the sweater's arm.*

SIMON (*laughing*): That's impossible. Nobody can do that. The hole's not big enough.

TOBY: It has to be. My head's in it.

SIMON: It can't happen.

TOBY: It's happened. *I can't breathe.* Get me out of here.

SIMON: How?

TOBY: Pull

SIMON: Like this? (*He pulls the sweater; it doesn't move.*)

TOBY: No, you're choking me.

SIMON (*laughing*): I don't believe it.

TOBY: I can't go to the airport like this.

SIMON: It isn't possible.

TOBY: Stop saying that! Where are you? I can't breathe.

SIMON: I'm going to pull it *up*.

TOBY: Do *something*. You'll have to cut

me out.

The horn honks.

Tell him I'm stuck.

SIMON: I'm not cutting my sweater. Stand still.

TOBY: I can't see.

SIMON: You don't have to see to stand still. OK – now I'm pulling up. Here goes.

He pulls the sweater up, off of TOBY.

TOBY: You saved my life. I could have died in there. (*He starts to put the sweater on again.*)

SIMON: Don't. I'll do it. (*He pulls the sweater over* TOBY's *head.*)

TOBY: Thanks.

SIMON: There. You're all set.

TOBY: I am.

SIMON: Shoelaces tied?

TOBY: I don't have shoelaces. I didn't forget anything, did I? I know I forgot *something*.

SIMON: No.

TOBY: Are you sure?

SIMON: I'm not sure; I'm not sure of anything.

SIMON *kisses* TOBY.

TOBY: This is ridiculous . . .

SIMON: I wish you wouldn't . . .

TOBY: Shh!

The horn honks.

SIMON (*shouts*): Coming!

TOBY: Well, I guess I'm ready.

SIMON: Yeah.

TOBY: Wait. My present! I bought you a present. Don't move. It's a surprise. (*He goes to the phonograph; takes a record album out, puts the record on – it is the song from the French movie . . .*) Couldn't resist.

SIMON: Bastard.

They embrace – a long kiss.

SIMON: You're going to miss the plane.

TOBY: No. (*He pulls away.*) Did I forget anything? I don't want to leave anything.

SIMON: You're leaving a lot.

TOBY (*starts to cry, then stops*): Hey, fella, no scars. Isn't that wild? No scars. How about you?

SIMON: None. A little more muscle.

TOBY: Figures.

SIMON: Are you gonna be all right?

TOBY: Who knows? (*He brushes SIMON's hair with his hand.*) Win a medal, OK? (*He goes to the door.*) I'll write. (*He turns to* SIMON.) I had a wonderful hepatitis.

He leaves.

SIMON *sits on the bed. He sees the guitar. He picks it up and runs out the door.*

SIMON: You forgot your guitar. Hey, Toby!

SIMON *is gone a moment, then he returns, with the guitar. He puts it down. The music is still playing. He turns and looks at his apartment, as*

the curtain falls.

ACCOUNTS

Accounts was first performed at the Traverse Theatre Club on 7 May 1981, with the following cast:

MARY MAWSON	Madelaine Newton
ANDY MAWSON	Kevin Whately
DONALD MAWSON	Cliff Burnett
JAMES RIDLEY-BOWES	David Calder
JOHN DUFF	Anthony Roper

Directed by Peter Lichtenfels
Designed by Andy Greenfield
Lighting by Colin Scott

At the Edinburgh Festival and at the Riverside Studios in 1981 the part of JAMES was played by George Pensotti.

The American premiere was at the Hudson Guild Theatre, New York, on 1 June 1983, with the following cast:

MARY MAWSON	Kathleen Nolan
ANDY MAWSON	Josh Clark
DONALD MAWSON	Kevin Conroy
JAMES RIDLEY-BOWES	Allan Carlsen
JOHN DUFF	Frank Girardeau

Directed by Kent Paul
Designed by Jane Clark
Costumes by Mariann Verheyen
Lighting by Phil Monat

Accounts

After two successful runs of *Rents* at the Traverse Theatre, Edinburgh, in1979, Thames Television provided me with a generous award to stay on at the Traverse for a year as resident playwright. Part of the agreement involved the writing and production of a new play. At this time, Chris Parr, who had directed the productions of *Rents* with such distinction, was artistic director of the Traverse. It was with his advice and encouragement that I started work on *Accounts*.

A half hour sketch for the play was performed by the Haltwhistle Young Farmers Club, and this experience helped me to authenticate the technical side of hill farming that is an important feature of the play.

The first full draft of the play was given to Chris Parr during 1980. This draft differed greatly from what was to become the finished version of the piece. The whole of part two was dumped in the bin. My original story had taken a melodramatic turn when the two boys had shot a vagrant mole catcher whilst they were out poaching! The disposal of the body and their guilty secret had become the prime events of the play. At this stage, their father was also a living character in the drama.

British Telecom had not got round to installing a phone in my Northumbrian cottage at this time (it finally took nearly two years of waiting!) and a whole series of telegrams and phone calls between my nearest call box in Kellah farmyard and the Traverse helped to determine the development of the play. It was during one of the phone calls, after I had trudged a mile across snow-covered fells, that Chris Parr suggested that it would be better if father had died before the action of the play commenced. We discussed growing up as boys without a father and thus a vital ingredient in *Accounts* was created.

Although Chris had been my help and advisor during the writing of the play, the first production was directed by Peter Lichtenfels, who was to be Chris's successor at the Traverse. Like *Rents*, the new play was revived for the Edinburgh International Festival in 1981, as part of the Traverse's programme. Immediately after the Festival, it transferred to the Riverside Studios in Hammersmith, London. This was the first time in my seven-year-old professional life that any stage play of mine had been seen south of Stockton-on-Tees!

Within weeks of the Riverside transfer, *Accounts* was under contract to BBC Radio for production in The Monday Play series, and to Partners in Production (PIP . . . an independent film making company) for production as a film for Channel Four's Film on Four series.

So within the space of a few months, *Accounts*, which had started out as a short scene for the Haltwhistle Young Farmers, had played on the stage in Edinburgh and London, been joint winner of the George Devine Award, and had been rewritten for radio and film. The experience of working in so many media was an important education for me.

In 1983, *Accounts* received its first American production at the Hudson Guild Theatre, New York, with an all American cast.

Michael Wilcox
1983

PART ONE

Autumn 1979

MARY (*from her journal*): Andy still cannot get used to Black Face sheep. He's pining for Swaledales. I told him that it'll take time, but his heart will mend. Donald is still back at Dean Burn in spirit. He says he can hear his father's voice calling sheep on the fell top. Yet it's two full years since Harry was killed. The boys were saying last night that he'd travelled north with the family. This morning I drove the Landrover into Kelso for provisions. It's a fair-sized town, bigger than Allendale with great buildings and a fine bridge. Yetholm WI are having a poetry competition next time round. I'll write mine in my journal. The year's starting to close in on us . . .

ANDY *and* DONALD *on the fell top.*

ANDY (*whistling instructions to his dog then calling to his brother*): Donald! . . . what's it like over by yon dyke?

DONALD (*off*): All clarts . . .

ANDY: What?

DONALD (*off*): Clarty man.

ANDY (*to his dog*): Haaaaaaaaaaaaaa . . . you rascal . . .

DONALD (*off*): Head them off . . . divven send them through here . . . (*Whistling.*)

ANDY: Ahhhh Patch man . . . ah-ah-ah-ah . . .

DONALD (*entering*): What are you playin' at man? . . . Gyp . . . (*Whistling.*)

ANDY: I thought yonder was short cut.

DONALD: Noooooo . . .

ANDY: Hell . . . let them be a while . . . byyyyyyy . . . but that's a grand view. Is that the sea, Donald?

DONALD: Aye . . . could be . . .

ANDY: Wind's getting fierce . . .

DONALD: . . . and Kelso's doon there like . . . in that direction . . .

ANDY: . . . a canny distance . . .

DONALD: Played against Tweed last season . . . with Hadrian colts . . . beat them . . . and in the Gala sevens . . .

ANDY: And it's all ours . . .

DONALD: What do you mean? . . . Just our bit's ours like . . .

ANDY: No landlords . . . no rents . . . no agents putting up prices . . . hanging round your neck . . . Da would be pleased . . .

DONALD: Da'd never have left Dean Burn . . .

ANDY: . . . never have left Swaledales . . . but these are wor fells . . .

DONALD: Not wors till we growed wi'em a while . . . till we're hefted like the sheep . . .

ANDY: . . . wors in the bank . . .

DONALD: We best drive 'em past yon rowan tree . . .

ANDY: Howay . . .

DONALD: It's ower clarty your way, man. We'll have to build ditches all over . . . it's useless there . . .

ANDY *and* DONALD *shelter from the wind by a stone wall. They drink from a thermos and eat their sandwiches.*

DONALD: It's no use increasing the sheep till the drainage is done, now!

ANDY: Maybe . . .

DONALD: I'm right . . .

ANDY: Now . . . do you want to hear my great idea?

DONALD: Gan on . . .

ANDY: I know you divven like cows . . .

DONALD: Not that . . .

ANDY: Hang on . . . now then . . . you know the burn pastures . . .

DONALD: Aye . . .

ANDY: It looks all stoney and useless . . .

DONALD: It is . . .

ANDY: Now if we were to clear that . . .

DONALD: Waste of time . . .

ANDY: Listen you! Now there's scope for increasing pasture down there, like . . . more hay . . . or maybes plant some beet . . .

DONALD: Down there?

ANDY: Aye . . . it's possible . . . now . . .

DONALD: Top soil's ower thin . . . Old Willie just had an occasional sick beast there . . . nothing for us, like . . .

ANDY: More feed would help if we're increasing the dairy herd . . .

DONALD: Who wants that?

ANDY: I do . . . this is my farm as much as yours. There's a lot of sense in a milking parlour.

DONALD: Now we're getting down to it.

ANDY: There's money in't. I could cope with many more beasts with a parlour.

DONALD: There's no sugar in this tea.

ANDY: Canny windy up here, mind.

DONALD: What were you up to last night?

ANDY: Not a great deal . . .

DONALD: Aye . . . but what?

ANDY: Went doon the toon.

DONALD: Kelso?

ANDY: Aye.

DONALD: Do you have to wake us up when you come in, like?

ANDY: I couldn't get my trousers off. I was hopping around in the dark and I landed on one of your boots. There's lasses in Kelso.

DONALD: Never!

ANDY: It's a remarkable fact.

DONALD: And bars?

ANDY: Few of them too. I scored, like.

DONALD: No doubt.

ANDY: She was a canny age . . . but better than nawt. Nineteen's supposed to be your prime. I don't want to let it pass by.

DONALD: Seventeen's your prime.

ANDY: Oh aye . . . that's more than you'd know!

DONALD: If you're coming in pissed each night, you best sleep in your own bedroom.

ANDY: Too cold. Let's gan o'er to Hawick the neet.

DONALD: Noooo . . . there's only one reason I gan there.

ANDY: Are you packing in rugby at Hadrian?

DONALD: I thought I could train at Tweed and travel to Hadrian for the games. I could, like. Pressures on for me to make a switch. More future for me as a player in the borders. No doubt about that. Playing for Tweed colts Saturday.

ANDY: Is that settled then?

DONALD: Aye . . . playing centre . . .

ANDY (calling his dog): Gyp . . . Gyp! Have you seen that circle? Them stones yonder?

DONALD: Aye . . . a canny few about . . . ower past yon gill . . . beyond the dyke . . .

ANDY: Aye . . .

DONALD: Canny few grouse . . .

ANDY: You check the stone walls up to the end of the old Roman fort. I'll start at the sheep dip and cut right up the fellside. I'll meet you ower yonder.

DONALD: Right.

They exit in different directions.

At the farmhouse. MARY *talking to* JAMES RIDLEY-BOWES.

JAMES: . . . so I've been disgracing myself around the flesh pots of Newcastle. Not really disgracing myself. Wondering whether I ought to. Wondering how to.

MARY: Harry took me into town once when we were courting. We went to a film and then went dancing. They were all the wrong dances. Not traditional, like.

JAMES: Most evenings I get back and flop into a bath and lie there for hours. And by the time I've got myself something to eat and got the fire lit I don't really feel like going out. At my boarding school the two worst crimes were smoking and talking to girls in the town. Lying, cheating, beating up people smaller than oneself were more or less tolerated. But fags and tarts, if I may use those dreadful expressions, were not on!

MARY: That's a long time ago, mind. Time now to set all that aside.

JAMES: Yes.

MARY: We used to have these great matches in the yard. Harry and me taking on the two boys. Cricket and football. I was canny at cricket. We used to have to sweep the yard first, mind. It was still awful messy. But the football was the worst. Sometimes in the most freezing weather we'd break out of an evening and fix up the lights and battle away for two hours or more and end up all clarts from head to foot with bleeding ankles and tempers flaring. It's a miss, like. Boys need a man.

JAMES: Yes.

MARY: At least you'll not be coming to put up the rent from now on. The boys will be sorry to miss you . . .

JAMES: Oh . . . not to worry. I'll be seeing Donald at the Rugby club one way or another. We've started training, tell him. Tell him Willie's dropped a stone on his foot stone walling . . . and Droop's been tossed by a bull. He's all right. – He says he feels like he did after the Hawick match last season.

MARY: James, I want you to know that you've been good for Donald . . . for us.

JAMES: Oh . . . well.

MARY: The boys were saying they'd not be seeing you so often . . . not now, like.

JAMES: I'd like to see you through the first year of the new farm. There's a lot can go wrong.

MARY: So we want you to call back when you're up this way. If you come this way.

JAMES: I will.

MARY: Harry's death is still with us. The boys are full of energy, but they lack all the wisdom of the land that Harry took with him. We still need a man around the place . . . at times.

JAMES: Well . . . I've got clients near Belford I've got to see before getting back to Ponteland.

MARY: They say it'll take at least two years before the phone's in.

JAMES: Thanks for the coffee and cakes.

MARY: You're welcome.

JAMES: Well . . . goodbye . . .

MARY: Goodbye . . .

MARY (*from her journal*): I seem to be losing touch with the folk from Allendale already. It's difficult for me to travel south to Northumberland to see them all. There's no telephone here and it's miles to the nearest call box. Secretly, I wonder if I'll ever settle here. It's for the boys, all this buying and moving . . .

JOHN DUFF, *the colts' coach at Tweed RFC, is on the phone to* JAMES RIDLEY-BOWES, *the colts' coach of Hadrian RFC.*

DUFF: How many pitches are you using this year?

JAMES: Same as last . . . but we're keeping the sheep away from the one down by the river this season . . . one of our lads . . . Skittle . . . was sent off last year for throwing sheep shit at Durham's full back.

DUFF: You need to crack the whip a bit, James. Hadrian colts are a wild bunch of hooligans.

JAMES: At least we don't steal sheep.

DUFF: So the dates in our letter stand, do they?

JAMES: Yes. We look forward to slaughtering Tweed after our triumph of last year.

DUFF: In all that wind, rugby was hardly playable. It wasn't a game at all, James.

JAMES: We train our lads to play in all weathers.

DUFF: Talking of your lads, now . . . let's get down to business.

JAMES: Yes.

DUFF: We've been approached by one of your lads.

JAMES: Donald Mawson.

DUFF: Aye. Now he wants to train with us but seems unclear in his mind whether he should be on our books or yours.

JAMES: We still think of him as one of us.

DUFF: No doubt. I remember him from last year. He caught the eye. There may be something there.

JAMES: We think so.

DUFF: I mean more than ordinary colts material. It depends on how he grows, how he develops. And the sort of coaching he receives.

JAMES: Are you suggesting that he'll do better in the borders than in Northumberland?

DUFF: Of course he will, James! How could you doubt it?

JAMES: I see. Carry on.

DUFF: If we're going to coach him, which is what he has asked . . . he approached us first, remember . . . we would want to play him as well. Maybe not in our senior colts . . . unless he made it on merit. No special favours for the lad.

JAMES: He'll have to make his own mind up. That's all there is to it.

DUFF: Aye, that's right. I just don't want you to think we've been poaching.

JAMES: I know you haven't . . . in this case. He could still travel down to us on a Saturday.

DUFF: It's not fair on the lad. If he's going to be one of us, he better commit himself the whole way. He's got to decide for himself.

DONALD *is stretched out at the farm house.* MARY *is setting the table for tea, which is a substantial meal.*
There's a blast of a shot gun, both barrels, from the yard. The rooks scream.

MARY: Dear God!

DONALD: Andy's having a bit of a blast.

ANDY *comes in with a shot gun.*

MARY: Warn us, will you!

ANDY: Rooks divven give ne warning.

DONALD: She said us, idiot.

ANDY *points the gun at DONALD and pretends to pull the trigger.*

ANDY: Pow! Pow!

MARY: Never point guns!

DONALD: Howay.

ANDY: Empty.

MARY: Give me that.

ANDY: I'm going to clean it. Leave it alone, man!

MARY: Father's gun that!

ANDY: Mine now!

DONALD: And mine.

ANDY: Shurrup, you bairn!

DONALD: Piss off!

MARY: I told you!

ANDY: My baby brother hasn't learnt how to pull the trigger yet!

DONALD: I'll wrap this poker round youse!

ANDY: Mam . . .

MARY: What?

ANDY: Has the *Hexham Courant* come yet?

MARY: When it does, it's me that reads it first . . . just like the old days.

DONALD: Oooo . . . hark at her.

ANDY: She's entering the nag of the month competition.

MARY: Do you want your tea in here or flung out in the yard?

ANDY: Flung out in the yard please. No . . . No . . . I meant in here! Mam's getting sprightly.

MARY: Be your age.

ANDY: I am. I'm being nineteen as hard as I can. Not always easy out here.

DONALD: You're right there, son.

ANDY: All right for you . . . you're still into sheep. I want something better.

MARY: What are you two on about?

DONALD: Not got into Black Face sheep.

ANDY: I should hope not.

DONALD: Blackies are thick . . .

ANDY: They are, like.

DONALD: Some angles your head's the same shape as a Blackie.

ANDY: You child!

MARY: I've been working on my poem.

DONALD: What poem?

MARY: For the Women's Institute.

ANDY: Gan on. Let's hear it.

MARY: Donald's been writing one as well.

ANDY: Donald?

MARY: Aye.

DONALD: No need to tell him!

ANDY: I didn't know he could write.

MARY: Read it out.

ANDY: Let's hear it.

DONALD: No! It hasn't had the finishing touches yet.

ANDY: Finishing touches! No time for them. Read it!

DONALD: No!

ANDY: Gi'us it!

DONALD: Gerroff man! Ahhhhhh . . .

ANDY (*reading the poem that he's snatched*): 'I love to walk the soddin' fells . . .'

MARY: Is that what it says?

DONALD (*snatching it back*): Give me that!

ANDY: '. . . soddin' fells . . . ' What's one of them, like?

DONALD: '. . . sodden fells . . .' It means they're wet, you ignorant worm.

MARY: What's the rest of it?

ANDY: Something about 'dingly dells' . . .

DONALD: What lies!

ANDY: And sheep that 'fall down wells' . . .

MARY: Sheep don't fall down wells.

DONALD: Billy Ferguson had one that did! It was a Swaledale!

ANDY: Of course it was! All Billy's are, you creep. If they'd been Blackies the whole lot would have fallen down the bloody well.

MARY: Language!

DONALD: You can all hear my poem when it's finished!

MARY: And mine.

ANDY (*producing a piece of paper from his pocket*): And mine!

DUFF *is at Tweed RFC on the phone to his wife.* JAMES *is at Hadrian RFC phoning his colts.* DUFF *is drinking whisky.* JAMES *is drinking beer.*

DUFF: I'm sorry . . . there's a committee meeting on . . . Helen, I know you've got supper ready . . . I know it's unfair of me, but you know how important this is to me . . . I know Duckling *à l'orange* is important too . . . of course you're not a widow . . .

JAMES: Hello Mrs Westerby . . . is John there, please? . . . hello, Snot . . . how are you? You played well last week . . . well I thought you did . . . I know you dropped an absolutely vital pass . . . Studs should have passed sooner . . . it was his fault rather than yours . . . now you mustn't let it get you down, Snotty . . . it's Stud's problem, . . . don't tell him that, of course . . .

DUFF: OK . . . OK . . . we'll make it four cans of lager . . . bottles . . . right . . . four bottles of lager . . . four plain crisps . . . *Look*, there's no lasses here, just big brute rugby players . . . Mavis might just as well be a big brute rugby player. Helen, I've got to drive to Aberdeen tonight to pick up some fertiliser. I've got to be back here for tomorrow's match! . . .

JAMES: Hello . . . Studs? . . . Ahhhh . . . now then, are you fit for training tomorrow night? . . . That was just a scratch, man! . . . What? . . . A great tough thing like you? . . . What's the matter? . . . Well get it cut short then they'll not be able to swing you round by it! . . . That was Snot's problem . . . he's never been good with his hands . . . You could have released the ball a couple of strides earlier . . . But you must come to training . . . tell her that you'll see Clint Eastwood on Friday night . . . Well that's too bad . . . she knew your Wednesday nights were booked before she started going out with you . . . be tough, Studs . . . don't be bossed around . . . What do you mean 'it's all right for me to talk'? . . .

ANDY *has met up with* DONALD, *who has been training, in the streets of Kelso.*

ANDY: It's only half past nine.

DONALD: Look! I've had a drink at the club.

ANDY: Why mannnn . . . take a look around the town.

DONALD: No! Let's go home!

ANDY: I'm not ready to.

DONALD: It takes an hour to get back. We've an early start in the morning. Market's tomorrow.

ANDY: I know that, young'un. There's folks I'm wanting to meet yet.

DONALD: Why mannnn . . . you've been on the town all night! You're reeking! I'll be driving you.

ANDY: You? You've not passed your test, son.

DONALD: You're not fit.

ANDY: It's me that's pickin' youse up the night. Anyways . . . I was hoping to happen on a lass.

DONALD: Ahhhh mannn . . . there's ne time for that.

ANDY: Doesn't take long.

DONALD: You're like a whippet . . . whip it in and whip it out.

ANDY: Maybe there's something for you.

DONALD: Like what?

ANDY: Like her daughter.

DONALD: Daughter! Who is this? Have you been breaking into the old people's home?

ANDY: No!

DONALD: I thought you said it was a lass you were after.

ANDY: She's nearly a lass.

DONALD: So was Queen Victoria. How old is't?

ANDY: Thirties maybes. You don't want to be that personal when you're screwing the arse off someone.

DONALD: So why divven you gan wi'hor?

ANDY: Mother kind of shoves her out of the way, like. Ahhh mannnnnnnn, do you not fancy it?

DONALD: Whyyyyyy . . . Maybe . . .

ANDY: Come on then.

DONALD: No!

ANDY: We're wasting time.

DONALD: Not with you there . . . I couldn't.

ANDY: I divven want to watch you wi'hor. I'll be busy.

DONALD: Not with your own brother. No, I couldn't. That would be in . . . in . . . inthingy.

ANDY: We sleep in the same bed at home.

DONALD: That's different. We're used to that, like.

ANDY: You are horny, aren't you?

DONALD: Shurrup man . . . they'll hear you.

ANDY: My brother's got a horn on!

DONALD: I'll bray youse!

ANDY: Oooooo . . .

DONALD: Where's the bloody Landrover?

ANDY: Ah-haaaaa . . .

DONALD: I'll fuck youse!

ANDY: Catch us first, little big horn!

DONALD *brings* ANDY *down and slaps his face.* ANDY's *surprised at his strength but shakes himself free.*

ANDY: Watch it, you!

DONALD: Let's gan!

ANDY: No.

DONALD: Give us the keys then.

ANDY: No way!

DONALD: You stay on . . . I'll go home. I'll pick you up early.

ANDY: At yon corner?

DONALD: Aye.

ANDY: Don't tell Mam.

DONALD: No.

ANDY *tosses him the keys.*

DONALD: Where is't?

ANDY: Beyond yon bridge end.

DONALD: Half-five?

ANDY: I've no watch . . . aye . . . half-five . . . or you could do the cows and make it half-eight? That would save you getting up so early. I'll make it up, like.

DONALD: Right . . . eight-thirty.

ANDY: . . . and Nellie's got an ulcer . . .

DONALD: . . . right . . .

ANDY: . . . and Maggie's got the shits!

DONALD: Behave now!

ANDY: Who me? Of course.

They split.

Some days later in Kelso.
MARY *is carrying a load of shopping back to her Landrover. She is approached by* DUFF.

DUFF: Mrs Mawson . . .

MARY: Yes . . .

DUFF: Can I help you carry that?

MARY: I'm managing . . .

DUFF: I'm John Duff . . .

MARY: Oh . . .

DUFF: I run the Tweed colts . . .

MARY: Oh aye . . . Donald said . . .

DUFF: I wanted to talk to you . . .

MARY: About Donald?

DUFF: Aye.

MARY: He's keen.

DUFF: Aye . . . we know that . . .

MARY: What do you want to tell me, Mr Duff?

DUFF: I . . . well . . . we hope you're settling in . . . that's it . . . he's a good lad . . . we want him to settle . . . with us . . . we might be able to make something of him . . . out of the ordinary . . . if he sticks with us . . . I'm in the fertiliser business . . . if you want to get in touch . . . there's my home number . . .

MARY: Donald has it . . .

DUFF: Are you in the Women's Institute?

MARY: Aye.

DUFF: I tell ghost stories! I get all dressed up for it!

MARY *exits towards her Landrover.*
DUFF *follows.*

On the fell top, ANDY *and* DONALD *are carrying bales of hay on their backs to feed the sheep. They are tired and sing phrases of 'Blaydon Races'.*

DONALD: 'All the lads and lasses there . . .'

ANDY: 'all with smiling faces . . .'

DONALD: '. . . gannin' along the

Scotswood Road . . .'
They exit.

Winter 1979

MARY *(from her journal)*: We have now been living on our new farm for three full months. So far we've been spared the worst of an early winter, which is a blessing in these parts. I think of our farm as being long, with high fells and the sheep, and low pastures with just a few beasts. Andy wants to increase the dairy side of things. The last farmer couldn't cope with that, although the potential was there. Andy says that with a milking parlour he can cope with many more beasts himself.

The wind has a different sound and feel to it here. I mean compared to our old home in Dean Burn in the Allen Valley. We are high here, more out-by. The wind sings with a sharper voice. It was blowing a gale the other night. Things kept falling off the inside of the slate roof onto the ceiling above my bed. Maybe the roof wants working on.

JAMES *is visiting* MARY MAWSON.

JAMES: You must make sure that there isn't a cash flow crisis in six months' time. That's the trick.

MARY: I know. We're planning on carrying a few more Cheviots. We're not exactly over stocked.

JAMES: A good idea.

MARY: And the boys are on about clearing what we call the Burn Pastures. That's down by the river beyond the first gate.

JAMES: I know . . . that's . . . ha . . . always been a problem. Old Willie stuck a sick beast in there occasionally.

MARY: They think it's wasted at the moment. Maybe they could plant out some beets or maybe a barley crop.

JAMES: Yes . . . oh dear . . . look . . . it's too stony . . . for the work involved . . . it's hardly worth it.

MARY: It was just an idea, like.

JAMES: Donald has deserted us.

MARY: Aye. I'm sorry.

JAMES: We could have done with him this season.

MARY: Tweed's a lot more convenient.

JAMES: It's a pity.

MARY: It's nawt to do with me, now. Donald is his own boss . . . except in the house.

JAMES: Yes . . . right.

MARY: And Andy wants to increase the dairy herd . . . get one of these new milking parlours.

JAMES: I see.

MARY: The byres will convert easy enough. With Andy taking care of the beasts and Donald away with the sheep, the boys'll not get under each other's feet. It's almost two farms in one, James.

JAMES: You're planning an additional bank loan for the milking parlour?

MARY: Aye.

JAMES: The fixed interest rate is a blessing, Mary, but don't overdo it.

MARY: I've always been a good accountant in the past.

JAMES: True.

MARY: The boys have a long time ahead of them. We must plan.

JAMES: Look, I hope you don't think I'm stepping out of turn. . .

MARY: No.

JAMES: If you feel unsure or worried about how things are going, talk to someone right away. Don't set things to one side. You've got to deal with problems right away. Forgive me, Mary. I'm interfering.

MARY: We need your advice.

ANDY *is on the telephone – a pay phone.*

ANDY: Hello? . . . Mrs Duff? Andy Mawson here. Aye . . . that's the one . . . I know I shouldn't . . . Howay . . . I had to phone you, like . . . couldn't help it . . . Is that miles out-by by any chance? . . . I've had some sleep . . . aye . . . about three hours . . . I know I'm not behaving myself . . . I know . . . it's more fun being bad . . . you know that . . . I didn't mean exactly that, like . . . I

didn't mean it . . . No . . . honest . . . I'm sorry . . . look . . . I'm sorry . . . of course I gan to church . . . what's that got to do with it? . . . right . . . you're right . . . I'm driving ower to Hawick this afternoon . . . I've got problems with my distributor . . . no I'm not going to the clinic . . . the distributor on the tractor . . . well you shouldn't read all these women's magazines . . . it's only townies get that, like . . . now . . . shall I look by? . . . It's ne risk if he's miles out by . . . Of course I'll make it snappy . . . if you want it snappy you can have it snappy, Mrs Duff . . . right . . . see

She has hung up suddenly.

Down at Tweed Rugby Club. JOHN DUFF *in his track suit. He has taken* DONALD, *all muddy and sweaty, on one side.*

DUFF: You . . . aye . . . you Mawson . . . here lad! How many games has it been now? How many?

DONALD: Seven or eight.

DUFF: You don't know exactly, Mawson?

DONALD: Not exactly.

DUFF: Now listen, laddie. You're holding the ball too long, like the Hadrian lads. You're part of Tweed now . . . remember? You cannot expect to barge your way through. The lads really tackle up here. None of your fancy Hadrian Academical stuff. When you get the ball in the centre say to yourself 'Can I make ten yards?' If you can't, pass it out straight away . . . in a flash . . . no hesitating. Now Fergus on the wing has a fair bit of pace . . . at least as much as you, Donald son. If he scores, you've scored because you've been part of that movement. And up here we don't like to see our wingers getting frozen and see the ball only twice in a match. Wingers are for using at Tweed . . . and if you get in the way of that you'll find yourself running the touch in no time . . . tries or no tries . . . Is that clear? Now what have you got to do?

DONALD: Get the ball out . . . unless I can make ten yards . . .

DUFF: Good! For your reward! *Ten press-ups.*

DONALD *is down in a flash doing his*

press-ups.

DUFF: 1 2 3 4 . . . that's it . . . 7 8 9 . . . up on you feet . . . *down again* . . . 5 for luck . . . 1 2 3 4 5 . . . *get up!* Now here's the second thing. Once you've moved the ball out, I want you to run round to support Fergus . . . aye . . . miss out the other centre occasionally like you did tonight . . . that was good, Donald. Young Willie will cover for you. You're vital to us, Donald . . . creating the overlap . . . running all over . . . you've got a future if you do what you're told. Understand laddie?

DONALD: Aye.

DUFF: I'll be watching you specially on Saturday. *Touch your toes!* 1 2 3 4 5 . . . Now away to your bath . . . *run! And keep it simple! . . . Hey Scottie . . . bring in those posts . . . no . . . the other ones . . . aye . . . no . . .* Jesus!

At the farm, MARY *has cornered* ANDY. *He is studying the plans for the milking parlour.*

MARY: There's no way we can afford another vehicle.

ANDY: He'll pass his test soon. Hell! He drives the Landrover more than I do. Coppers'll get him one of these days.

MARY: I'm going to put a stop to all that too. It's about time someone put their foot down in this house.

ANDY: Howay and see the plans for the milking parlour.

MARY: What do you think I've been looking at all day? And don't try changing the subject, Andrew Mawson.

ANDY: What subject?

MARY: You know what's on my mind.

ANDY: Really?

MARY: Do you think I haven't heard about your carrying on?

ANDY: What do you mean?

MARY: The folk at the WI were full of it. Talking away when they thought I was out of ear-shot.

ANDY: What were they saying, like?

MARY: Unrepeatable things! About other folk's wives . . .

ANDY: Just a bunch of old gossips. I don't know why you bother with them.

MARY: You'll land my family in trouble before you're through. Can you not stick to courting like the other young men do?

ANDY: What other young men are you on about? Nawt different about me. Maybes I'm a little more imaginative than some . . .

MARY: That's the least of it from what I hear. And it's affecting the farm . . . and us . . .

ANDY: How's that?

MARY: Milking the cows later and later.

ANDY: It always gets done.

MARY: And all this talk of raising another £50,000 for the milking parlour . . .

ANDY: It's done! Bank's agreed the principle at least. Things just need signing.

MARY: You'll get no signature from me the way you're carrying on.

ANDY: You'll benefit too. You know the money side of things. You said it was canny enough when we all discussed it.

MARY: Only if we get enough back from the increased milk yield to pay off the loan. It's getting things balanced that matters. It's risks like we've never faced before. Risks of not paying rent as tenants but owning things with none to bail you out if things slip. And you're playing about as though you owed nothing to anyone. Father would have whipped you and thrown you out by now!

ANDY: Like hell he would!

MARY: His insurance money and the compensation is all tied up in the loans. Remember that! We may own a farm now but we've no cash to speak of. So end this talk of new cars.

MARY *leaves in distress.* ANDY *follows her.*

ANDY: We want the milking parlour!

DONALD *and* JAMES *are together in Kelso finishing fish and chips.*

JAMES: Duffer's been doing well . . . scored twice against Percy Park.

DONALD: Aye.

JAMES: . . . and Pud's still getting into trouble. He will allow himself to get so worked up. They all know about him . . . the opposition . . . and they work on him on purpose . . . just trying to get himself sent off or something daft. We had this lady referee the other week and all the lads were frightfully well behaved. They couldn't stand the idea of getting ticked off by a mere woman. But Pud just did the same old business . . . scrapping away in the loose mauls.

DONALD: He's thick.

JAMES: She gave him such a dressing down. Pud just stood there . . . shell-shocked. God! He was absolutely useless for the rest of the game. We had to take him off! Poor Pud.

DONALD: I miss the lads, like.

JAMES: Get yourself down sometime. They keep asking after you.

DONALD: Aye.

JAMES: You're looking fit.

DONALD: Aye. Training's hard up here, mind.

JAMES: If you decide you've had enough at the end of the season, you can always come back to us.

DONALD: I'm taking my driving test Tuesday. I'll be getting a car sometime . . . driving legally soon, like. Do you want us back?

JAMES: Yes.

DONALD: I mean . . . you personally? Have you missed us?

JAMES: Yes.

DONALD: I'm not yet settled, James. I still think myself back to Dean Burn. Things is different here. The air. The fells. The wind. It tires you more than it did at home . . . harder somehow. Winter's been canny mild, mind.

JAMES: Plenty of hay in?

DONALD: Enough. Maybe more than enough if it carries on the way its going. It's good, like. But on the fells it's ower boggy . . . marshy, like . . . and it's easy to get lost when the mist comes down. And your instincts don't take you home some nights. Not straight away. We're not with the land yet, James. It's hard.

JAMES: You and Andy should get your own two-way radios . . .

DONALD: No. We don't do things like that, James.

JAMES: Is there anywhere round here I can have a pee?

DONALD: There's a canny wall round there.

JAMES: I don't think I should.

DONALD: The river's a walk off, but it would take no harm . . . even with a bladder like yours.

JAMES: Look . . . oh . . . well . . . keep a look out . . . whistle if anyone's coming . . .

JAMES *goes to pee.* DONALD *screws up his chip paper and lobs it like a grenade, whistling as it flies through the air.*

(JAMES *rushes back.*) God . . . I can't see anyone . . . bloody hell . . . I've pissed all down my leg!

DONALD: I didn't mean to whistle . . . it just kind of came out!

JAMES: I'm bursting! Help!

DONALD: Come on with me. I'll show you where.

JAMES: Hurry!

DONALD: Tie a knot in it.

JAMES: We might never get it undone!

DONALD: *We?*

DUFF *is telling stories to the Women's Institute. He is dressed like a borders character from a Sir Walter Scott novel.*

DUFF: . . . now Billy Macrae lived at Glen Cune and he was the meanest man in the valley. He never settled his bills. He was never known to give gifts at any time of the year, even to Old Tilly, his wife. And folks couldn't understand how Old Tilly had stood for all her husband's cruelty all those years. And they grew old together, and yet he still would beat her with his stick when he fell into one of his foul moods. Now I'll tell you the strange things that happened.

One day, Tilly was away in the wood gathering sticks. And it was a dark day with the north wind blowing. And she thought she heard a voice. 'Tillllllllyyy

... Tillllllllyyy ... pick them berries ... the berries by yon mountain ash ...'
And she staightened her aching back to look around. But there was no soul to be seen! And there by the mountain ash she saw the deadly nightshade gleaming!

And Billy Macrae ... he died that week. There was no money for his funeral and they buried him in the darkest, dankest spot in Studholm Churchyard. And within the year, a mountain ash grew out of Billy's grave and folk said its roots were feeding on Billy's bones and it was his only generous act in a long black life! And the tree is still there to be seen!

And Old Tilly lived another twenty years and folk said they'd never seen her so happy.

And we know why ... good ladies ...

Spring 1980

MARY (*from her journal*): Spring's setting in early this year. The weather's been exceptionally mild. One of my new excitements at Comb Law is discovering what there is planted in the garden round the house. There's been snow drops all over, sometimes packed so close that bulbs have been forced out of the ground by their neighbours. These I've gathered carefully and re-distributed. It's a wonder that bulbs so freshly planted have the energy to flower so quickly. There's an abundance of crocuses. The trouble was avoiding treading them down by accident. And there's been a shrub bursting cherry pink with colour that caught me entirely by surprise. The flowers have come before the leaves and seemed, on the cold morning that I found it in bloom, to be a miracle.

The new milking parlour is all but finished with the mild weather.

There has been sad news from nearby. A tractor overturned and crushed the lad from the next valley. Strangely, his grandfather died in the same spot in similar circumstances many years back ...

One evening at the farm house. ANDY's *busy with the 'Farmers' Weekly'.* MARY *comes in to get the table prepared for tea.*

MARY: Do you want feeding or not?

ANDY: 'Corse!

MARY: Shift yourself then.

ANDY: Oh Mammmmm!

MARY: Over to the sofa! Howay!

> ANDY *shifts.* DONALD *enters all mucky from the byre with his boots still on.*

MARY: Out of here with your boots all clarting the place up!

DONALD: Oh aye.

He leaves.

ANDY: Where's the embrocation, Mam?

MARY: What do you want that for?

ANDY: My thigh's playing war.

MARY: It's over by the coal bucket where Donald left it last time.

> MARY *goes back to the kitchen.* ANDY *fetches the embrocation, drops his jeans by the fire and rubs some on his thigh.* DONALD *comes back with his boots off.*

DONALD: That's mine, man!

ANDY: Took a bit of a tumble the day, like.

DONALD: Don't use any more. I need that.

> DONALD *takes the bottle. He pours some on his hand.*

You divven want to get this near your balls. You catch fire!

ANDY: Mine catches fire without that, like.

> DONALD *suddenly attempts to get the hand with the embrocation inside* ANDY's *pants.*

Howay. You bent bastard! Get stuffed you! You poof!

> MARY *comes in.*

MARY: What are you playing at? Disgusting! I'm not standing for it!

ANDY: He's been queer all day, him.

DONALD: Get lost!

ANDY: Something's up.

DONALD: Aye ... something is!

MARY: Get decent the pair of you! (*She*

goes out.)

ANDY *gets back to the sofa with his 'Farmers' Weekly'.*
DONALD *slips a book out from his overalls and tries to read it privately.*

ANDY: What's that then?

DONALD: What?

ANDY: The book, man.

DONALD: Nothing much.

ANDY: Let's have a look.

ANDY *manages to get the book off* DONALD.

DONALD: Get lost you!

ANDY: Hey lad! How sly can you get? The Swaledale catalogue!

DONALD: Give it here!

ANDY: Where did you get this?

DONALD: Borrowed it.

ANDY: Who off?

DONALD: None of your business! A friend!

ANDY: What friend's this?

DONALD: Give it here!

MARY (*off*): Stop shouting!

ANDY: Who lent it you, like?

DONALD: James.

ANDY: Oh aye. So you've been hiding it.

MARY *comes in.*

MARY: What's this racket then?

ANDY: Donald's been hiding the Swaledale catalogue so he can have it first.

DONALD: Mam, tell him to give us it.

ANDY *is reading it.* MARY *snatches it.*

ANDY: I was reading that!

DONALD: I was first!

ANDY: You're all schemes and plans you. Sly . . . a sly brother!

DONALD: Can I have it, Mam?

MARY: I want to have a look.

DONALD: Tea's burning!

MARY: Help!

She rushes to the kitchen. The book is

flung onto a chair and falls to the ground. Both brothers dive for it and they start to fight over it.

DONALD: Fight you for it!

ANDY: Cumberland wrestling rules!

DONALD: Right!

They fight.

ANDY: Bastard!

DONALD: You fart!

ANDY: Bloody little turd!

DONALD: You smelly sock!

ANDY: Y-front!

DONALD: Snot!

ANDY: Acne!

DONALD: Ahhhh . . . that's my arm . . . ahhhhh!

ANDY: Is it really? How insignificant . . . how worthless . . .

DONALD: Ahhhhh . . . ahhh man!

DONALD *manages to get out of it and ends up on top of* ANDY, *with* ANDY *flat on his back with his arms trapped.*

DONALD: Divven move or I'll gob on you!

DONALD *starts to trickle spit out of his mouth and then sucks it back just as it is about to fall on* ANDY's *face.*

ANDY: Don't . . . ahhhh . . . gob-shite . . . ahhhhhhh!

DONALD *lets the dribble go too far and* ANDY *has to take it in the face.*

DONALD: It's raining . . . raining . . .

ANDY: I'll get you . . . ahhh . . .

DONALD: Oh dear, . . . you're getting wet . . .

MARY *comes in.*

MARY: Get up the pair of you . . . *get up*!

They get up.

ANDY: I'll not forget that . . . you shit.

MARY: I'll not have that word in my house!

DONALD: It's usually me underneath you, isn't it. Things are changing now. My turn now!

MARY: Fighting and carrying on at each other's throats! I'll not take this from either of you!

DONALD: It's not me . . . it's him!

MARY *clouts him.*

MARY: Now sit down!

ANDY: Hee-heeee . . .

MARY *clouts Andy.*

MARY: And you!

The boys sit down obediently at the table.

MARY: Now I think we'll have grace.

ANDY: Oh Mam . . .

DONALD: What is it?

MARY: Hands off! Liver hot pot . . .

ANDY: Ugh!

MARY: Shurrup!

DONALD: Shurrup Mam . . . I'm prayin' . . . Dear God . . . thanks for Mam's stew . . .

ANDY: . . . it's hot-pot . . .

DONALD: . . . and for my queer brother . . .

MARY: Donald!

DONALD: . . . and help me to recognise chronic liver fluke infestation when I see it!

MARY: That wasn't very nice.

DONALD: Amen!

ANDY: Amen!

DONALD: Say amen, Mam.

MARY *serves out the food.*

MARY: Cut the bread please, Andrew.

DONALD: Ooooo . . . Andrew!

ANDY: Bonny-bum-Donny . . .

DONALD: Sling ower the bread!

ANDY: Hey lad! Is that all I get?

DONALD: Pepper . . . pass the pepper!

MARY: Pass your mother the salt please, Donald.

DONALD: There you are.

ANDY: There's the pepper, Mam.

DONALD: Do you want some bread?

ANDY: There's the butter like . . .

MARY: Don't rush it! Eat it slow!

DONALD: I'm starving.

ANDY: I'm ravenous.

DONALD: He's always stuffing something . . .

ANDY *gets out the Swaledale catalogue.*

DONALD: Swaledales! You best get into Blackies, Andy lad.

ANDY: I'd love to start Swaledales on these fells.

DONALD: Canny expensive . . . take years . . . hefting them from one generation to another . . . building up the flock . . .

MARY: And it's not just the sheep that stray till they're hefted. I know what's gannin' on. And we'll have no reading at table!

ANDY: There's no harm in't. I'm going to hold up a photo of one of the tups and I want you to guess what price it fetched at auction.

MARY: Put that away!

ANDY: Father used to do this each year!

ANDY *holds up one of the photos of a tup, covering up the details with his other hand.*

ANDY: How much? . . . howay . . . how much?

DONALD: £800 . . .

ANDY: Mam?

MARY: Not at table.

ANDY: Gan on.

DONALD: Gan on, Mam.

MARY: Errrr . . . £660 . . .

ANDY: Not bad . . . Donald's got it . . . £800 . . . What about this'un?

DONALD: Hold it closer . . . errrrrr . . . £1350 . . .

MARY: £500 . . .

DONALD: I'm good me, you know.

ANDY: How do you do it, lad? You're bang on again . . . £1350!

DONALD: I look at the wellies.

ANDY: Tups divven wear wellies, man!

DONALD: Noooo mannnn. In the pictures there's the wellies of him that's holdin'

138 GAY PLAYS

tup . . . and those are Eddie Pemberton's wellies and I remember the sale and it went to Colonel Netherton's farm out by Lazenby for £1350. Ower-priced in my opinion. That tup couldn't screw a yow if it tried!

ANDY: My legs are aching something rotten.

DONALD: And have you got sores in your mouth and is your nose running?

MARY: Send for the vet! Sit down you two! There's more to come yet.

ANDY: What is't?

MARY: Jelly.

DONALD: I love jelly.

ANDY: I hate it!

DONALD: I'll have yours.

ANDY: Noooo . . . I'll eat it.

MARY (*serving it out*): Get on then before it melts.

ANDY: Jelly doesn't melt . . .

DONALD: . . . it kind of wobbles to death.

MARY: Donald! Your hands are filthy!

DONALD: They were clean a minute ago.

ANDY: He's filthy all over, him!

DONALD: Shurrup!

MARY: Hold your tongue!

ANDY(*holding his tongue with his fingers*): EEERRRRRRRRRRRRRRR . . .

DONALD *flicks a spoonful of jelly right into* ANDY's *face.*

DONALD: Haaaaa . . .

ANDY: Pig!

MARY: Stop it!

ANDY *picks up a handful of jelly and flings it at* DONALD.

ANDY: I'll kill you!

MARY: Sit down!

DONALD (*who is at the other side of the room*): Truce! I declare a truce!

ANDY: Well I don't!

MARY: Sit down and finish your meal.

ANDY: Come here, Donald!

DONALD: On one condition!

ANDY: Oh aye.

DONALD: If I come back to the table and try to finish my jelly, do you promise to leave us alone?

ANDY: Gan on then.

DONALD: No . . . no . . . I want a promise. Do you swear?

ANDY: I promise I'll let you finish your jelly.

DONALD: You heard that everyone?

DONALD *goes back to the table.*

Now then . . . please note that I'm going to eat most of my jelly but I'm going to leave just a little bit 'cos Andy said there was a truce till I'd finished my jelly BUT I'm *not going to finish it*! Is that clear?

ANDY: I've not forgotten that now.

DONALD: That's good.

MARY: I think I'll clear the table.

ANDY: Let it be. I've not finished yet.

DONALD: Neither have I. In fact there's things I want to say.

ANDY: What things?

DONALD: Thoughts I've been having.

ANDY: Thoughts?

DONALD: Now you've got your milking parlour.

ANDY: Gan on then.

DONALD: We could be making more money.

MARY: We need to!

ANDY: How, like?

DONALD: We're still not using our resources. If you've got resources it's daft not to use them.

ANDY: Parlour's using our resources.

DONALD: If the milk yield stays high enough . . . aye . . .

ANDY: Well then?

DONALD: There's tourism.

ANDY: Howay to hell!

DONALD: There's grants to be had. James was telling us.

MARY: James?

DONALD: There's folk that want to visit

the borders. We could improve our property using other buggers' money. We can't keep raising loans. It's thousands more with the parlour to pay off.

ANDY: It pays for itself, idiot.

DONALD: The Nicholsons of Hartley Shield made above £10,000 doing almost nothing with bed and breakfasts and such like.

MARY: Almost nothing! Workin' her fingers to the bone more likely!

ANDY: And folk trampling over their property . . . their dogs frightening the sheep.

DONALD: The Burn pastures has beaten us! We wasted days slogging away trying to clear the rocks and that. We'll never make awt out of that unless we use our heads. We'd best leave it as it is and get planning for a camp site . . . maybes a caravan park. Why mannnn . . . it's out of sight of us, isn't it? And the extra money would be useful at the tup sales. We're hill farmers at heart . . . not dairy men. It's sheep we know about. And the cash would be useful for other things. We need a new Landrover.

MARY: We're not affording another Landrover and there's an end of it!

DONALD: If we don't exchange it soon it'll not be worth anything, and prices is soaring!

ANDY: What are tourists going to come here for?

DONALD: Because we advertise. Pony trekking. Fishing.

ANDY: Why mannn . . . they're just . tiddlers, man.

DONALD: There'll be more grants maybes for stocking the river. We'll get a reputation. It'll not cost us much. Your way of making money's expensive . . . creating huge debts for us. My way's using our heads and making money out of what's here.

MARY: I couldn't cope with the fuss and the people and all the coming and going.

DONALD: I'm frightened we'll not be able to repay the loans.

MARY: Divven fuss about that. That's my worry.

ANDY: Donald . . . if you start something like that, it's stuck there with you. And it grows and grows and it suffocates the life out of you, and the family and the beasts. We'd all suffer. All your talk of resources! Isn't the happiness of this family a resource? And our fells to walk on at will . . . without other folk . . . and ponies . . . and the mess of the campers . . . and the litter and other folks' drunkenness and the disturbance of it all? Resources isn't just for making money . . . it's for making lives better.

DONALD: You're sounding like Da.

MARY: No hurt in that.

DONALD: When you owe thousands for the farm and thousands for the parlour resources *is* for making money!

ANDY: Not your way!

MARY: What's that?

ANDY: What?

DONALD: I cannot hear awt . . .

MARY: Shurrup . . .

They listen. Sound of fire in the distance. DONALD rushes out into the yard, then flies back into the house.

DONALD: Byre's ablaze!

ANDY: You get the beasts out . . .

DONALD: Mam . . . take the Landrover and seek help!

MARY: Where's the keys?

ANDY: Catch!

He throws her the keys.

DONALD: Howay!

They rush out.

PART TWO

Spring 1980

MARY (*from her journal*): The boys have been working themselves near to death trying to cope on the fells and keeping the milking parlour going. I wanted them to have help in, but they were both against the idea, for this year at least. They seem to have a fear that if they give one inch of their territory away, they've lost something for good. Since the fire, the milk yield has been right down, with the shock of it and the smoke getting to the cows. Andy's not been able to increase the herd as much as he should, which may be a blessing as far as the labour is concerned. But the shortage of cash, which I had bargained on from what we all thought would be extra milk sales, is playing war with the loan repayments . . .

The farm one evening. ANDY *is servicing his fishing rod and reels.* MARY *is clearing away the tea things.*

DONALD (*off*): Mam . . . *Mam*!

MARY: What?

DONALD (*off*): Where's your hair dryer thingy?

MARY: What are you doing in my bedroom? Get out of there!

DONALD (*off*): Where's the hair dryer?

MARY: In the box under the bed.

ANDY: Folks say Greenwell's Glory's canny. Have you still got any of those Scottish Field magazines, Mam?

MARY: There's a couple by the coal bucket . . . gave the rest to the WI jumble sale.

ANDY: I never had time to read them. You might ask, like.

MARY: I pay for them.

ANDY: We all pay . . . comes out of farm money.

MARY: Me that gets them in.

ANDY: What's that idiot up to?

MARY: Just getting himself tidy.

DONALD *comes in. He's bathed and done his hair. A clean shirt is hanging out and he's trying to get cufflinks in unsuccessfully.*

DONALD: Could you do these, Mam?

ANDY: Poufffff . . . what is that smell? Ughhhhh!

DONALD: I found some Brut up there.

MARY: That's years old that!

ANDY: Father's!

DONALD: Smells canny to me. Better than smelling like a rancid udder.

ANDY: Where did you get them from?

MARY: These were your father's cufflinks.

ANDY: Let's see.

MARY: They were a wedding present from your Uncle Joseph. They're silver, mind.

ANDY: Who said you could wear them?

DONALD: No point in just leaving them in the drawer for ever.

ANDY: You should still ask.

DONALD: Mam doesn't mind. Mam gave them to me.

ANDY: Oh?

MARY: Now . . . there's something for you too.

ANDY: Like what?

MARY: I thought you could try his engagement ring.

ANDY: Can't you just leave his things together, without interfering? It's ower early to start splitting things up, like.

MARY: Three years is long enough. It's best to make use of things.

ANDY: I'm the oldest. You should have asked me first.

DONALD: What's special about being the oldest, like?

ANDY: You should have asked us.

MARY: I should have asked you together.

ANDY: Aye . . . that would have been better, like.

MARY: I'm sorry, now. I was wrong. Howay and get dressed, Donald.

DONALD *leaves.*

I never realised you'd care so much.

ANDY: I do care. I still have the feeling that Da will come walking through the door. When I hear the tractor pull into the yard, I expect to hear him come banging his way in.

MARY: You need to start going out more . . . like you used to. With a bit more sense, maybes . . . but you've gone too far in the other extreme.

ANDY: Don't start on us.

MARY: You've been working ower hard. You need company . . . other folk. I'm getting away more than you now.

ANDY: Don't go on.

DONALD *comes back in.*

DONALD: Where's the shoe polish?

ANDY: What a little tart you are. Why won't you tell us where you're going?

DONALD: 'Cos I didn't want you onto us all day long.

ANDY: Where are you going, then?

DONALD: Edinburgh.

ANDY: For the night?

DONALD: Not the whole night . . . I'll be back late on.

ANDY: Edinburgh! How?

DONALD: He's picking us up.

ANDY: Who?

DONALD: James.

MARY: James?

DONALD: There's an evening of rugby films.

ANDY: I thought you were sick of rugby.

DONALD: Sick of Tweed, more like. How does that look, Mam?

MARY: Very good.

ANDY: You don't look like my brother at all.

DONALD: I don't want to look like a walking hay stack . . . not in Edinburgh. Doesn't matter in Kelso . . . but they might think you're daft in Edinburgh.

ANDY: They might still.

MARY: I wish someone was coming to take me out for the evening.

DONALD: Have you ever thought of getting another husband, Mam?

ANDY: Howay! Divven put ideas in her head, man Donald!

DONALD: She's not entirely past it yet, are you Mam?

ANDY: Shurrup!

DONALD: You should know about that, like.

MARY: That's enough!

ANDY: Stupid little bugger!

ANDY *attacks* DONALD, *wrenching his shirt and messing up his hair.* DONALD *swings at* ANDY, *who parries the punch.*

DONALD: You're mad!

ANDY: Bastard!

DONALD: You've snapped Da's cufflink! Look what you've done! It's broken, man! Look!

ANDY *rushes from the room in distress.*

MARY: Don't be hard on him, son.

DONALD: What am I going to do?

MARY: Come here. Let's have a look now. I'll have that mended in a moment.

She fetches her sewing basket and sets to work sewing the link together.

This'll do for now. We'll get it mended properly later.

DONALD *is almost in tears, but doesn't want his mother to see.*

JAMES (*off*): Hello!

JAMES *enters.*

JAMES: Hello Mary . . . excuse me barging in.

DONALD: Not quite ready, James.

JAMES: Right.

MARY: That's fettled it. Now off you go and get your jacket.

DONALD *goes.*

MARY: This has caught us all on the hop.

JAMES: Sorry about that.

MARY: Donald sprung this expedition on us. Are you going to be late?

JAMES: Not if we hurry.

MARY: I meant coming back.

JAMES: Oh . . . ha . . . I thought we'd stop and have fish and chips in Dalkeith. Very important, fish and chips in Dalkeith. We'll be back before midnight.

MARY: Only he's got an early start in the morning.

JAMES: Yes . . .

MARY: His turn with the cows . . . getting them started at least.

JAMES: Right.

DONALD *returns.*

DONALD: I'm ready. Bye, Mam.

JAMES: Goodbye.

They go.

MARY: Behave now!

DONALD (*off*): Try to!

When JAMES's car has left the yard, ANDY comes back into the living-room. He says nothing. He returns to his fishing gear.

MARY: . . . Mind . . . there's something about fishing in Horse and Hounds.

ANDY: Where is't?

MARY: In my bedroom.

ANDY: I'll seek it later.

MARY: Still early.

ANDY: Beasts can look after themselves tonight . . . I've finished work.

MARY: I've a proposition to make to you.

ANDY: What?

MARY: Let's drive down to Allendale for the evening.

ANDY: Allendale!

MARY: Aye . . . you drive down . . . we'll have a drink or two . . . see our friends . . .

ANDY: . . . takes an hour and a half . . .

MARY: That just about gives us time.

ANDY: Give us an hour maybes . . . by the time you're ready to set out.

MARY: Canny chance of drinking after hours!

ANDY: What's come over you, Mam?

MARY: I'll drive back, mind . . . no arguments about that! *And* you come when I tell you! Do you promise?

ANDY: Aye . . .

MARY: . . . and no stopping over the night!

ANDY: No.

MARY: Well get yourself ready, lad. I'm not going out with the local scruff. Get washed and shaved . . . and there's a clean shirt in the drawer.

ANDY *runs upstairs to get ready.*

. . . and I'll be ready to leave in ten minutes.

DUFF *entertaining the ladies at another Women's Institute meeting.*

DUFF: . . . and Lord Belister held a great banquet on New Year's Eve and his servants were sent out far and wide to gather food and fuel. And singers, dancers and acrobats were engaged to entertain the guests. Then . . . when the feast was at its height . . . the Grey Minstrel entered . . . and the lord commanded him to sing. And he sang the songs of the great borders families, and the great cattle raids, and the heroic deeds of generations. And the guests were bound in a spell by the stranger.

But the other artists were jealous and they spread rumours that the Grey Minstrel was a spy sent by Lord Belister's enemies to observe the strength of the castle. And before dawn, the Grey Minstrel vanished from the castle and Lord Belister set the hounds loose in the misty darkness. And the whole company waited on the castle walls, listening to the baying hounds. And they heard the death screams of the Grey Minstrel as the hounds tore his body. At dawn they found his bloody remains.

But the Grey Minstrel's ghost still haunts the grounds of Belister. And when his song is heard through the mists, or his grey form is seen, whoever then is Lord at Belister is sure to die violently!

JAMES *and* DONALD *with fish and chips in Dalkeith.*

JAMES: C . . .

DONALD: E . . .

JAMES: N . . .

DONALD: T continued.

JAMES: . . . oh . . . CENT . . . R . . .

DONALD: . . . A . . .

JAMES: . . . have you got me . . . hold on . . . ha . . . L . . . CONTINUED! L continued . . . God.

DONALD: L . . .

JAMES: Oh heck! . . . Oh heck!

DONALD: You've had it, man!

JAMES: Ohhhh what about CENTRALLIFICATION?

DONALD: No such word.

JAMES: Ohhhhh Y . . . I suppose . . .

DONALD: That makes you a DOPE!

JAMES: I'm not a DOPE am I?

DONALD: You were a DOP to my DO . . . you lost the last'un . . . so that's your E . . . sorry James . . . you're a DOPE!

JAMES: I am rather sometimes.

DONALD: You are tonight, like . . . no offense, mind.

JAMES: What's your fish like?

DONALD: Canny.

JAMES: The whole world should know . . . that fish and chips in Dalkeith *can* be fun!

DONALD: Your turn to start.

JAMES: P . . .

DONALD: R . . .

JAMES: . . . I . . .

DONALD: The great thing about tonight is that we've talked about nothing serious. What is it? PRI . . . oh aye.

JAMES: OI? Challenge!

DONALD: No man . . . PRI . . . C . . .

JAMES: Oh Donald . . . what are you thinking of?

DONALD: Nothing much.

JAMES: No doubt . . . K continued . . .

DONALD: PRICK continued . . . what more is there? . . . er . . . L . . .

JAMES: Oh *no*! Ohhhhh . . . do you spell PRICKLY with an -EY?

DONALD: Nope!

JAMES: Can you be PRICKLED?

DONALD: Improbable, I should say.

JAMES: Oh you can PRICKLE someone. I PRICKLE; you PRICKLE; he she or it PRICKLES . . .

DONALD: Only if you were a horny blackberry.

JAMES: Look . . . this evening I've been a CLOT, a TWIT, a FOOL and, that ultimate humiliation, a DOPE . . . please, this once, let me PRICKLE . . .

DONALD: Gan on then . . . but don't start with a P again . . .

JAMES: Oh hell! Where can you pee in Dalkeith?

DONALD: Not again.

JAMES: I'm full.

DONALD: There's dustbins down that alley . . . doubt if they're big enough, mind . . .

JAMES: Whistle properly this time . . . remember the Great Flood of Kelso . . .

DONALD: I'm coming too . . . gan on, man . . .

They disappear up the alley.

Later that spring

On the fell top. ANDY *has been drawing drainage plans.*

ANDY (*shouting*): Donald!

DONALD (*way off*): Hello . . .

ANDY: How far is't from here to the gully?

DONALD (*off*): Which gully?

ANDY: Far'un . . .

DONALD (*off*): 150 . . .

ANDY *makes a note. He starts making all sorts of calculations about the drainage, then packs it in. He gets out his food and pours himself a coffee from the flask. Eventually,* DONALD *arrives.*

DONALD: Thanks for waiting.

ANDY: Still hot, like. Do you want yours now?

DONALD: Aye . . . gan on . . .

ANDY *pours him some coffee.*

ANDY: Canny few ditches needed . . .

DONALD: Is it worth draining?

ANDY: Huge grant, man . . . mustn't miss our chance . . . may not last . . .

DONALD: Young Farmers is doing a play for the competition.

ANDY: Oh aye.

DONALD: Thought I might take a look in.

ANDY: Aye.

DONALD: Fancy it?

ANDY: Maybes.

DONALD: I wonder if there's bodies in yonder moss.

ANDY: Bodies?

DONALD: Aye . . . it preserves them. They never rot. It's the peat. They found this gadgy once . . . with a rope around his neck. He'd been dead for hundreds of years. All black he was. I saw his photograph . . . black as leather. And all the wrinkles on his face and his hair and whiskers were plain to be seen. Divven take all the sarnies . . . eh! You've had all the tomato ones!

ANDY: Cheese'uns there.

DONALD: You must have started early on the bait.

ANDY: Need to with you around.

DONALD: If we drain the fell o'er there . . . and the moss dries out . . . who knows what we may find?

ANDY: Cake's canny.

DONALD: How many drainage thingies do we need?

ANDY: *Tiles*, man.

DONALD: Drainage *tiles*.

ANDY: Thousands . . . hold on . . . where's some paper?

DONALD: I got none.

ANDY *finds some paper in one of his pockets.*

ANDY: This'll do . . . eh . . . look at this!

DONALD: What is't?

ANDY: My poem! Remember our poems . . . last winter?

DONALD: Hold on now . . . mine was . . .

ANDY: Hey laddddd . . .

DONALD: Shurrup man . . . listen . . .

When I'm mixin' Nelly's feed

I think on buns and cake and breed
But when at neet ah stuff ma belly
Oot o'ma heed gans poor old Nelly.

. . . something like that . . .

ANDY: Is that poetry, like?

DONALD: 'Corse it is . . . what's yours then?

ANDY: Ohh no . . .

DONALD: Gan on . . .

ANDY:

The sigh of the wind
The bleat of the sheep
The curlew's complaining
The deer that do leap
The sky larks a-chattering
The gentle hare-bells
All are a-singing
The song of the fells.
The frost in the winter
The drifting of snow
Logs for the fire
A warm place to go
Tractor in mornings
With hay for the sheep
Songs in the evening
And early to sleep.

DONALD: Not exactly early to sleep with you bouncing around all night.

ANDY: What do you mean me?

DONALD: Good poem, though . . . I like the drifting snow and logs for the fire.

ANDY: Have you finished stuffing your face?

DONALD: Aye.

ANDY: Now . . . we need to pace out from yon dyke end to the far ditch.

DONALD: Hold on . . .

ANDY: What do you mean?

DONALD: We'll have a race to the dyke.

ANDY: Which part of the dyke?

DONALD: Where the gate used to be.

ANDY: All right . . . go!

DONALD: Come back here! None of your cheating. Now get in a line. Not that sort of line! Now stay by that bit of grass.

ANDY: I'm ready.

DONALD: To your marks.

ANDY: Get back . . . gan on . . . six inches!

DONALD: To your marks . . . get set . . .

ANDY: . . . howay . . .

DONALD: *Go!*

DONALD *races off with* ANDY *in hot pursuit.*

ANDY (*off*): Come back . . . *cheat!*

JAMES *is talking to* MARY *at the farmhouse. They have spent hours going through the accounts and are now waiting for the boys to come home.*

JAMES: My parents were in India, you see. I went there a few times, but mostly I spent my holidays with an aunt in Tunbridge Wells. When I was seven I decided to take matters into my own hands. I knew there was an orphanage run by nuns at the other end of town. And I'd read all these books in which parentless children had the most marvellous adventures. I was especially fond of one in which the parents were killed by Red Indians and the little boy was taken away alive to be brought up like an Indian brave. Anyway . . . this summer afternoon Aunt Sylvie was busy watering the garden so I took off all my clothes and walked naked through the streets of Tunbridge Wells and strode up to the front door of the orphanage and reached up to the great iron knocker. And this old nun opened the door . . . and she stared at me in astonishment . . . and I said, 'My mother and father are dead . . . take me in!' And she screamed out and I thought My God she sounds just like Aunt Sylvie . . . and before I knew what was happening I was whisked into this room, surrounded by a whole flock of nuns, wrapped in a blanket and perched on a table. And as I looked around at them I realised that I'd made the most ghastly error. I had swopped an old aunt, who I was experienced at making a fool of, for a whole gang of aunts . . . and there wasn't a dirty or free child in sight . . . and not a hint of adventure. So I came clean and told them where I lived. And I was taken at reckless speed through the streets in the back seat of a great black car . . . with half a dozen nuns on top of me. Aunt Sylvie was hysterical when we

arrived. Police were everywhere. And I suddenly felt naked for the first time that day. Aunt Sylvie punished me by forbidding me to have a bath that night . . . which was marvellous . . . ha . . .

MARY: Donald has told me how much you enjoy bathing in the plunge with the other lads after training . . . It sounds like a sheep dip . . .

JAMES: Yes . . . and the water is deliciously muddy . . .

The boys arrive back.

MARY: They're in.

JAMES: Good.

MARY: I'll get some tea going.

She goes off to the kitchen. ANDY *enters. He is very scruffy after a day's work on the fells.*

ANDY: Oh . . . hello . . .

JAMES: Hello.

ANDY *collapses on the sofa.*

Where's Donald?

ANDY: Puttin' dogs away.

JAMES: Busy day?

ANDY: Aye.

JAMES: What's the fencing like out-by?

ANDY: Canny . . . mostly . . . dykes down in places like . . . been stone walling a canny few times . . . drainin' at the minute like. I'm knackered me.

DONALD *enters.*

DONALD: Mam's making some tea . . . hi.

JAMES: Hi.

DONALD: Better wash my hands.

JAMES: No.

DONALD: What?

JAMES: No need . . . I mean . . . no need to wash them just because I'm here.

ANDY: Spends all day washing hisself.

DONALD: Do I nick!

DONALD *leaves as* MARY *enters with tea.*

MARY: There you are now.

ANDY: Thanks, Mam . . .

MARY: Andy generally sleeps for an hour

when he comes in from the fell top.

ANDY: Divven tell him all our secrets.

MARY: There's yours now.

JAMES: Thank you.

ANDY: Drainage tiles is going to cost a bit, mind. Canny few needed. Got to do it, like . . . if we're going to take on more sheep . . . got to . . . going to be a job getting the JCB up there an' all . . . heck of a lot of work, like.

DONALD *returns*.

MARY: Now that we're all together . . .

ANDY: Ha'd on . . . what's this then?

DONALD: Shut up.

MARY: This is serious now.

ANDY: Gan on then.

MARY: James and me . . . we've been going over all the accounts . . . all afternoon.

ANDY: Oh aye.

DONALD: Shurrup man!

MARY: It's time to face up to the facts of life. Do you want to hear it from James or me?

DONALD: Let James tell us.

ANDY: Aye.

JAMES: Oh . . . well . . . ha . . . bad news I'm afraid . . . not disastrous.

ANDY: Get on with it man James!

JAMES: You've been unlucky. Right! There isn't enough cash to pay off the interest on the various loans that you have outstanding. Even though the interest rates are fixed and highly advantageous. It's really the fire that's caught you out.

ANDY: Milk yield's been poor. I know that.

JAMES: Not just poor, Andy. You're not getting enough cash back from your milk sales to keep yourselves afloat. And . . . just wait a moment . . . and . . . you've made a tactical error in not accepting the insurance offer made to you over the damage to the byre.

ANDY: How's that, like?

JAMES: You seem to have got it into your heads that the byre was worth what it might have become if you'd been able to

develop it to extend the milking parlour. It only becomes an asset on that sort of level after the work has been carried out. At the time of burning it was just a byre and has to be valued as such.

ANDY: After tup sales we'll have money.

JAMES: You can't wait that long. Anyway . . . by then the debts will have grown fantastically. When things start to slide . . . they just get out of control so fast with such large loans involved.

DONALD: What are we going to do?

ANDY: We're not selling up. Never!

JAMES: I'll tell you what you've got to do.

MARY: Tell us.

JAMES: One . . . settle the insurance claim straight away. Accept what the loss adjusters have offered. If you agree to that, I'll phone through to the company and get them to send you a cheque by return.

ANDY: Ha'd on! What if we hold out a bit longer . . . till the tup sales?

JAMES: To put it simply . . . the receivers are going to move in on you . . . *soon*. If you want to hang on to your farm, you've got to take my advice.

MARY: Carry on.

JAMES: Secondly . . . this is going to hurt . . . are you ready?

ANDY: Aye.

JAMES: You've got to slaughter the whole of the dairy herd and take the Common Market golden handshake. You'll make a lot of money that way. Far more than the value of the cattle. Then you sell the milking parlour equipment. It's almost new and you should get a reasonable price. If you do all that you'll eliminate one loan altogether, you'll pay off all your outstanding interest payments . . . and . . . ha . . . you'll even have some extra cash in the bank . . .

ANDY: We'll think on't!

JAMES: All the figures . . . and letters . . . are over there. Your mother has been through the whole lot with me and will explain anything you don't understand.

ANDY: We'll think on't.

JAMES: You must act fast. I mean this week!

ANDY: Hell man!

JAMES: Bluntly . . . you're not bloody
tenants anymore! You're bloody
landowners! And you've got to behave
as such!

DONALD *rushes from the room.*

ANDY: Right! That's enough! You've said
your bit! That's enough!

JAMES: Yes . . . I've said my bit.

MARY: Now . . . I've got food to prepare.

ANDY: I'm starving, Mam.

MARY: Of course you are. They've
worked damned hard, James.

She goes to the kitchen.

JAMES: I know. It's a good farm. You've
just got to get things right.

ANDY: Aye.

DONALD *returns. He has a hastily
wrapped package.*

ANDY: Are you OK?

DONALD: Aye . . . I reckon.

ANDY: That's good now.

DONALD: I've got James a present.
There you are.

JAMES: No need.

ANDY: What is't?

DONALD: Take it . . . please.

JAMES: Thank you.

DONALD: Open it.

JAMES *opens the package.*

JAMES: Oh.

ANDY: Da's cufflinks!

DONALD: Aye.

ANDY: You shouldn't! They're not yours
to give!

DONALD: They are mine! Mam said they
were! They've been mended . . . after
you broke them!

JAMES: That's very kind, Donald. I think
these should stay in the family.

MARY *enters.*

ANDY: He's given away Da's cufflinks!

JAMES: No.

DONALD: Take them . . . please.

ANDY: They're not yours to give.

DONALD: They are!

MARY: I think that's very generous.

JAMES: I can't accept them.

DONALD: Why not? Why not?

JAMES: Here . . . please.

DONALD: They're yours now!

DONALD *runs from the room again.*

ANDY: I'll gan after him.

He goes to look for DONALD.

JAMES: I'm terribly sorry.

MARY: It's not your problem. None of this
is your problem.

JAMES: Do you mind if I don't stay for
tea?

MARY: You're very welcome.

JAMES: I've got to see people in Keilder
about some trees.

MARY: Stay a while.

JAMES: I'm going.

MARY: Come back tomorrow . . . or the
next day . . . please.

JAMES: They want me to get through a
pile of work by the end of the week,
Mary. There's just a chance of a
partnership if I play my cards right.

MARY: My family needs you. I need you.
Please come back . . . soon.

JAMES: I'll try. You can always get
Donald to phone my Ponteland flat in
the evenings.

MARY: Stay for something to eat.

JAMES: I'm going.

MARY: Take these.

She gives him the cufflinks. He leaves.

A week later.

DUFF *is training his colts from the
touchline under floodlights.*

DUFF (*shouting*): Out to Willie . . . out
. . . *out* . . . catch the bloody thing,
McAndrew . . . what were you doing
last night? Good Jemmy . . . *good boy*
. . . fall . . . fall . . . *fall* . . . *yesssssss!*
Heel . . . *heel* . . . now out . . . *out* . . .
ohhhhhhhhh deeeaaaaarrrrr . . . Right

. . . hold it . . . *hold it*, ref! OK lads . . . now I want to make a couple of changes.

Puffin . . . you go stand off . . . aye . . . swap with Stoney . . . aye . . . that's right, lad . . . and Mawson . . . Donald man! Wake up, son . . . you go out on the wing . . . you'll do less damage there . . . Monkey, you go centre . . . aye . . . where Mawson was . . . now we'll have five minutes hard play . . . then we'll call it a day . . . Right-oh ref . . .

MARY (*from her journal*): We signed all the necessary papers today. Andy sat up half the night going through all the loan agreements and bank statements and letters. He looked like a condemned man the next morning, but had made his mind up for what was best. The day they led the beasts to slaughter, Andy lay on the sofa and wouldn't speak to anyone. The ladies are having a fancy dress party next month . . .

DUFF *on the touchline.*

DUFF: *Come here, Mawson!* Aye . . . *you*, son . . . *run*, you young bugger!

DONALD *comes off the field, covered in mud.*

Oh my God . . . what am I going to do with you? *Eh? Eh?* Tell me what's to be done. You're playing like a beginner, Mawson. What's happened to all the promise of the start of the season? You may think this is one of my famous jokes, but you actually looked like a rugby player last autumn. Is it my fault? *Eh?* Have I rubbed you up the wrong way? Are you at war with me? Is that it?

DONALD: You're picking on us.

DUFF: Picking on you? Why should I do that? 'Cos you're English? Is that what you're thinking?

DONALD: You said it.

DUFF: I've coached the others since they were bairns. They've all had a bollocking from me many a time. You're sulking! You're letting down your team mates. Did you do this at Hadrian? Eh? Eh lad? Are you the sort that lets your mates down?

DONALD: No.

DUFF: I've a mind to put you in the

reserves on Saturday. I actually thought there was a place for you in our sevens side. Aye . . . I was thinking of playing you at Hawick. You'd like that. Eh? Would you? Would you?

DONALD: Aye.

DUFF: Tell you what I'm going to do. I'm playing you in the senior colts on Saturday up at Gala if you promise to give me all you've got for a change. Is that a deal? Is it?

DONALD: I'll try.

DUFF: Promise?

DONALD: Aye . . . am I on the wing or what?

DUFF: No . . . outside centre . . . now then . . . no birds . . . no booze . . . no dirty books . . . now get in that bath . . . run . . . *run*! I'm after you!

DUFF *chases after* DONALD.

JAMES *is on the phone to* MARY, *who has called him from a call box.*

JAMES: I can't come tonight . . .

MARY: Can you not . . .?

JAMES: I've been travelling all day . . . out by Nenthead . . . through to St John's Chapel . . . I don't want to start heading north . . . it's all . . . ha . . . too exhausting . . .

MARY: The boys would love to see you . . .

JAMES: I'm in the bath . . . or rather . . . out of it . . . and I've just piled in a load of clothes that need washing . . .

MARY: Into the bath water?

JAMES: Well . . . the water wasn't *that* dirty . . . that's the way I always wash my things . . . think of the energy I'm saving . . . I've got to do it tonight. I think you've been making all the right decisions lately, by the way . . .

MARY: Can you make it by the end of the month . . . to check things over for us?

JAMES: Of course . . .

MARY: Promise?

JAMES: Well . . . good heavens . . . I'll do my best . . .

MARY: Will you get a message through . . . when you're coming?

JAMES: I'll try . . . I'll get in touch with Donald at Tweed on training night . . . OK?

MARY: Thank you . . .

JAMES: Look . . . I've got to go now . . . I've got reports to write for tomorrow . . . my lords and . . . ha . . . masters expect me to work for a living . . . for them I mean . . .

MARY: Right . . .

JAMES: 'Bye . . .

He hangs up.

MARY: Goodbye . . .

She puts down the receiver.

ANDY *has been visiting* MRS DUFF *but is confronted by* JOHN DUFF *as he leaves the house.*

DUFF: Come here you!

ANDY *tries to make a run for it, but* DUFF *is too fast and brings him down with a rugby tackle.*

Where are you going, son?

ANDY: Piss off!

DUFF: Do you want your fucking head pushed through that wall? Do you? Eh?

ANDY: Ahhhhh . . .

DUFF: Shut it! I've been looking forward to catching you on the job. It's you that's been drinking all my beer and eating all my crisps . . . eh? All the junk I've been carrying out for her! You're just a bloody kid, aren't you, son? I thought maybe she had something going with the postman or the gamekeeper . . . but it's just kids she's been going with. And what's your name, son? Eh?

ANDY: Andy . . . ahhhh . . . let go of us . . .

DUFF: Andy what?

ANDY: Mawson . . .

DUFF: Brother of Donald Mawson?

ANDY: Aye . . .

DUFF *lets him go.*

DUFF: Shit! Shit! Shit!

ANDY: What's the matter?

DUFF: You fucking Mawsons are everywhere! Buggering up my colts!

Screwing up my home! Will you get off my back! Get back south of the border you fucking English cunts! If I catch you within 100 yards of my house again, Andy Mawson, I'll break your fucking legs!

ANDY: I used to play rugby . . .

DUFF: I don't care if you were captain of the fucking Lions! Just get out of my life!

ANDY (*from a safe distance*): Goodnight Fluff!

He runs. DUFF *chases him off.*

At the farm, MARY *is just finishing work on* DONALD's *sheep costume for the Young Farmers' play.* DONALD *is in his underpants.*

DONALD: Have you finished, Mam?

MARY: Nearly. Where's Andy?

DONALD: Still bathing.

MARY: Do you know your lines, now?

DONALD: Aye . . .

MARY: Try this . . .

DONALD *gets into his sheep outfit.*

DONALD: Baaaaa . . . baaaaaaaaaaaa . . . aye, it's canny!

ANDY *enters. He's just been washing his hair.*

ANDY: Ha'd on . . . I'll just fetch out the dogs . . .

MARY: Get your costume on . . . I want to see the pair of you . . .

ANDY *goes off to get into his costume.*

MARY: What time have you got to be there?

DONALD: Seven-thirty . . . it's the last but one rehearsal, this, you know.

MARY: Hang on a minute . . .

She adjusts the costume.

That's more like it, now . . .

ANDY *enters in his Stinkhorn the Bull outfit.*

ANDY (*singing*):

I don't need a pig or a foal
I don't need a hedgehog or a mole
I don't need a chicken or a sow

All I want is a smelly old cow . . .

It's the shudder of her udder
And the tickle of her hide
It's the blaring of her moo
That gets me inside
So prick up my ears
And up onto my toes
Any old cow
And away I goes . . .

DONALD: He's a right show off him you know . . . he's called Stinkhorn . . .

MARY: I'm not surprised . . .

ANDY: Watch out now or I'll toss you into the yard!

DONALD: Tossing's all he's good at!

MARY: Let's hear your song now . . .

DONALD: Oh Mammmmm . . .

ANDY: He sounds like a Blackie . . .

DONALD: Shurrup! I'm a Swaledale . . .

ANDY: Aye . . . a Swaledale yow!

DONALD: Not my fault I'm a yow . . .

MARY: Howay!

DONALD (singing):

Farewell to all our friends every market day
Farewell to sheep and hens
All going away away
Food for the family
Roast beef and pork
Oh what ways to end our days
On the end of a knife and fork . . .

ANDY and DONALD (singing and dancing their rehearsal steps together):

Don't let the knackers get you down, friends
Let's all be happy for tonight
We'll sing a rousing chorus
With market day before us
And we don't give a damn what the farmer does
They can send our children to the butchers
We don't mind our bollocks cut away
They can fatten us and kill us
Roast us and grill us
But we'll dance shout and sing
HIP HIP HOORAY!

MARY: Who wrote all that stuff?

DONALD: Duff the Fluff.

MARY: Do you want to know a secret?

DONALD: Aye.

ANDY: Gan on.

MARY: Don't tell anyone, mind.

DONALD: 'Corse not.

MARY: He's been writing to me.

ANDY: Duff?

DONALD: What about?

ANDY: I don't want to know.

MARY: Things.

DONALD: What things?

MARY: Oh . . . this and that.

DONALD: About rugby?

MARY: Not really. He stops us in the street. He even wanted to carry my shopping.

DONALD: What does he say in his letters?

ANDY: Divven ask.

MARY: He wants to take us out!

ANDY: Is that it?

DONALD: Never!

MARY: He wants to meet us and that!

DONALD: He's got a wife, Mam. Ask Andy!

ANDY: That's all finished with.

DONALD: What do you say, Mam?

ANDY: Do you want us to fill him in, like?

DONALD: Aye . . . we'll see him off!

MARY: No . . . I've sorted it out . . . it's no problem.

ANDY: Why tell us?

DONALD: Let her.

MARY: No one else, is there.

ANDY: Sorry.

MARY: I just don't want you to think your Mam's past it. I could still have another bairn, you know.

DONALD: You're not going to are you, Mam?

MARY: I said I could . . . I'm not going to, like.

ANDY: There's still life in the old cow yet.

MARY: Shurrup, Stinkhorn!

DONALD: James has invited me to the Hadrian fancy dress party.

ANDY: Oh aye.

DONALD: Shall I go like this, Mam?

MARY: Aye . . . you look canny. You best get along now.

ANDY: Aye.

MARY: Mr Duff says he's interested in the Landrover . . . if the price is right, mind.

ANDY: I'll sort it.

They exit.

MARY (*from her journal*): The boys did well with the Young Farmers. They didn't win, but we all had a great laugh. There were folks from all over there, and we've made a lot of new friends. Donald is wearing his sheep costume to Hadrian's fancy dress disco . . .

After the Hadrian fancy dress ball, JAMES, *dressed as the Emperor Hadrian and* DONALD *in his sheep outfit are eating fish and chips on the way home to* DONALD's *farm.*

JAMES: Damn . . . too much salt.

DONALD: This vinegar's full of water.

JAMES: Those blasted disco-whatsits are too . . . ha . . . loud.

DONALD: Can I not stay the night at Ponteland? With you, like?

JAMES: No!

DONALD: Save a long journey.

JAMES: You've got to start work early.

DONALD: No cows anymore.

JAMES: You've got to get back tonight.

DONALD: You've got the morning off tomorrow. You told us.

JAMES: I'm not taking a boy back to my place for the night. OK?

DONALD: Don't call me a boy! I'm old enough to get my head shot off in Northern Ireland. OK?

JAMES: I'm taking you home.

DONALD: I want to spend the night with you.

JAMES: No!

DONALD: Is that all you can say? Do you not want to. like?

JAMES: This conversation never happened. Right?

DONALD: Of course it happened.

JAMES: Let's get back to the car.

DONALD: I don't want to get in.

JAMES: Don't be difficult, Donald.

DONALD: You don't want to understand anything, do you!

JAMES: Are you ready?

DONALD: Aye . . . take us home! Thanks for the chips, anyway!

JAMES: I can't do any more . . .

DUFF *and* ANDY *have met up in a local bar. They've had a few drinks.*

DUFF: So that just about concludes the evening's business, Andy.

ANDY: Aye. It's a fair price.

DUFF: Aye. Now . . . I've got another proposition to put to you.

ANDY: Aye.

DUFF: Next season I'm looking for people to take an interest in the lads who're just starting out. They need an older person to give them a bit of encouragement on training nights and help with the fixtures.

ANDY: I've forgotten about the game, man John.

DUFF: You used to play. I know that. I've checked you out. James from Hadrian says you were a promising youngster.

ANDY: Did he say that, like?

DUFF: Aye. Now when the new season starts, come down. You'll know a lot of the senior colts from the Young Farmers. You can train with them for a couple of sessions. Then you take on the wee laddies. I'll give you a hand. We need new blood at Tweed. There's room for you . . . if you're willing.

ANDY: I'll think on't.

DUFF: You belong to us, now . . . you Mawsons. You may be bloody English but you're bloody Scots too!

ANDY: Allendale seems a canny way off now, like.

DUFF: It's another world. You're wi'us

now, laddie! You'll have the summer to think about it.

ANDY: Aye . . .

DUFF: There's time yet this season . . . to get acquainted. Take a look down at Tweed sometime . . .

ANDY: Maybe . . .

DUFF: We *need* Donald next season . . . he's been difficult. Sort him out, Andy.

Early summer 1980

MARY (*from her journal*): Lambing has gone well, without many losses. I still have it in mind that one day I'll move back to Northumberland. Perhaps when the boys are married and no longer have the need of me the way they do now.

There seems to be something dead in my heart. I keep thinking that I ought to want another man. But just can't bring myself to it. I feel young . . .

Harry's ghost is always going to be with us. There's a lot of his things safely stored away in the attic. The boys wear his clothes quite happily now.

The boys are playing dominoes in the farmhouse.

ANDY: Are you knocking?

DONALD: Ha'd on . . .

ANDY: You've got to, like . . .

DONALD knocks. ANDY lays down another domino.

ANDY: La-la-laaaa . . .

DONALD: Hell . . .

ANDY: Still knocking?

DONALD (*knocks*): Gan on . . .

ANDY (*laying another*): Te-he-heeee . . .

DONALD: What you got there, like?

ANDY: Wait and seeeeee . . .

DONALD knocks again. ANDY lays his last domino.

ANDY: Out! Three-two to me!

MARY enters dressed as a witch for the WI fancy dress party.

MARY: Good evening little children! He-he-heeeeeeeee . . .

ANDY: Aaaahhhhhhhhhhhhh . . .

DONALD: You never told us the VAT man was coming!

ANDY: What shall we do?

MARY: Fee-fie-fo-fum . . .

DONALD: I'll stick a thistle up your bum!

MARY: Has anyone seen my broomstick?

ANDY: Aye, it's away ower the fell top.

MARY: Look. I'm being serious. I must have it. Look! Come on.

DONALD: I haven't touched your broomstick.

ANDY: It might be in the bathroom . . . I was cleaning mud off my wellies with it.

MARY: May your wellies leak for ever!

MARY goes to seek the broomstick.

ANDY: The Women's Institute has a lot to answer for . . .

DONALD: Want another game, like?

ANDY: Not really.

DONALD: Just because you're winning.

ANDY: Don't fancy it right now.

DONALD: What are you doing tonight?

ANDY: Stopping in.

DONALD: That's something.

ANDY: Mam's away with the Datsun.

DONALD: Aye.

MARY comes in with her broomstick.

MARY: Andy!

DONALD: Oh gawd!

MARY: Pin me up round the back.

ANDY: Oh aye.

DONALD: Are you sure the WI will recognise you instantly as being a character out of Scottish history, Mam?

MARY: Of course they will . . . there's witches in Macbeth you know . . .

ANDY: Canny few gannin' the night an' all.

MARY: Mrs Forbes is going as Sir Walter Scott . . . and Mrs Kingdom is Robert the Bruce.

DONALD: She ought to gan as the spider.

ANDY: I pity anyone going for a late night stroll in Yetholm!

MARY: Now you two behave yourselves.

ANDY: Divven drink ower much.

DONALD: . . . and divven waste ower much on the raffles!

MARY: Hocus Pocus Malus Locus . . .

DONALD: Help! I'm turning into a frog!

ANDY: That's all you ever were.

MARY *goes.*

DONALD: Let's have baths.

ANDY: Divven feel like it.

DONALD: I'm feeling a bit knackered, mind.

ANDY: I think I have the answer.

DONALD: Oh aye.

ANDY *produces half a bottle of whisky.*

DONALD: Where did you get that?

ANDY: It was . . . a sort of present.

DONALD: Who from?

ANDY: An admirer . . .

DONALD: No chance! They must be myopic!

ANDY: Oooo . . . long words . . .

DONALD: We play this word game . . .

ANDY (*pouring two glasses*): Who?

DONALD: James and me . . . finished with him now . . .

ANDY: I thought we hadn't seen much of him lately . . . Let's drink to wor farm . . .

DONALD: The farm!

They drink.

ANDY: Do you reckon Mam was hot for James?

DONALD: Not the sort of person you can easily get hot about . . . not in my opinion . . .

ANDY: Nothing doing there?

DONALD: Na!

ANDY: How are you getting on with that Duff down at Tweed?

DONALD: Not good . . .

ANDY: Packing in down there?

DONALD: Doubt it. Too old for colts

next season. Plenty of other teams. Be finished with him. I spat at him actually. He was driving this new car . . . and I was walking up to the club house and he comes up behind us and I never heard him and he hoots and I jumped, like . . .

ANDY: Aye . . .

DONALD: . . . and I kind of swung round and there was Duff sat behind the wheel of a great white Ford . . . and I just stared at him . . . a really vicious stare, like . . . like this . . . and he's got this cassette blaring away with bagpipes or some such shit . . . and I spat a great gob of hockle splat on his bonnet . . . and he went pale and I thought he was going to run us down . . . but he backed down, like . . . wouldn't speak to us all evening, like . . .

ANDY (*topping up the glasses*): Tomorrow . . . I've got a plan . . .

DONALD: Oh aye . . .

ANDY: Down Burn Pastures . . .

DONALD: Aye . . .

ANDY: There is a case for it now . . . now the beasts are away . . . ne good trying to plant beets or barley crops . . . better now to look into that plan of yours . . . the camping and caravaning and all that . . .

DONALD: Aye . . .

ANDY: Makes more sense now, like. Worth looking into at least.

DONALD: Can't afford to waste what we've got.

ANDY: No promises, mind . . . but worth looking into.

DONALD: Have you talked to Mam?

ANDY: Not yet.

DONALD: Maybes we'll get another car . . .

ANDY: Have to sometime.

DONALD: You've been hogging the Datsun!

ANDY: Have I hell!

DONALD: Aye . . . you have . . . keepin' up with all these old wifies you're so keen on.

ANDY: What lies!

DONALD: Surprising what you hear in

the bath at the club.

ANDY: Let's play cards.

DONALD: Divven want to.

ANDY: Play snap!

DONALD: No.

ANDY: So what are you so keen on?

DONALD: What do you mean?

ANDY: You heard!

DONALD: More interested in tups than yows just now like . . .

ANDY: That's exactly what I meant.

DONALD: Do you mind?

ANDY: Not really.

DONALD: That's that then.

ANDY: Aye . . . it is . . . I suppose you'll be blaming me?

DONALD: No.

ANDY: Good . . . let's gan poaching!

DONALD: Cannot poach your own pheasants!

ANDY: Bloody miles to the next bugger's.

DONALD: Let's take another dram.

ANDY (*pouring*): Aye.

DONALD: Maybes you should sleep in your own room . . . from now on like . . .

ANDY: Right . . .

DONALD: OK . . .

ANDY: Canny cold . . .

DONALD: Can be . . .

ANDY: No need for rules . . .

DONALD: Not really . . .

ANDY: I'll get the gun . . .

He fetches it.

DONALD: What for?

ANDY (*checking and loading it*): Got an idea . . .

DONALD: What is't?

ANDY: Come out in the yard.

DONALD: Why?

ANDY *fetches over the torch and gives it to* DONALD.

What's the plan?

ANDY: I'm going to blast the rooks.

They've been ower noisy in the mornings . . .

DONALD: Leave 'em be . . .

ANDY: They'll all be in their nests now. A couple of blasts'll shake 'em up a bit . . . aye . . . that'll fettle them . . .

DONALD: Howay man! They're just rooks man Andy . . .

ANDY: They're vermin! They've got to be kept down. We're the masters of this farm. They got to sing to our tune from now on!

ANDY *goes to the door.* DONALD *is unwilling to follow.*

ANDY: Howay!

He goes into the yard. DONALD *follows.*
Silence . . .
The blast of both barrels.
A furious, terrified squawking of crows.